1985

THE GOOD LIFE AND ITS PURSUIT

THE GOOD LIFE

AND ITS PURSUIT

EDITED BY JUDE P. DOUGHERTY

PARAGON HOUSE

New York

The editor and publisher are grateful to the Philosophy Education Society, Inc. for permission to reprint the articles by Ivor Leclerc, Robert Solomon, and Roger Sullivan which first appeared in the *Review of Metaphysics* and to the International Cultural Foundation, Inc. for permission to reprint the other articles utilized in this volume which first appeared in the *Proceedings* of the International Conference on the Unity of the Sciences, Volumes II-X.

Paragon House Publishers, New York
© 1984 by Paragon House Publishers.
Printed in the United States of America
90 89 88 87 86 85 84   5 4 3 2 1

Library of Congress Cataloging in Publication Data
Main entry under title:

The Good life and its pursuit.

    Includes bibliographies and index.
    1. Ethics—Addresses, essays, lectures.   2. Happiness—Addresses, essays, lectures.   3. Values—Addresses, essays, lectures.   4. Science—Social aspects—Addresses, essays, lectures.   I. Dougherty, Jude P., 1930-   .
BJ1012.G65   1984   170   83-62067
ISBN 0-913729-00-0

CONTENTS

PART II

Determining Moral Norms

PART III

Contributions of Science and Technology

INTRODUCTION

JUDE P. DOUGHERTY

I

The theme of this volume is an ancient one. Plato and Aristotle addressed it, so too did the Stoics and the Christian writers, both Greek and Latin, who followed them, not only in time, but often in doctrine. There is a long line of texts in Western literature which speaks to the topic and which often is as relevant today as when it was first written. Descriptions of human nature, discussions of happiness, of virtue, of means and ends, of personal and social goals, and of law are as instructive today as they were when they first appeared in antiquity. The twentieth century is more conscious of method than the Greeks, but the ancients no less than we distinguished between the ontological source of principle, principle itself, the application of principle, and the role of observation in both determining and applying principle. The essays which follow in a large measure presume classical learning both with respect to content and method, but they extend ancient discussions as required by modern problems and address them in a contemporary idiom.

Aristotle was convinced that the good life, at least in a general way, is describable. He was certain that through systematic inquiry it is possible to determine what is best both in the order of ends and in the order of means. Good laws and customs as well as one's personal happiness depend upon such knowledge. Aristotle's writings also make it evident that systematic moral inquiry rests on or presupposes certain other and more fundamental knowledge. Moral philosophy presupposes an ontology and presupposes an acquaintance with actual social structures and practices. Philosophy, particularly metaphysics, provides the indispensable generic principles for the acquisition of wisdom both speculative and practical. History, on the other hand, lays bare the particular, displays continuity, shows implications and, in doing so, provides a laboratory for the testing of ideas. This essay and this volume are concerned with both sources of moral knowledge.

Philosophers in recent decades, particularly in Anglo-American circles, have tended to eschew both metaphysics and the past. With evangelical fervor they have denounced the inherited in favor of an order yet to be created out of new materials supplied by the natural and social sciences. The reforming spirit of much twentieth century philosophy has found it easier to place greater hope in the future than in past accomplishments only dimly perceived and appreciated. The theses to be advanced here are that moral science is indeed possible and that a knowledge of history is indispensable to moral inquiry.

II

Though a multitude of viewpoints are reflected in the essays which follow, for my part I am willing to argue that the first prerequisite of an adequate theory of the good is a realistic epistemology. A theory of the good must be grounded in the conviction that reality is intelligible, that things and social processes are the cause and measure of our knowledge of them. Such a theory of knowledge avoids the extremes of empiricism, which denies the power of intellect to rise above the particular fact, and rationalism, which places the conditions and measure of knowledge in the intellect as subjective forms of the latter. Aristotle's realism not only allowed him to overcome the difficulties inherent in Plato and the sensists, but it also enabled him to avoid the error which was to appear much later in rationalism, namely the error of regarding essences, or things in themselves, as unknowable, and thus of denying to the intellect the power to control itself by reference to reality.

Aristotle's theory of knowledge is inseparable from his theory of becoming, and while it is doubtful that he utilized fully in his ethics all the insights provided by his metaphysics, he did leave a legacy of certain concepts indispensable to the development of moral and political theory. These are the notions of "substance" and "final causality" and the related notions of "potency" and "act." In an attempt to understand change, Aristotle distinguishes between the relatively permanent essence and its modifications. Becoming is understood as the gaining of further actuality. Through its activity a substance emerges from isolation and enters into relation with other substances, either passively receiving their influence to which it is actively open, or acting in ways ultimately determined by its essence. Each entity tends toward further actuality beyond what it already has. For Aristotle the whole of reality is shot through with the distinction between potentiality and actuality, between what is still only able to be and what actually is. The potential is related to the actual as the imperfect to the perfect, the incomplete to the complete.

Equipped with these insights we cannot only understand what a thing is viewed statically, but we can understand it viewed dynamically—that is, as subject to change. Change is rendered intelligible in terms of the end of change. That toward which a thing is essentially tending is judged to be its proper good. There is a relation of fitness. Goodness is not to be identified with any goal; it is a fulfillment, and thus is founded on the essence and its tendencies. By good we mean what is fit for a thing, what is due its nature, the further existence that will complete its basic tendencies, and its incidental tendencies as well, so far as these do not conflict with the former. Thus the valid ground for desire is that the thing desired is prescriptively required by the nature of desiring it.

A teleological concept of nature, supported by a realistic epistemology is therefore the basis of the unity of "being" and "ought," of "fact" and "value," of "nature" and "goodness." The ontological and moral orders are ultimately one. A basis for values exists only in the tendency of something incomplete to complete itself. In apprehending a tendency we grasp something of what the entity is tending towards. The essence of a thing implies the goal of becoming.

Here it is important to acknowledge that essence is not something which we first understand by itself—and from which we infer tendency. We experience beings and infer something of their essences by observing them in the process of fulfilling these tendencies. Things are always in a state of becoming or development. Essence herein conceived is not an immutable substrate, nor is it subjectively created by interest; nor does it represent a kind of shorthand by which we keep in mind properties, or observations, we cannot now conveniently articulate.

Essence is rather given in experience and discovered upon reflection. It controls our endeavor to distinguish between the peripheral and the central, to discover the order and cause of the properties which the sciences catalogue. In answering the question "What is it?," essence marks the thing off from other entities. And most importantly for value theory, essence in its tendential aspect implies what is suitable to it.

In these considerations, we can observe the ground work of a theory of the good. It consists in advice (1) to look to man's nature to determine what is good for him, and (2) to look to social structures, given both through experience and through history, to determine which are conducive to man's communal well-being. No conclusions are ready-made. This is evident both in Aristotle and in Aquinas as the latter appropriates the philosopher's insights developing his own moral philosophy. To suggest dependence is not to ignore a difference in starting points and emphasis between the two. Aristotle's ethical quest begins with a man already in society with given mores. Those mores, which have in a large measure already formed him, play a major role in determining the value schema he finally produces. Aquinas, on the other hand, begins with the conviction that the divine intellect is the root of a natural order which the human intellect is able, with appropriate effort, to perceive. What this order is remains to be discovered. All relevant sciences are to be employed as this order is explored. Both Aristotle and Aquinas place a heavy emphasis on reason. Joseph Owens has shown that Aristotle identifies right reason with practical wisdom. In his famous "Treatise on Law," Thomas tacitly identifies law with reason; elsewhere, he develops a methodology which reason is to follow. Thomas's amplifications are interesting because they take Aristotle to a logical conclusion.

In utilizing Aristotle it is significant that Aquinas draws no clear-cut distinction between natural and civil law. His famous definition of law, while formulated to be predicative of all law, is primarily a definition of civil law. Where so-called natural law leaves off and civil law begins, there is no hard and fast line. True, there is this difference: civil law is articulated in some fashion by the state, whereas natural law is not. Yet the difference is not determinative. Natural law can be articulated by a church or an academic community before it is reflected in the ordinances of a community. By whom it is articulated is not a significant distinction, nor is it significant that the state does not articulate all that is affirmed by the community of scholars. What deserves emphasis is the fact that law, natural or civil, is the product of reason figuring out what is good for men taken individually or as members of the community pursuing common interests. This suggests that the principal difference between natural law and civil law is the difference between the constant and the variable.

Aquinas, like Aristotle, recognizes that there are certain constants in man, and that these can be discerned. These constants are the grounds for those normative enunciations which will remain the same from generation to generation, or for that matter, whenever and wherever man is found. The variables are cultural, economic, and topographical. The proportion between the constant and the variable is not worked out, but Aquinas is not generous in mentioning constants. The assertion that the natural law in immutable can easily misrepresent Aquinas's position. As he presents his views in the "Treatise on Law," most of the content of the natural law is variable, which suggests that one should be careful in emphasizing content, if, in fact, law is something that is constantly evolving.

This can be stressed, for there is evidence to believe that a careful reading of Aquinas will show that too much is made of the distinction between natural and civil law. Aquinas, in the Treatise, is affirming principally that law is rooted in something other than the will of the legislator. Where he distinguishes between the immutable and temporal aspects of law, he is recognizing that in certain basic features, man is everywhere alike. But the emphasis in this treatise is upon reason as the proper way of finding out what is good for man. Aquinas is more concerned with methodology than with content. It should be clear that not everything that is legislated or determined to be law by a law-making court is in fact to be treated as law. Aquinas will not give the force of law to those enactments which clearly fly in the face of reason and experience. One may assume, however, that when legislative bodies are interested in determining the equitable, and conditions are propitious, they will in a large measure, perhaps as far as humanly possible, succeed. This is not to ignore that much legislation is a tissue of compromise, often reflecting conflicting and contradictory insights and principles. Free intelligence and good will produce good law, not inevitably, but for the most part, and this law is continuous with the dictates of nature, or natural law if you will.

It is worth stressing that reason, for both Aristotle and Aquinas, is not to be identified with deduction. The natural law is not to be deduced from intuitive or antecedently known principles. Anthropology and cultural history will play a major role in the ethics of both. Here, the moral philosophy of an Aristotle or Aquinas is to be contrasted with the purely formal ethics of Kant, where anthropology has little or no role to play. It is through induction, not deduction, that the moralist is aware of certain constants in man. It is through induction that the philosopher can generalize about man in a changing environment. How much permanence and how much change are, again, questions to be settled by reference to the data of the sciences.

III

Turning to the use of history in the determination of moral norms, "history" is employed in the two senses. First there is the history of ideas as disclosed through the texts in which those ideas were initially articulated or restated, and, secondly, there are those attempts commonly made by historians to capture context and to interpret the past. Emphasis must be placed on the documents by which great thinkers of the past have recorded their thought, but narrative history is not to be neglected, for it alone can provide the setting, display the implications, and trace the development of thought.

The use of the past is, of course, only instrumental, but in moral philosophy it has particular weight. The subject matter of philosophy, unlike that of the natural sciences, remains static. Human nature and fundamental social structures remain constant, whereas, in a sense, the "nature" investigated by the physical sciences does not. Nature, of course, *is* constant. Whatever our theories to account for the present, we do not witness an evolving nature. But the "nature" which is the object of science does in fact change. As a result of the perfection of instruments and techniques of observation and measurement, we have a whole new world before us, unknown to the ancients. We have more things to know about. Radio telescopes, particle accelerators and electron micro-scopes have expanded the limits of the natural world. The character of science itself, in its quest to understand in the light of causes and principles, has not changed. Neither has the character of philosophy, in spite of attempts to render it more precise or more empirical. The ancients were as careful in observation, precise in distinction and as acute in reflection as we are now. They reached generic truths about human nature, human goals and the means to achieve them, which are not to be gainsaid. This is not to say that there has been no progress in philosophy, when philosophy is taken as the aggregate of individual effort. But to know whether an inquiry has advanced, one needs to know what has been said before, and not just immediately before. We cannot, with credibility, use Hume as the starting point of our understanding of the problem of causality, nor in agreement with James, say, that since Kant no one has felt the need to take up the question of God's existence nor can we begin moral inquiry with the presuppositions of Kierkegaard.

Ideas have a life of their own. Like institutions which span the centuries, they are not simply the now, their present articulation. Their development, expansion, and refinement can be traced, their inner logic witnessed as it unfolds across time. Implications are not seen all at once, depths not plumbed in an instant. Just as a craftsman may spend his entire life in the construction of a great edifice whose completion may be generations away, so, too, the philosopher may be an unobtrusive workman in the construction of an outlook. As a craftsman serves best when he knows the purpose of the work as a whole, so, too, the philosopher serves best when he is not a naive accomplice but has a grasp of the entire enterprise. When one can see ideas with their implications spread out across history, one is positioned to judge and evaluate. One knows the time-tested, the certainties, which can be passed on with a degree of confidence. There is much in philosophy which has withstood the test of time. Thus the teacher can recommend with confidence classical texts and witness, with silent pleasure, the student responding with awe and appreciation to the reading of Plato, Aristotle, Boethius or Augustine.

A respect for the history of thought can yield a confidence in the fruit of the philosopher's present work. When contemporary inquiry duplicates ancient solutions the perennial or timeless character of philosophy is vividly evident. There is no law which compels the intellectual to be a revolutionary, in spite of frequent posturing which might suggest the opposite. If one is convinced that to have scientific knowledge is to understand "what is" by means of its causes and in the light of generic principles, then to master the "what is," to describe it accurately, to understand why it is that way and no other, to relate that knowledge to other and more general knowledge, is to have achieved scientific knowledge of the object in question. Perhaps one of the greatest failures of modern philosophy is the failure to perceive itself either as a science or as a wisdom. Philosophers have chosen to be reformers, skeptics, and, recently, conversationalists. But where the Greek view of intellect prevails, where nature is regarded as intelligible, and the human mind as powerful enough to ferret out the secrets of nature, a lofty view of philosophy can still prevail. As a science, philosophy is productive of wisdom. To say "wisdom" is to imply objective standards from which to judge.

To possess wisdom is to possess a particular frame of mind, namely the habit of viewing in the light of the most general principles or schema of reality. To approve, for example, of acts of self-discipline, both moral and intellectual, because of their long range beneficial effect on conduct, is to give evidence of an understanding of human nature and of the requirements for self-perfection. Theories of being or theories of reality determine one's understanding of human nature, and both, in turn, determine one's grasp of morality.

The Socratic search for wisdom requires a tripartite explanation: man is to know himself in relation to nature, to himself, and to the Divine. For Socrates these descriptions are not separated from one another. While there is a place for the piecemeal and detailed inquiry which characterize much day-to-day philosophical work, the technique of accomplishing that piecemeal analysis does not lead to an appreciation of philosophy itself. Something more fundamental is presupposed. That something is the kind of inquiry characteristic of Aristotle's *Physics* and *Metaphysics*.

Not surprisingly, when philosophy adheres to its ancient vocation, when it regards itself as the pursuit of wisdom and not as mere technique, it is not only true to itself but is most marketable in the contemporary college and university. Incorporated in the attitude recommended here is not only a respect for the history of thought but a recognition of the centrality of metaphysics. If one can be provincial in time as well as in place, one can be myopic in taking a special report for a general account.

There is another vice to which the English speaking seem particularly vulnerable. Many philosophers speak as if philosophy had not emerged in the Greek isles twenty-five centuries ago, but only in the twentieth century and in the English speaking world at that. Absence of linguistic ability is as much a curse as an ahistorical mind. The former is frequently the cause of the latter. To be steeped in the history of philosophy requires a mastery of classical and European languages. The sabbatical trip to English-speaking

Oxford frequently confirms previously adopted outlooks rather than opens one to alternative approaches.

If one begins with the Greeks, as I believe one should, one finds in classical texts not only a tested pedagogical tool but also a being-centered, not a knowledge-centered world. While the mind's capacity to know is taken for granted, a knowledge of nature is not. Nature is to be explored, to be systematically explained. Nature controls and directs inquiry. How inquiry is possible is itself a second-order question, a question not to be avoided, but nevertheless not a primary one. The other-directedness of the classical outlook can also serve as a much needed antidote to the subjective and inward looking propensities of the contemporary mind disposed to confuse the psychological with the ontological.

IV

There is perhaps no domain where these basic distinctions of classical learning are more needed than in the field of ethics. True, the twentieth century has made us conscious of a multiplicity of distinctions. Value theory abounds. If, in the middle decades of this century, philosophy was frequently presented as nothing more than symbolic logic or as an analysis of language, scientific or ordinary, this trend has been supplemented, if it has not given way, to another which attempts to make philosophy relevant by having it address the preoccupations of the day. We now have the rush to add ethics courses on environmental issues, animal rights, and obligations to future generations, as well as biomedical ethics, legal ethics, business ethics, and a score of other specialized inquiries.

Need attention be called to the ambiguity which surrounds the use of the term "value judgement"? The term is employed in many contexts and, even in a single context, it can have a plurality of meanings. As used in moral discourse, the term may connote a subjective prizing or, conversely, the recognition of an objective ontological structure. It may be used to designate persona preferences or to refer to social customs. It may suggest an ethical judgment or merely the preferences of the marketplace. It may mean the systematic study of what ought to be done. It may mark the culmination of a line of inquiry, such as the study of the family, and consist of the results of that line of inquiry: a series of do's and don'ts, or principles which might be considered a family ethic. These principles may even win common assent.

But the application of principles is another thing. A parent may well agree that certain do's and don'ts are solid principles and yet be unable to translate them into action. The parent may, in the prudential order, fail in the application of principles to which he subscribes. Failure is possible because two types of intelligence are involved. The derivation, enunciation, and defense of principle is one thing; the application of principle is another. The prudential decision is fraught with a contingency that does not characterize the generic moral principles.

The use of the word "values" to designate moral norms or a set of principles is of relatively recent origin. Contemporary usage is in fact foreign to the classical mind, and, perhaps, even to the modern mind. For the classical mind—and on this point Aristotle may be taken as typical—some things are prized in themselves, that is, as ends; other things are prized for their utility, that is, as means. That which is prized for itself is primarily responsible for the other prizing. Prizing is the recognition of worth. To evaluate is to take an ontological measure. Since men are fundamentally the same, they have fundamentally the same requirements and, therefore, will measure in fundamentally the same way. Alike in their common desire for happiness, men may sometimes differ about the means for the attainment of happiness, but there is, nevertheless, enough agreement about ends that there emerges a science which investigates and weighs materials as instruments for the achievement of those commonly recognized ends. Aristotle insisted that through systematic inquiry it is possible to determine what is best in both the order of ends and the order of means. The matter may not lend itself to specificity, but generic principles can be discerned.

General rules governing conduct may be enunciated because men have similar needs and achieve fulfillment in substantially the same way. But having acknowledged the role of principle, one must also recognize the individuality and precariousness of practical judgment. There are no rules respecting the application of rules. To judge in the light of principle is fraught with danger. One can be certain that the principles to which one adheres are objectively correct and yet be less than sure that one is doing the right thing. Many who emphasize the subjective do not in fact make the distinction between speculative and practical wisdom; they desire in the practical judgment a certitude which is not to be found, a certainty characteristic of the speculative alone, and then conclude that principles themselves are transient and subjective, arising only in the problematic situation.

Others who emphasize the subjective deny the ontological grounding of principle because they deny the reality of structures apart from the mind. In this view, things have no natures; rather, reality is a process. Inquiry creates the substances it deals with. Thus if there are not structures independent of the mind, there are no goods independent of the evaluative process, no objects which may be regarded as excellent in themselves. This outlook flatly contradicts the classical one that excellence follows being and, in making values subjective, tends to denigrate the inherited. It is often associated with Descartes who, with considerable justification, is called the father of modern philosophy.

Descartes called for the reform of the whole body of the sciences. All the vast accumulation of knowledge and tradition which was the heritage of European culture, all the ideas and beliefs which men acquire from experience and literature, and the contact with other minds were to be set aside as an impure and uncertain compound of truth and error, and to be replaced by a new knowledge of mathematical certitude which was derived from the infallible light of pure reason. This attitude of mind produced an extraordinary impression on the thought of an age. It was responsible for the formation of those abstract ideas—reason, science, and progress— which were enshrined by the Enlightenment. The West has yet to free itself from the Cartesian spell; vestiges remain. The contemporary academic mind typically places itself in an adversarial role, construing itself as a critic of the establishment, be it civil or religious, rather than a transmitter of a time-tested or classical heritage.

The neglect of the past is particularly dangerous in the realm of morality. For it is in the past alone, which displays values incarnate, thereby preventing a subscription to a romantic future where everything is a possibility. We have seen philosophers, cut off from the lessons of history, emphasize a bright future, belied by everything that has gone before. The possible world of the future is, in fact, an ideal world, not the real world with its limitations. An emphasis on progress, meaning a repudiation of the past, goes hand in hand with boundless hopes for the future. Those American philosophers who have played down the value of history have been the most extravagant in their praise of science and the world it is supposed to deliver. Viewing the history of science as a history of progress, they have emphasized change at the expense of permanence, uniqueness at the expense of a recognition of commonness, the here-and-now at the expense of the time-transcending.

If there is no concept of nature, human or otherwise, then everything is possible. If all values are determined in the situation, if there is nothing but prudence, then speculative wisdom is rightly ignored. But I am convinced, that the fundamental Aristotelian distinction between speculative and practical wisdom can be ignored only with peril. Speculative wisdom is carried in traditions. It is borne by principles honored in the homes, in the common education, and in the customs and rituals of a people. A close-knit group, bent on preserving itself in a larger heterogeneous society, instinctively stresses the importance of rite. Ethnicity requires attention and effort if it is to be preserved. Many rites may not be intrinsically important. But the unimportant has a way of adding up to a culture, to a way of life. Rites performed in the home, consciously or unconsciously, determine the attitudes of the young.

A further observation on decision making: the prudential judgment is made in a changing situation, but having acknowledged the importance of circumstance and the uniqueness of situations, a note must be added. In one sense, situations are unique, but in another sense, few situations are truly unique. They resemble each other. Thus the person with some experience, whether it be gained from previous similar encounters or gained by observing the behavior of others, directly or through history, is able to acquire a habit of right judgment. If in the early years of life or the early days on a job, the apprentice is in the company of people who consistently make good judgments (assuming a degree of reflection on his part) he will learn and habitually perform likewise. He will assume normalcy for his own good and for the good of the community.

Those common truths are worth mentioning because there has been a school which has denigrated the role of habit. Kant insisted that an act in order to be truly meritorious must be done not only in the line of duty but with proper motivation. The Kierkegaardians want every act to be made within the context of fear and trembling. Neither approach is speculatively warranted nor practically possible.

If it is good that a person perform a good act, it is better for that person to acquire a good habit. A good act is momentary and passing; a good habit is relatively permanent and is integral to the character of the person. Character is nothing more than the sum total of habits acquired over a lifetime. Habit disposes, facilitating a line of action deemed suitable. Habits can be bad as well as good; men can be vicious as well as virtuous. Both Plato and Aristotle gave considerable thought to the means of inculcating virtue in the young. A correct early education is recognized as all important because of its lasting effects.

Another problem, too large to explore here, but nevertheless one which demands attention in this context, is the role of authority in perpetuating a code or morality. Examining the mechanism by which values are transmitted, cultural history shows that Eastern vehicles of transmission are different from those which have served in the West. The contemporary failure to recognize the need for some vehicle assumes that each individual is capable of creating a morality for himself. If it sometimes takes a lifetime for the trained academic to establish a code of morality, it is unlikely that the manual laborer or office worker is apt to do so without some help. Appeals to community standards are often futile in a heterogeneous society. In the West, at least until recent decades, religion, particularly Christianity, provided an authoritative guide for the overwhelming majority of people, even if it sometimes spoke with a divided voice. But religion of late has been relegated to the church and to the home and has ceased to be an intellectual force in the life of the nation. In the East, Confucianism similarly supplied an outlook for large numbers of people. Both Christianity and

Confucianism have existed for millenia and they may continue to exercise an influence in the future. But the present, for both East and West, is a period of moral anarchy. Outside the Soviet bloc, few governments would dare promulgate a code of morality, though the many programs that governments endorse presuppose a moral outlook. Perhaps the only authority available is that of the classical tradition itself. There is a line of texts from Plato to Yves Simon which carries the best that man has thought about the good life and its pursuits, texts which, happily, are accessible to young minds even as they are perpetual fonts to which the trained return for refreshment. Through attention to those texts, the inherited, the permanent past, can become a standard against which the changes of the present can be measured. Learning is no substitute for personal moral behavior, but right action presupposes speculative wisdom which only the tutored mind is apt to possess.

Lest it be overlooked, I must add that the tutored mind is not simply a metaphysical or a past-oriented mind. The tutored mind is conscious of inheritance, but it is also a mind aware of possibilities, possibilities presented largely through a knowledge of science and technology. From Hesiod to John Dewey, the West has been convinced that material progress is possible, as one generation builds upon the accomplishments of another, appropriating ancestral insight and art. Lately that faith in the power of reason has been challenged by those who speak of the limits of scientific inquiry and the end of progress. But is it confidence in the intellect that has been shaken? Is it not, rather, that we have become dramatically aware that science and technology divorced from moral control can be used most inhumanely. Aristotle remarked that man is the only animal who can become through his choices less than he is by nature. A pumpkin can never be less than a pumpkin, but a man can be less than a man. The problem presented by science and technology is not so much a cognitive problem as it is a moral problem. Improvements in material life do not entail moral advancement. Yet the type of reflection recommended here is not directed solely to an examination of the structure of the free will act and the metaphysical roots of moral norms. The instruments of action must also be examined. Thus it is not inappropriate in a volume devoted to the good life and its pursuit to find discussions of the nature of science and technology and of the criteria and strategy by which the sciences proceed to their conclusions. The role of technology in the achievement of personal and social goals, while not primary, is too real to be ignored. Discussions of the common good most certainly rely on a knowledge of concrete possibilities which only the sciences can give.

The tutored mind must run on all five cylinders, virtues identified by the Greeks long ago. It must be at once a mind governed by the habits of understanding, science and wisdom and also of art and prudence.

PART ONE

THE QUEST FOR HAPPINESS

1

HAPPINESS AND THE GOOD LIFE

IRWIN C. LIEB

I

This paper orders and comments on some notes on the theme that a good life is, or ought to be, happy, because there would be an injustice if it were not. There have been many formulations and discussions of this theme. Some of them are broad and cosmological; some are ethical and formal; some are personal and poignant. There is, for example, Anaximander's notion that the opposites repair their injustices to one another in due season and Kant's argument that we can hope that a good person's desire to be happy will be fulfilled; there are the stories of Job and Dostoyevski, and the histories of martyrs and victims who have suffered and sacrificed their lives. The common theme in these formulations is that the universe is or should be ordered so that the deep desires of good persons shall not be unfulfilled. The notions which are most important for this theme are the notions of human nature, the contingency of the satisfaction of human desires, and the idea of an agency which can affect the contingency of what occurs or otherwise assure us that there will be conditions under which persons will be fulfilled.

This theme is so deep in thoughtful feeling that it, or something like it, is sure to be true. Our deepest thoughts and feelings cannot be separated from the world which has made our minds and sensibility. Still, the theme is general and indefinite, and many specific formulations of it are neither sound nor good spirited. What soils many of them is a note of commerce, contract or exchange, as if there were an implied agreement that if we live in certain ways, we will get what we want most in return. Something of this note remains even if we do not choose to make our lives good just because we want our desires satisfied. The note then is that our desires ought to be satisfied, if not because we are deserving, then as fitting bounty and blessing. The basis of the commercial note is the fact that our actions are means to ends, either our own ends or the ends of others, or both. The questions, therefore, are: whether we can take account of the fact that our actions are means, without becoming crass about the principle that good persons ought to have their lives fulfilled; and whether we can account for the pain and other unhappiness which has often occurred in the lives of persons who are good. The answers to these questions depend on our understanding the means and ends of action and the notion of a fulfilled life. The crucial issue in understanding them is understanding the difference between what constitutes a life and is inside of it, and what conditions a life and is outside of it.

II

In all our actions we aim at something. Usually, we aim to do two sorts of things. First, we seek to form the action itself and, second, we try to have our action become part of the occasion for there being consequences which we also intend or hope to have come about. These two are often considered together and rightly so, for our notion of competence in action is that we shall not only know how to do what we want to do, but also shall know, intend and approve the consequences of our actions. When it is important for us to distinguish between our action and its consequences, the distinction is usually between our agency and the agency of others. Our action is what we do, and the consequences of our actions are what others do because of us. It is only in certain kinds of cases that we are responsible for what others do; it is only using suppositions about agency that the actions of others are also ours.

The distinction between our agency and the agencies of others need not lead to a narrow conception of action, or to a conception of a narrow life. We needn't, for example, think that all we can do is will, want, or desire, making our motive or intention the only thing that can be good in our action. Our actions can be more overt than deciding or willing and still be owed to our agency, even when they involve other things and other persons who have agencies of their own. The conception of action we need, then, is one in which we are agents throughout. We are not to see ourselves as persons who start an action and have it go its way, moved by our causal push. We are not the cause for which our action is an effect, different from ourselves. Instead, we are engaged in our actions through the whole of what we do. We are not behind them or under them; we are in them as we produce them and thereby continue ourselves.

A general summary of this Leibnizian conception is that we make our own lives and that the fulfillment or lack of fulfillment which occurs within them is owed to our own causality. Our lives occur of course in circumstances which are not all of our own making. There are contingencies in the world around us and in our lives as well. But the question whether our lives are good or fulfilled or not is a question of our agency and not of the circumstances under which our lives are constructed, or even of the contingencies which occur within them.

Aristotle, I think, takes a similar view and examples which may be persuasive can be drawn from his texts. When Aristotle considered whether we can ever be assured that a living man is happy, he asked whether one can be happy if he is poor or ill, or if some calamity befalls him or his children. His answer is that in such circumstances one man might be happy and another not. The examples make emphatic a distinction between our lives and the circumstances in which our lives are constructed. They suggest to me that often, perhaps always, when we talk about what will make us happy we are talking about the circumstances which surround our lives and which enable, encourage and help to sustain us in the lives we decide to lead. What will make us happy or what we require for our happiness is matched to the kinds of lives we think we have. In citing our requirements, it is as if we were saying that we could not or would not lead certain kinds of lives unless there were certain conditions about us in which we could take certain satisfactions. The examples also suggest that when we talk about deserving certain things, we are thinking that, depending on how persons make their lives, the circumstances of their lives should be such as to provide them with what they want.

The reflection which follows on these examples, and which may seem to some of you harsh, is that a good life is defined from the inside out. Constructing and conducting such a life requires of course contexts of circumstance. But the fulfillment of our lives depends on what is inside of them and on what comes out of them through our own agency. Concerned for such fulfillment, we would be misguided in thinking that others or the world at large can provide anything material to our lives. We would be misguided to think that we deserve anything because of the lives we live. A good life is defined from inside of it, and it is as good as a life can be. Any other good that comes into it does not make the life more fulfilling or fulfilled, though it may make it more pleasant and satisfy some of our desires.

To develop this conception of a life lived from the inside and to remove some of the seeming austerity of the conception, two issues should be discussed—what place the desires whose dissatisfaction would test and strain us have in the conduct of our lives, and how a life that might be good is itself defined.

III

In the theories of human action which call for a demanding structure for our lives and which also suppose that we have a claim to have some of our desires satisfied, our nature is thought to have two parts; one part is subject to the demanding call for definition, and the other is the seat of rational desires. Of course, the two are thought somehow to be connected so that it is then thought that if we are, through one part, responsive to the requirements on life, some of the deep desires of the other part deserve to be satisfied as well. Why? Because the desires are founded in our nature and are not gratuitous, and because the call to define our lives is not a desire of ours. It is a requirement. What requires it therefore, or what we may hope has an interest in the requirement, will dispose circumstances so that our desires will be satisfied. And why should that be so? Because it would be unfair or unjust if those who define their lives suitably are—perhaps because of doing so—deprived of the satisfaction of their reasonable desires, especially if those desires are, even if contingently, satisfied in persons who do not define their lives as they are called upon to do.

This petition for justice or fairness is profound. It recognizes, as any sound account of good and satisfaction should, that the basis of obligation is not desire, or the kind of desire whose urgency can be quieted. It also recognizes that we nevertheless have needs, urgent wants and reasonable desires, and that it is as whole persons, and not in one or the other of the parts of us, that we are to be fulfilled. Still, the petition seems to me misconceived, because it divides us into parts, each of which has separately to be responsive to distinct demands, and then it hopes, and without reason, that there is something apart from us which has an interest in one of the demands and which is also powerful enough and fair enough to see to some satisfaction for the other.

It is a mistake, however, to think that if we were so divided we could nevertheless be a single being, capable of agency in single actions and in a single life. It is also a mistake to misconstrue the contingencies of the world by supposing that some of them need not be contingencies because something might assuredly determine what they will be. A theory of action which divided us so and then hopes for an adjustment of the circumstances in which we act tampers with human agency, with the outcome of action, and mixes up assurances and chance. It would be sounder to hold that we are single, undivided beings but that we can seem to be divided because our actions are like vectors which resolve the fact that, as we act, we have to address the different aspects, the different realities which are the enduring contexts of the world. These aspects, these realities help, as we will see, to define a kind of life. They can help us first, however, to locate the supporting and unsettling ways in which desires are part of our lives.

It is obvious and often noted that there are grades of desire, or grades leading to desire. These are called needs and wants; so thus, there are needs and wants and then desires. The three are distinguished in several ways. They are like items in a matrix which has a number of coordinates; they are located at different places along different defining lines. We can note, for example, what sorts of items are needed all the time or repeatedly, and those which are called for or may be called for only now and then. We can also locate items as being more or less general, so that some may be satisfied in any number of ways while others call for very specific satisfactions. Then too, we can locate items on a coordinate which goes from our natural selves to the selves which we try to construct in answer to our conceptions of ourselves. Some items then are needed or wanted in order for us to be or to continue to be, while others, further along the line, are wanted or desired as we are or are becoming the persons we conceived ourselves to be. Parallel to this line there is another line, on which we locate the agencies which can or should respond to our needs, wants and desires— nature or the world at large for our need, institutions or institu- tionalized persons for needs, wants and some desires, and then specific individuals, mated to desires for which only they can provide our satisfaction. There are perhaps other coordinates which it would be useful to draw. But even these show some interesting points about needs, wants and desires and their place within our lives.

An array of needs, wants and desires, along the coordinates I have mentioned, would make clear the major differences between them, in what they are in themselves, in the order of their occurrence, bearing and importance, and in the calls we make upon others for their satisfaction. Each and all of them show our insufficiency and contingency, and yet all also show that we are capable of acting and that we may even develop desires about the ways in which our needs and wants are to be satisfied. We may therefore try to think of the lives we can construct which will lead to the satisfaction of some or many of them, and to think, as well, of the kinds of persons we are, desiring as we do the satisfaction of our array of wants and desires.

There are, I am sure, many close and intricate connections between our having desires and our being persons who are not only alive but who shape and direct our lives. The most general connection we should notice is that many persons suppose that, in a life directed by rational desires, we are well advised to respond to the urgent immediacies of need and want within our interest and in satisfying those desires of longer range which arise from the gentler aspirations of our minds. Many persons, that is, think that we should respond to immediate need out of our concern that other needs and wants shall also be satisfied; we try then to civilize our needs and invest in our response to them the constancy of the responses we are also making to the continuing desires of life.

All this seems fine and almost ideal, and it is: it is the art of measurement which Socrates contrived in an argument against Protagoras. It is an elevated and sensible utilitarianism, but it is not sound for a reason which can be expressed in either of two ways, from one or the other of two points of view. In one formulation, the reason is that the stabilizing, long, continuing and cultivated desires which are thought to structure and civilize life are so unlike desires, they are so different from desires, that it is a contrivance to think that they are continuous with our natural needs and wants; it is also a contrivance to think that if they were refinements of our native animation, they would have any normative authority for the construction of our lives. The second and stronger formulation is simply that a life which we can have is not directed to the satisfactions of needs, wants and desires; a life that we can have is not an ingenious plan to satisfy some maximal number and attractive array of needs, wants and desires. It is not that such a life does not aim to satisfy them. It is aimed to do something else instead, and to satisfy needs, wants and desires incidentally, in the course of doing what we aim to do. It is not true, of course, that what we aim to do is incompatible or even uncongenial to satisfying our wants, nor

is it true that what we can aim to do is not focused through our
wants and enriched by their satisfaction. What is true is that the
structuring, animating aim of life is not an object of desire: we can
make our own lives but we cannot yield for ourselves the satisfaction
of our insufficiencies. The structuring, animating aim of life has
therefore to be defined for us by a reality apart from us. It does
not derive from the spring of life itself; it is derived from realities
apart from us, realities with which we are inescapably involved,
and toward which, in a life that we possess, we take our aim and
thereby have our lives.

It remains, of course, to say how a life that we can commend
can be defined. There is one kind of important objection, though,
which should be considered briefly before providing an outline of
the construction. The objection is that if what defines a life is not
itself desired, if it is not based in the springs from which we act, it
will be something outside of us entirely, without a purchase on the
natural direction of our energies. The only means, then, of making
something so alien into an aim of ours would be to have it imposed
on us, and perhaps with sanctions, so that we would be coerced to
have an aim which does not derive from our natures and which we
have to take as our own, not freely, or perhaps not for commendable
reasons.

The themes in this objection are, of course, those which
were considered by Kant when he thought about the possible
heteronomy of the demand of duty. The resolution which he offered
for them was that there is a second and distinct self and that it is
drawn to the injunction of duty by the admirability of duty. In this
profound resolution, the difficulty is again that there are two selves,
not one. One self aims at the satisfaction of its needs, wants and
desires, while the other is motivated by its image of a moral
principle. Unfortunately, there can be no communion and no
consonance in the activity of these two selves; they do not and
cannot coincide.

There is no easy adjustment of the picture which is
presented to us in this objection, because even though the picture
is too focused and too sharp, something like the notes and distinctions
which are made in it should indeed be drawn. The best course in

altering the picture, perhaps, is to see that, mistakenly, the picture represents us as engaged in single actions, in actions one by one, as if we were not already acting in the world, and as if each action came out from inside of us because of an inner motive and that each projected an outer aim. The fundamental mistake in the picture, then, is that it is not a picture of us as engaged in a continuing and active life; it is a picture of actions which are so distinctively and separately motivated that they cannot be actions in the world.

The change in the picture which I think we should make is to see ourselves as always engaged inwardly and outwardly; we are not at each moment wholly inside ourselves and apart from things, and we do not then make fresh entry into the world by an odd combination of motivation and causality. We are always in the world in which we act, continuing our activity, though there is always something of us inside and in reserve. The problem of acting and living a fulfilling life is to make action out of the activity of our aliveness, or to make our aliveness into a life.

The world in which we live is not a sheaf of transience. Enduring realities define its stabilities, its equalities, its ongoingness and its unity as a world. We have no alternative, if we are to act, but to take account of these realities. It is as we do this that we construct our lives, though the realities do not prescribe in definite principles how exactly we are to live. Even so, as having selves, we cannot avoid the construction of a life. The great trick which the world can play on us is that if we try thoughtfully to plan to enjoy and satisfy the vitalities of our being alive over an indefinite period of time, we may also have a good and fulfilling life; the poignancy of the world can be that we can have a good and fulfilling life which is not filled with the satisfaction of our vitalities.

This substitute picture acknowledges that there is something given which we have to take account of in the construction of our lives. To define a life is, again, not simply to plan on satisfying our needs, wants and desires, as these may happen to arise. The substitute picture notes that the realities which define a life are already, or have already, been taken into account by us when we think how to construct our lives. There is no question of our being thoughtful and our having then to have a separate motivation for acting thoughtfully. The disputed distinction between two selves, then, is paralleled in the new picture by the distinction between being alive and having lives, and the parallel to the imperative for morality is the realities which structure both us and the world in which we act. There is no strong comparison, however, between the definite directive principle for the morality of a single act and the principle upon which a fulfilling life is made. That is because a life in the making is fuller than a single act, and because it has no single maxim.

IV

How should we understand the construction of a life? By a life, I mean directing our aliveness into action. None of us, then, strictly has or can have a life, for we go from aliveness to direction and back again. More loosely but still usefully, though, we think of our having a life, even when there are times when we are merely alive, if our undirected vitalities are encased or bordered or are to be followed by periods of direction. There are of course many conditions for having a life, and there are many conditions on the lives we have. The condition on our having a life which is most important for our discussion is having a comprehensive aim, and the note which is most important about having a comprehensive aim is that it is defined by a basic reality. We have of course to have specific aims in singular actions; we want to do this or that; we aim to act in a certain way. But even in single actions, we cannot be without a comprehensive aim, because the configurations of actions, the extensiveness, the bordering, the unity and the comparability of actions are fixed by basic realities. When we act we adjust to them, and action as action is directed, more or less knowingly, by our acknowledgment of them.

    This notion, this outline, is a familiar one. Many thinkers

have held that our lives are directed toward a fundamental reality, and because of the bearing of that reality on everything else, we take account of everything else in a certain way. The prevailing rendition of this tradition is that there is a single reality and that our aim is directed toward it and, in the light of it, thereby toward all the less fundamental and derivative, contingent realities. So, for example, Jewish, Christian and Moslem theologies have held that God is the fundamental reality, that he is the Creator of everything, including what is contingent, and that we take proper account of Him and of everything else when we do His will in the world. Plato supposed that we aim at the Good in all our actions, and that the Good illuminates the nature and value of all we specifically do. Aristotle thought that because of our natures, and within their limits, we imitate the Unmoved Mover. For other thinkers, there are different single, fundamental realities. The structure of all these accounts is formally much the same, including the dependence on the fundamental realities of the being of what is contingent in the world. The differences in the accounts are mainly in conceptions of what we are, on how we are dependent on or otherwise necessarily affiliated with the fundamental reality, and on the fields of its action and our own. The basic reality serves as our aim as we try to be or act like it, as we try to do what it enjoins us to do or judges what we do. Having to have such an aim and having it reflectively or self-consciously, then, has nothing to do with having to satisfy the wants and desires we may come to have for this or that, beyond those that are necessary for our lives themselves.

This formal scheme of having to take account of a polar reality is, I think, inescapable. My own view is that there is not one fundamental reality—that the supposition of one is not ample enough to explain or account for the necessary features of the world and for its contingencies—but that there are four equally final realities, God being one of them. The supposition of there being more than one such reality, however, does not change the formal scheme we have been talking about. If there are two or more such realities, they have to be together and have, with derivative realities, to constitute the world. It must be the case then that each and all of them provide access to the other finalities and to everything else—so that there can be different kinds of lives focused on and through one or another of the realities; all the lives will be equal in standing and all can be equally fulfilling or unfulfilling.

For any single kind of life, or for any of the kinds of the lives that there might be, we have the kind of life that we do because we take account of the bearing upon us of the basic realities, and because we try to construct actions in which the subordinate or supervening unities, provided by these realities, order by type the contingencies within our actions themselves. The contingency of actions is what the filling for actions will be, and it is also in the effect of our agency on the necessities and in their effects upon us. There have to be contingencies because things like us have agency. The contingencies are not altogether controlled by the necessities. Though one or another of the necessities might constrain our agency, contingency cannot be entirely removed.

We live outward in our agency, and our lives are ours in the measure in which our vitalities are controlled, in the measure in which they are directed. Our control of them, our direction of them, is qualified by the attention we also give to the actual and probable effects on us of the contingent companions of our activity. These may cause pleasure for us or not, and they may or may not cause us to change the pace or even redirect the immediate aim of our action. But even so, so long as we possess our lives, we cannot help but try to create inside of them the unities which the necessities, as independent of us, impose upon our lives. We try, that is, so far as we can, to make what is outside of us inside our lives as well, and in all our actions, our effort to do this can always be better.

There is no assurance, and there is no final measure, that we have ever acted as well as we might have, that we have done all that we could have done. Because of being constructed, because of the contingencies in them, our lives cannot contain within themselves the unities of the necessities themselves. The cosmos alone is large enough to contain them as distinct and outside one another. Our incorporation of them in an action and in our lives subordinates them to one another. There can be no perfection in the small. The world is against us—but that is what it is, for it to be a world.

We may, we often do, yearn for a small and simple theater in which to act, in which all that can occur is under our control. There, we think, we can act so well that we could not have acted in any better way. We can also imagine or remember times so filled with torment and constraint that there seemed no possibility of action or worth or dignity. No matter how constructed or constrained, however, no world removes the generality which enters into action, so that we could not have acted better than we did. There is no sharply lined limitation on our abilities. And the sight that we could have acted better is the sight and affirmation that we have our lives and can shape them. He who says that he could not have done better acknowledges that his action has been at a point coerced, that what comes into it has, at a point, forced him to respond. The issue is not small: it is about shaping into action whatever comes within the ken of life; it is about the fact that no matter the weight or even the brutality of what enters our lives, so long as we have our lives, we can also act.

What is poignant for us, then, is that no matter how we try, we always could have acted better than we did. We can therefore never be completely satisfied. We always could ask more of ourselves, or something different from ourselves. That, however, does not mean that what we have done is without value, or that there are no conditions under which we deserve good or support. The arena of deserving, however, is among our fellow human beings, and only then within the domain of actions directed to a specific, common aim. We deserve commendation or blame, we are justified in having expectations about what others will do, only as we and they are concerned to do something together. Thus we always should or we never should treat a friend, a wife, a colleague or a person in a certain way. We have no covenant with the basic realities, however, and there is no deserving in connection with them and with their defining our lives. We are, for example, not covenanted with God in a common aim for an important good. There is therefore no deserving between man and God. Deserving occurs within the arenas of specifically directed actions. The basic realities define the arenas but are not participants along with us in the construction of specific actions; there is nothing that they and we together try to do, and there is no insufficiency in them that we can complete.

It is necessary that there be contingencies, but there is no necessity for there being the contingencies that there are. Our needs, wants and desires are evidence that we are contingent and dependent beings. They may or may not be satisfied through the sufferance of the world, through the interest and agency of others, or through our arranging that the world shall satisfy us. However, the satisfaction of our insufficiencies cannot be our aim. We can only aim at what we can do. Even when our aims are specifically directed to doing what we hope will have the consequence of satisfying our desires, we aim beyond those moments, and we have no final assurance that what we hope will occur will occur in fact, even if we discipline our wants and desires and make them fitting to our final aim. The world may not satisfy us even if we do not ask for much.

The fulfillment of our lives, then, so far as we have them, cannot depend on our getting what we want. It must therefore depend on how we have our lives and on the use we make of them, and that will be in the full use of our lives, directing all that we have of them toward the only realities at which we can finally aim. In such an aim, however, we never can succeed—saints torment themselves with their sinfulness, and there is no redemption for a failure. Still, lives that are lived in such fullness are as full as lives can be. The fullness they have is a measure of what comes out of them; it is not a measure of what comes into them from something else, and there are no goods that can be added to them as goods which we deserve. The common and familiar sense that good lives are fulfilled is therefore sound—but not sound as a doctrine of lives filled with good and satisfying things which have been bestowed on us. Good lives are good as lives, full of life as being ours, and they may or may not contain much that persons who do not have those lives think of as being good. This doctrine is stark and stands in patience even to malicious agency and the harsh strokes of other contingencies. Nevertheless, it seems to me true; specifically, in summary, it seems to be true to hold that:

(1) Our needs, wants and desires testify to our contingency and insufficiency.

(2) All we can do is, of course, done through our own agency.

(3) Therefore, we cannot, of ourselves, satisfy our own needs, wants and desires, though we may act on other things to see that some of what we need is provided for us.

(4) Whether or not our insufficiencies are satisfied depends on the nature of the things we act upon and the agencies of others. These agencies may or may not be directed in our behalf, and it is only in the limited circumstances of shared ends that we deserve the attention and support of other agencies.

(5) Therefore, so far as our lives are possessed and directed by us, they cannot be aimed at the satisfaction of our needs, wants and desires. When they are dominated by these, we are searching, petitioning vitalities and our aliveness is not directed by us; without directing our aliveness, we do not have our lives.

(6) Having a life, directing one, is aiming to deal with everything that comes within our ken in the light of basic, necessary realities. Formally, it is to incorporate in what we do the kinds of unities that the realities, as pertinent to us, possess and provide. Satisfying our needs, wants and desires occurs, when it does, in the course of directing our vitalities into actions and our actions into lives.

(7) Taking account of the basic realities is not an imposition upon us or our lives. It is a condition of having our lives; that is, directing them to the degree that we have them. The Platonic version of this thesis is that he who knows the Good will do it.

(8) We cannot succeed in doing all we should; we never altogether succeed in possessing our lives. This, however, is not the reason we do not ultimately deserve to have our needs, wants and desires satisfied. The reason is that there is no deserving between us and the basic realities; we and they are not aimed together at a still more comprehensive and common end.

(9) The fulfillment of lives, however, does not consist in having good things intrude on our lives, as if these things were to

fill them up. We have no control of what intrudes on us, not even the basic realities control the intrusion upon us of contingent things.

(10) Our fulfillment consists instead in the full control of our lives and in their full expenditure in acting so as to take account of everything. Fulfillment, therefore, depends upon ourselves. And if that is so, we can fulfill ourselves in the best of worlds, and could do so in even the worst of them.

2

WHAT IS HAPPINESS?

NINIAN SMART

A weakness of utilitarianism, as classically expressed in modern Western philosophy, is that the concepts of happiness and its converses, unhappiness and suffering, are not very subtly analyzed. Since our culture in the West is largely utilitarian in its actual ethos, this is a defect which ought to be remedied. Moreover, analysis will reveal an ironic fact: that it is not possible to put morals (or economics, etc.) on a scientific basis without turning up a question of criticism. Or to put it in another way: the pursuit of analysis will point to value questions which inevitably arise about what true happiness may consist of, and, conversely, true suffering and unhappiness.

Still, the first thing to be done is to be cool in trying to reveal the lineaments of happiness as it is seen through the glass of language. Such portraiture will help to clarify our thinking and perhaps our ambitions. Thus I shall begin with the analytic task. I shall begin in a most elementary and basic manner, because the concepts we wield are so familiar, so close to us, that, like our eyelashes, we rarely see them. And it is easiest to see them in a mirror.

First, what or who can be happy? Primarily persons are happy. Animals we sometimes think of as happy or unhappy. By some analogy we can speak of arrangements as being happy, or events. "When is the happy event due?" we enquire of the pregnant mother. We suppose that the arrival of the child will be happy-making, and likewise a happy arrangement which in some sense or other makes the parties to it happy. But primarily it is persons who are happy or unhappy.

It always seems to make sense to ask "Why is he happy?" "Why is he so happy?" or "Why is he unhappy?" and so forth. Incidentally we may note here that happiness seems to be a matter of degrees, though like some other degree concepts you can be perfectly happy, or so it is said. This means, I presume, that there is nothing more in that connection which you would wish to have or do. There is then a notion of "enough" and a notion of "supreme" (supremely happy persons are roughly speaking perfectly happy, though maybe the converse might not be the case).

The question "Why?" brings us to the question of intentionality. For when we ask why someone is happy, we mean roughly, "What is it that makes him happy?" This in turn usually means "What event or situation is it that makes him happy?" Conversely we say, "he is so happy because his son has just come home after all those years," or "he is happy because he has just signed a contract with a publisher for his novel," or "he is unhappy because the doctors have just told him that he has to undergo chemotherapy."

Of course there is a funny or not so funny sense of "happy" meaning roughly "drunk." A person has the mood of happiness, but the reason has to do with the state of his bloodstream and brain: it will wear off in the morning, when, so to say, the person returns to reality. Alcohol can produce the mood, but not the realities of what makes a person happy.

It is partly a matter of mood. Perhaps it is also a matter of illusions. After all, the fact that happiness has a focus—the event or state of affairs which brings about happiness, at least on a short term basis—means that you can be genuinely happy because you have the wrong information. A woman may be happy because she hears, but hears, erroneously, that her son is coming home after many years away. Drugs often produce illusions about one's powers and the like, so a drunk person may be rationally happy about some achievement but wrong about the achievement. Thus we can speak of artificiality of mood and illusion about the object—two different causes of short-term distortion concerning happiness. It is like fear. If I confront a horrifying monster it is reasonable enough for me to be afraid. But it may be that the monster is unreal, perhaps an illusion induced by some drug. Conversely, after having an adrenalin injection, I may have great sensations of fear, but no object to pin my feelings upon. One is a distortion of mood, the other is a distortion of object. Both are intimately bound together, because feelings and dispositions to have feelings are coordinated in the normal and well-trained person to proper objects of those feelings.

So far then we can say that happiness is a matter of degrees—it can be more or less intense; that happiness involves an object or circumstance (or set thereof); and that there is at first sight a proper or normal kind of response to those objects.

I have spoken of events and circumstances as reasons or objects which make a person happy or unhappy. As for circumstances, the most important and typical may be work and marriage. Thus a person may be happy or unhappy in his job, or happily or unhappily married. Typically such judgments imply a long-term disposition. It is a bit of a paradox to say that a person is happy in his job but only spasmodically, or for one hour a week. But there are unusual situations which could make such statements intelligible. Again it would be odd to say that two people were happily married for the first few hours of their marriage. We normally mean by "happily married" that the persons in question have been together over a reasonably long period.

Such senses of happiness can be called "contextual," and they are typically dispositional. So we may judge that happiness is often of this sort. It may be that happiness *tout court*, which represents a judgment on a person's whole life or at least his life up to now, or a stretch of it, is in a wide sense contextual. A person is happy with his life, as distinguished from his marriage or his work. But it is obvious that for most people it is not possible to be happy in general if one is unhappy in something so central as work or marriage. This is perhaps why we think of integration as being important, for in part it is shorthand for a certain harmony between important aspects of one's life—family life, work and so forth. Someone who is happy in his work but yet the work interferes with the happiness of his marriage is courting a serious lack of integration in this sense.

I have so far supposed that there are reasons or contexts for happiness. The question "What makes him happy?" has as an answer the outlining of such reasons. But is it possible to be happy for no reason at all? Is it possible just to wake up feeling happy but without knowing what it is if anything which makes one happy? I think our notion of happiness can embrace this—does embrace this indeed. But yet subtly there is a pleasing, satisfying context. It is hard to conceive of a situation where a person wakes up happy and then slowly begins to be aware that his dear, dear wife died the day before, that he was arrested overnight for drunkenness and so on. It is true he may be just waking up from a blissful dream. After all the subconscious mechanisms of a person's mind might restore the beloved in sleep. Still, it is here of course another case of context: The happy feeling as the person wakes up is after all related to an object, a context. Still, there may be a sort of *joie de vivre* which makes a person happy without any specific object or context being present to him. Let us for the sake of distinctions call this sort of object-less joy *bliss*. The question "Why is he blissful?" perhaps nudges us in the direction of causes rather than reasons— say some substance rather than some context which brings about bliss.

It is, incidentally, true that sometimes the feeling of bliss is ascribed a central role in religious experience. The bliss of the mystic may lie at the heart of the ineffable. Such intensity and refinement of feeling is not itself context-less. So one must note that the cause-reason distinction does not tell us everything. Also, there are, of course, different sorts of bliss. But for the moment let us neglect all that and think of bliss as a short-term feeling which for the purposes of this argument is object-less.

So far we have analyzed happiness as object- or context-oriented. It is also most typically dispositional and long-term in character where the context is broad, as in marriage or work, or general, as when one is speaking of happiness *tout court*. Much of philosophy has been concerned with this last sense: what after all is it that makes a person happy? Is it true that we can call no man happy til he be dead—for the judgment about happiness should in principle be a judgment about a whole life?

Now here, of course, we immediately meet with the thought that one man's meat is another man's poison: that surely the ingredients of happiness must vary from person to person. Even so, some generalizations may be possible, for two reasons. The first is that human nature in regard to vital motifs in life is somewhat similar from individual to individual and from culture to culture. All people have sooner or later to die. Sex, for example, is a vital ingredient of personal living. Cruelty brings suffering through torture, deprivation, humiliation, insult—and if insults vary from culture to culture, and hurts may depend on individual circumstance, still they have an organic similarity. So, first there is a certain standardness of human psychology and response. Second, even where there may be variation in a person's tastes, circumstances, hopes and fears, we can make a distinction between form and content. Thus it may be thought a good and satisfying thing that a person should develop and exercise his talents. What those talents are depends on the individual. So we can accept the formal recipe "develop a person's talents" as an educational prescription, but note the variations and particularities of content.

Does this imply then that it would be possible to write a standard book on how to be happy—*Teach Yourself Happiness*, let us say? Maybe there would be merit in such an exercise, in the sense that people could be led to analyze the objects and contexts of their happiness in a realistic way and so develop strategies of action which would be more likely to conduce to happiness. But of course we are inclined to smirk a bit at the thought of *Teach Yourself Happiness*. Why the smile? I think one reason is that we know very well that happiness is not to be directly aimed at. It is like the case of Zen in the art of archery. It is a matter of hitting the target without aiming.

The point here is at least twofold. On the one hand, one cannot pursue happiness directly. One can only aim at happiness-creating ends, the objects and circumstances which are reasons for happiness. And then in any case they may not quite seem so felicity-inducing as might have been expected. So first the pursuit of happiness is at best indirect. On the other hand, happiness is a matter of happenstance. That is, one needs a certain degree of good fortune. Thus though you may in fact expect great happiness from the fact that you are about to marry the person whom you would love to marry, you cannot protect yourself from disaster: he may die in a year, or his character may not be as you thought it was, and he may change in unanticipated ways. So there are reasons why you cannot quite teach yourself happiness. You have to pursue it at best indirectly. Then you need fortune. It is not totally in human control.

Also there are complications at the individual level. Thus you may pursue avidly those things that you think will bring you happiness. But this becomes essentially a selfish enterprise. This being so you may come to lose friends, and the respect and love of other people. So it would seem that happiness itself contains, so to speak, traps. It lures you on, but if it lures you too much, it must evade your grasp.

Our remarks so far, however, already suggest something about politics and economics. In so far as public policy ought to aim at improving the quality of life, as we say (and this in part means, one hopes, increasing happiness or at least diminishing unhappiness), then the indirectness of happiness—the logic of its object and context orientation—means that the maximization of happiness as a goal is merely a formal one: materially, policies should aim at those institutions which increase felicity and at those forms of production that facilitate ends that typically bring happiness or diminish unhappiness. This is the argument for wealth, that it multiplies possibilities for men and women to gain what they wish to gain without the grinding poverty and hazards which bring in their train all those obstacles to felicity which mankind knows so well. For various reasons the removal of evils is easier than the promotion of goods.

This is the argument for negative utilitarianism, namely the view that policy should aim at the diminution of suffering rather than the maximization of happiness. Though in this form the policy cannot be ultimately defended philosophically (doomsday by destroying all humans in the twinkling of an eye would diminish suffering, wipe it out in fact, but we would scarcely commend it as a political aim), it does point to an important fact: that suffering is more easily identifiable and obstacles to happiness are more basic. Thus we all agree about cruelty as an evil, but are less clear about the worth of toys, however joy-making they may be to children. And if a person suffers from a painful and debilitating disease it cuts off all possible achievements and constitutes, in the main, an obstacle to all forms of happiness. So, as a rule of thumb, there is something to be said for the precept "try to remove clear evils rather than to promote debatable goods."

But it may be thought here that it is possible to attain a sort of happiness even under the most painful adversities. In fact, if faced with the right heroism and spirits, pain itself may be an ennobling thing, and it may gain a kind of positive value (often, though, it is difficult or impossible for a given individual to face pain with the right heroism and spirit). Of course, this does not mean we should encourage suffering in order to multiply chances of such nobility. But the possibility of such nobility ought to be taken seriously for a special reason.

It gives emphasis to an aspect of the dictum, regarding happiness, that one man's meat may be another's poison. Or rather it may illustrate the converse: one person's poison becoming another's meat. For it shows that not only is it important to look upon the objects and contexts which make a person happy or unhappy in the light of normal human reactions (whatever they are, for much will be culturally determined). We must also look upon the objects and contexts of a person's moods and feelings in the light of how he regards them. Thus a worldview or a particular chain of circumstances may alter the perspective of the agent. The giving up of material things by the monk or the yogi may be seen by him in the context of devotion to God or to the quest for realization. For him these may yield the highest sort of happiness, different from worldly happiness. Again, a particular sequence of events may seem to a person to be his destiny, and this already makes a difference in their meaning for him.

Thus we may see a certain hierarchy at work. Above the objects and contexts as seen from a common sense perspective lies another layer of meaning.

It is because of this that the possibility of the criticism of common sense ideas of happiness can be undertaken. Or to put it another way: there are more, and there are less, profound ways of estimating the values which make persons happy. We sometimes through deeper experience come to see the shallowness of what we earlier took for happpy times or circumstances. It is possibly "I thought I was happy but I did not really know what real happiness was like." Real happiness is not just here more intense happiness, but happiness as it were within a differing perspective, rooted in other objects, other circumstances.

It is typical of religion, whether it be a traditional one, or one of the secular quasi-religions, to proffer a critique of the common sense world— to offer more profound values, to speak of the transcendental lying beyond this world, to suggest that we may be in the grip of a false consciousness which does not penetrate to the true nature of our genuine alienation.

Moreover, and here is an even more radical thought, it may be that there are some things more important than happiness. Thus the person who sacrifices his life to save another, or lays down his life for his country, cannot be said to be prizing his own happiness as the ultimate value. He finds the call of duty greater than that of the pursuit of happiness. How can altruism prize happiness? Well, of course it can in the following sense, that altruism is without meaning unless it is action on behalf of the other, so it is perchance the other's happiness which is prized. Happiness reigns: whose happiness remains somewhat in jeopardy and dispute. (And here again is a nice trap for the selfish: not saving another being may be an act that haunts the selfish man to the end of his days—his selfish cowardice ruins any chance of true happiness). The question of the possible non-ultimacy of happiness, though it can be resolved in the manner I have just indicated in favor of happiness's ultimacy, suggests that there is an extra reason beyond those to which we have earlier referred why you cannot necessarily get happiness, that there is no sure way to "teach yourself happiness." It is not just that aiming at happiness is a kind of absurdity because you really have to aim at gaining happiness-making things and eliminating obstacles to happiness and causes of unhappiness. But there is, further, no guarantee that those objects of your immediate concern may not themselves have an independence of the concept of happiness which means that they may forever carry the seeds of collision with happiness. Thus you love someone, you cherish that person, but the need to do it—which is a kind of moral demand, but more, a deeply felt existential demand—means that you may be forced to sacrifice many a happiness-making thing on his behalf.

So far I have been looking upon happiness as something which may belong to the individual. Can it, though, be a group property? We think so sometimes—we think that those past times, when life was for the most part carefree and prosperous were happy times for all of us. We also think of an occasion as happy: a nice wedding party, let us say, when folks were happy together. But, though there is a use for this idea, it is reasonable to look upon happiness and unhappiness essentially as properties of individuals. Concern to help others, either positively or negatively, is basically a concern to help others achieve, so far as possible, a kind of happiness and to avoid unhappiness. Because the common sense values of the world may come under a kind of higher criticism, it may often be that there is a true comfort which one individual may bring to another which transcends suffering. This no doubt is part of the power of love.

From a practical point of view, then, the pursuit of happiness is a severely modified policy: for one thing, one cannot teach oneself happiness with any guarantee of success, for reasons which I have outlined. And it may be too that the very prizing of others—the love which is part of the fabric of the worthwhile life—may mean a collision between one's own aims and the deeper demands of others.

Incidentally it is worth noting that unhappiness, such as sorrow for the death or misfortune of another, is not something which can be transmuted by some worldviews, some faith, into happiness. Or if it can be there is I think a certain falsity. What is it to love another if the disappearance of the other is no wrench, is no cause for sadness? But it may be that sorrow can itself have a kind of value: it is the tribute of devotion to the person lost; it is a true grieving which is part of the acknowledgment of the other, a kind of mute communication. And if we think, as we may, that the loved one has gone to some higher place, then the sorrow is indeed tempered by the faith. But it is not washed away. It is only made a little more hopeful.

The present analysis of happiness, which builds into it the possibility of a critique of the values commonly seen as happiness-making, suggests a role for religion and ideology in the contemporary world: for much of secularism, whether seen in the consumerism of the Western world or the pigs with haloes and pig-iron with glory which figure in socialist propaganda, point to a shallow set of human goals. Let us deeply respect the freedom and the modest prosperity which alleviate so many causes of unhappiness. It is a great achievement of social democracy to gain both at the same time. It is no mean gain for humanity that many great evils have been eliminated in some societies, while hope is growing in the still impoverished world that a similar global prosperity may at last lie within our grasp. All that is to the credit of modern times. But though we may praise some of our modest secular gains, let us not for a moment forget that a life which is saved remains a life still to be lived through. So the transcendental perspective is a point from which a critique of the secular can be generated. (In this way, religion becomes for us a challenge rather than a credo, a set of questions rather than a string of dogmas, a kind of dazzling enigma from beyond.)

Sometimes in reflecting upon happiness it may be useful to picture not only the Zen archer, hitting the target without aiming. It may also be useful to think about the figure of Christ on the Cross and of the Bodhisattva, whose compassion is flecked with the knowledge of suffering. Christ reminds us that, mysteriously, other persons may call us to throw away even our own happiness; the Bodhisattva may remind us that even those who have happy circumstances and may even have ultimate bliss within their grasp know that the joys of life have to be lived in a kind of sorrow, the sorrow of other sorrow, the sorrows, that is, of other living beings. It is perhaps for this reason that perfection is often thought to lie in another world, not this. Or at least it lies in other times, beyond the present which we know.

3

HAPPINESS AND THE IDEA
OF HAPPINESS

MASATOSHI MATSUSHITA

I t is strange and interesting that the idea of happiness has developed in the West and not in the East. It does not mean that the East is indifferent to happiness. Perhaps the quest for happiness is a part of human nature and so no human being can be entirely indifferent to happiness. The difference between the East and West is not about this fundamental human nature but about the idea of happiness. It is well known that the idea of happiness was well explored and established in Western philosophy in early periods and has always been an important subject of philosophy. Perhaps the most outstanding example is Bentham, who insisted that the purpose of government is to seek the greatest happiness of the greatest number. This particular philosophy is called utilitarianism and has been well established in Britain and the United States. However, the idea of the greatest happiness of the greatest number is not limited to this particular school of philosophy. Whether it is expressed as by utilitarians or not, the idea of happiness is always implied in the Western philosophy.

Take for example the ideas of liberty and equality which are the fundamental assumptions of democracy. Why do we seek liberty and equality? What for? Liberty and equality are distinctly social; but we must clearly remember that the entity which enjoys or is supposed to enjoy liberty and equality is distinctly individual. When we say "we" enjoy liberty and equality, it means that a collection of individuals, individually and collectively, enjoys liberty and equality. Then, why does he or she have to enjoy liberty and equality? Simply because liberty and equality are enjoyable and pleasurable. Individuals seek liberty and equality not because they are good in themselves, but because they are enjoyable and pleasurable; and "enjoyable" and "pleasurable" are identical to happiness. That is why, perhaps, the Founding Fathers definitely used the words "life, liberty and pursuit of happiness" in the Declaration of Independence.

The idea of happiness is very closely connected with Western or modern civilization. I do not think that it is correct and fair to say that Western civilization is "material" while Eastern civilization is "spiritual." Civilization is essentially "spiritual" whether it is Eastern or Western. The difference between Eastern civilization and Western civilization is that there is some element in Western civilization which stimulates material civilization which is absent in Eastern civilization. What is this "some element?" Most philosophers of history attribute this element to Judeo-Christianity, especially its idea of creation. One almighty and omniscient God created the universe. God must be rational, otherwise "God" cannot be God. If God is rational, the universe must be rational. Therefore, the universe is worthwhile for rational research. This is the assumption of science, and science has brought about modern technology. This is the reasoning of the philosophers of history. I am quite willing to agree that the Judeo-Christian idea of creation by one God is responsible for the rise of science and scientific thinking. However, the fundamental character of modern civilization, which we often call "material civilization," is not science or scientific thinking but technology. It is true that technology is an application of science. Therefore, it can be said quite safely that the modern material or technological civilization could not have existed if there had been no science. However, it does not follow that science or scientific thinking necessarily produces technology or technological civilization. The motive for science and scientific thinking is the seeking of truth. It does not call for its usefulness. The motive for technology is to create usefulness, and usefulness is not always identical to truth. There may be some truth which is useful, while there may be some useful things which are contrary to truth. So these two ideas are entirely different and distinct. Therefore, it is not true that science necessarily produces technology.

What is chiefly responsible for Western, modern and materialistic civilization is the idea of happiness. Judeo-Christianity is closely related to Western civilization, but it is not the direct cause of technological civilization. Very often Judeo-Christianity has acted as an element checking technology. Let me briefly explain why the idea of happiness is the cause of the Western, technological civilization. As man is a complex being, he does not act with one single motive. He acts with self-interest, but this fact does not exclude his selfless motive. A businessman works hard to make money. However, if he believes that he is also working for his country or for the world, he will be more enthusiastic about his work. Thus it is dangerous to attribute one's particular action to only one motive. I am not in a position to insist that the idea of happiness is the sole cause of Western technological civilization. Perhaps the only valid methodology is a negative test, which means that without the idea of happiness the modern technological civilization in the West could not have arisen. If we limit our argument to this extent, we are on safer ground and can advance our argument with more confidence.

We define happiness as the fulfillment of desires. When we are hungry, we desire to eat. If we succeed in eating, we are happy. When we want to love, we are happy if we find the right mates, etc. So happiness is the fulfillment of desires. We all have desires, and we all want to fulfill desires. In order to successfully fulfill our desires, we can not afford to leave the matter to chance. We must control social and material conditions to fulfill our desires. If one is convinced that the fulfillment of desires is not only desirable but also justifiable or even moral, he will try his best to create and control social and material conditions to fulfill his desires. If he, on the other hand, is convinced that the fulfillment of his desires is a necessary evil and essentially immoral, he will be inclined to control his desires rather than the social and material conditions. As human beings are fundamentally identical, the peoples in the East also

want to fulfill their desires. However, they have been more inclined
to control their desires rather than to control social and material
conditions, because they do not believe that the fulfillment of
desires is a virtue. On the contrary, they are more inclined to
believe that the fulfillment of desires is something to be avoided.
They are more concerned with social stability. They find themselves
valuable when they believe that they are a useful part of the
community to which they belong.

For instance, the purpose of marriage is the stability and
preservation of the community, and not the happiness of the
individuals who are to marry. In the West this kind of idea is
unthinkable and absurd. To them, marriage is definitely for the
happiness of the individuals who love each other. Stability and
other social values might come as a result of the marriage, but that
is only a result of happy marriage. The primary purpose of marriage
is definitely happiness. Western peoples do not doubt the right-
eousness of their idea. Marriage in the East is entirely different.
The primary purpose of marriage in the East is to preserve the
tradition of the family, which is the foundation of the community.
The happiness of married individuals is desirable because it would
ultimately contribute to the stability of the community; but it is
not important in itself. I am trying to explain the difference between
marriage in the East and marriage in the West. In explaining the
difference, traditional Eastern ideas and customs are used to contrast
with Western ideas and customs. Modern ideas and customs in the
East, especially in Japan, are more Western than Eastern. So it
may be argued that what I have explained is not applicable at least
to Japan. I frankly admit that the argument is true to some extent.
However, I do not think Japan is so completely modernized or
Westernized with regard to marriage as is generally assumed. In
spite of the fact that the so-called "nuclear families" are increasing,
the traditional marriage is still the rule and not the exception.
Moreover, because the Western marriage system, free marriage,
does not necessarily bring about good results, there is a new trend
among young people toward a preference to the old traditional
marriage system. Therefore, it is not true that the change from
Eastern to Western is a natural and inevitable course.

The difference between East and West with regard to

happiness is not limited to marriage. The difference is very great and the contrast is sharp even in the field of business, which is generally regarded as dry. Western people regard their jobs as contracts. They have a very strong sense of "pacta sunt servanda," so a breach of contract is exceptional. I think that this kind of mentality is largely responsible for the rise of capitalism. However, they feel quite free to change their jobs, if this is in accordance with their contracts. Since employment contracts are usually free, Westerners often change their jobs. They change jobs because the new jobs offer larger incomes than the old ones. Why do they prefer jobs with larger incomes? Larger incomes mean greater happiness. This does not very often happen in the East, especially in Japan. Japanese employees feel they are morally bound to companies, government organizations or other people who employ them. Therefore they are unlikely to change jobs simply because new employers offer larger incomes. This means that they are quite willing to sacrifice their happiness for what they regard as moral obligations.

The idea of happiness has brought about a brilliant technological civilization in the West, and this idea has spread all over the world. In other words, the whole world has been Westernized to some extent. This tendency has been called "progress" and has been regarded as unqualified goodness. Recently, however, people have become, and are becoming increasingly more skeptical about progress. They no longer take it for granted as unqualified goodness. They are reconsidering the traditional Oriental cultures which they totally ignored in the past. I think this is a good and hopeful tendency. It means that the West has the will to learn. However, it is strange that these people have not yet realized that the essential defect of the Western civilization is neither the idea of progress nor liberty, but the preoccupation with the idea of happiness. Let me repeat very definitely that seeking happiness is a part of human nature. Therefore, there is no way to escape from the rule. We, as human beings, are bound to pursue happiness with or without the Declaration of Independence. Our question is whether we should simply recognize it as a fact or justify it morally. This alternative is not arbitrary. Since we can not escape from human nature, we have to recognize things as they are. To recognize things as they are is not to justify them morally. There are many things which are moral and immoral, but there are many other things which are non-moral. Now, human nature in itself belongs to this third category. The question of morality arises when we are compelled to choose between the abuse and restraint of human nature. Therefore, neither the absolute denial of happiness, as advocated by some sects of Oriental religions, nor the justification of happiness is right. In this respect the beatitude in the New Testament is a very balanced teaching concerning happiness. It does not deny happiness in its ordinary sense. Neither does it justify it as utilitarian. It simply teaches what we should do first. I do not think the beatitude, like other teachings of Jesus, is the monopoly of Christians. This is exactly what all human beings should do, regardless of nationality or religion. The fundamental idea is neither to seek happiness nor to deny it, but seek something higher and leave the result to someone higher than us.

4

THE METAPHYSICS OF
THE GOOD

IVOR LECLERC

I

In the inquiry into this topic it is desirable at the outset to enter into some linguistic examination, for this will facilitate, not only the avoidance of possible confusions because of the diversity of senses in which the word "good" is used, but also the recognition of where exactly lie the philosophical issues with respect to the "good."

In its predominant usage the word "good" (as also ἀγαθός, *bonus*, and their cognates in modern European languages) is an adjective, but the English word, on which we will here concentrate, sometimes also occurs in an adverbial and in a substantival usage. The *Oxford English Dictionary* (O.E.D.) defines good as: "The most general adj. of commendation, implying the existence of a high, or at least satisfactory, degree of characteristic qualities which are admirable in themselves or useful for some purpose."[1] Of particular significance in this are: (1) the generality of the adjective; (2) that it is one of "commendation"; (3) that the object of the commendation is certain "characteristic qualities"; (4) that the adjective does not connote the attribution of the qualities absolutely, but rather relatively, comparatively, in degree; and (5) that the qualities are distinguishable in respect to being admirable either (a) in themselves, or (b) as useful for some purpose.

In this characterization of the adjective its philosophical relevance is signified by its generality. But wherein exactly that generality lies becomes a question. Does it pertain to the factor of "commendation," or to the "qualities"? It might be to the former, since the word "good" always implies "commendation." But on the other hand, "good" also carries the connotation of the qualities in question being ones of "worth," i.e., they are "worthy of commendation." That is to say, it is the qualities which, by their "worth," elicit the commendation. However, to pursue this we have to take account of some complications in regard to the meaning of the word "good."

Some of this comes to the fore in an examination of the word "worth." "Worth" means "having a specified value," originally a pecuniary value, the word later coming also to be used in a generalized sense of "the relative value of a thing in respect of its qualities or of the estimation in which it is held."[2] Highly relevant here is the word "value," a synonym of "worth"—more especially relevant because of the prominence of this word in philosophical discussions of the "good." The noun "value"—deriving from the Old French *valu*, past participle of *valoir* (from Latin *valere* "to be strong") meaning "to be strong, to be of worth"—in its earliest usage in English meant *the amount* of some commodity, medium of exchange, etc. which renders it of worth.[3] Thus the word "value," like "worth," and "good," also entails in its connotation the relative or comparative. This is signified too in the word which has in the last hundred years come into use as the name for the "general theory of value," viz., "axiology"—from ἄξιος "weighing as much, of like value, worth as much as, hence generally, worth, worthy."[4]

It is important to note some differences, as well as similarities, between the words "good," "worth," and "value," for these will turn out to be of philosophical significance. First, the word "value" is used both as a noun and as a verb; "worth" as a noun and as an adjective; and "good" as primarily an adjective, but also sometimes substantively. Secondly, there is a peculiarity of the word "good" distinguishing it from the other two—as a consequence of which "worth" and "value" cannot be accepted as exact synonyms of "good." The connotations of both the words "worth" and "value," as we have seen, entail their being relative, comparative, not used in an absolute sense. The same holds in respect of the word "good" as an adjective, as has been brought out above in the consideration of the O.E.D. definition of "good." But this word has the peculiarity that when the adjective is used substantively, it becomes absolute. One instance of this is when the adjective "good" is used as plural, with the meaning of "good people"; here "good" (used with the article) is absolute, e.g., in the statement, "where the good cease to tremble." Another instance of the absolute sense is the plural adjective, "goods," meaning initially "property, merchandise, etc.," but extended also to non-material properties, etc. A third, and main, instance of the absolute use is that in which the singular adjective is used with the meaning of "that which is good (in various senses)," e.g., "he became a power for good," "for the good of mankind."

This absolute sense is of special significance philosophically. We get an intimation of this by considering a statement of the form "X is good." An instance of this would be "Jack is good." This statement is ambiguous. The word "good" here could be an adjective used predicatively, the statement meaning "Jack is a good person"— the adjective carrying the implication of the person being relatively or comparatively good. But the word "good" in the sentence could be meant as a predicative noun, in which it has an absolute sense. Another instance of this form of statement would be "pleasure is good." This could mean that pleasure is "a good thing (attribute, condition, etc.)." But "good" could be intended here as a noun. Now, this could mean that pleasure is "a good," one among others. Or it could mean that pleasure is "the good," unconditionally. It is to be noted that in the latter sense, of "good" with the definite article, the word "good" has a distinctively philosophical meaning. It is to be noted also that this sense of the noun "good" is not captured by the nouns "value" and "worth." One could meaningfully say, pleasure is "a value," but not that pleasure is "the value," or "the worth," for the words "value" and "worth" are relative and comparative, by contrast with "good" in the sense under consideration, which is absolute.

These considerations become especially pertinent when we take account of point (5) above, that the qualities commended as "good" are to be distinguished as commendable—either in themselves or as useful for some purpose—this distinction being alternatively referred to in philosophical discourse as respectively "intrinsic" and "instrumental." It is this consideration which more particularly brings us to the philosophical issue in respect of "good."

II

The central philosophical issue is that concerning the nature of "good." The word "good," as the most general adjective expressing qualities of "worth" or "value," covers a wide range of specific qualities, such as "excellence," "superiority of kind," the connotation including qualities such as "commendable," "admirable," "appealing," "agreeable," "enjoyable," "gratifying." It also includes such as "useful," "advantageous," "beneficial," "adequate," "effectual," "suitable," "competent," etc. This last group clearly pertains particularly to the "instrumental" sense of "good," that of "good for" something. The others, especially "excellence," "superiority," could be "intrinsic," but they could also be meant in an "instrumental" sense.

Philosophically the issue is what it is in all this variety of qualities whereby they connote "goodness," i.e., the quality or condition of being "good"? What, fundamentally, is meant by "good," "goodness"?

We can narrow down the search for an answer to that question by noting that the instrumental sense of "good," that of "good for," points beyond itself to ends or purposes sought to be attained because of their "goodness." These, however, might themselves also be "good" in an instrumental sense, but since a *regressus ad infinitum* must be rejected, we must come to some or other "good in itself." It is therefore to the meaning of "good" in the intrinsic sense that we need to direct our attention.

Now in our earlier analysis of the *O.E.D.* definition of

"good" we noted a certain polarity: on the one side is the feature of "commendation," and on the other the objects of this commendation, the "things" which are regarded as "good." We then raised the question, with regard to the generality of "good," whether it pertained to one or other of the two sides. We can now more sharply focus the issue by asking whether the things are commended because they are "good," or is it the case that "goodness" resides on the side of the "commendation"?

The latter is the position taken by thinkers, such as Ralph Barton Perry in his *A General Theory of Value*, who hold that the commendation is a function of "interest," "desire," "feeling," etc., of the subject. That is, this theory is that a thing is "good" by virtue of its being the object of interest, desire, etc. Now it is significant that in the argumentation for this theory, it is the word "value" which is predominantly used rather than "good." The argument is that the object is "valued" by a subject, and that accordingly the object has a "value" by reason of the act of "valuing"; that is, a "value" is placed on the object by the subject. The inference then is that the object cannot be "intrinsically good."

In the argument it is "value" as a verb that is predominant—"value" as a noun derives from the verb, which expresses the act of "valuing." The subject "values," which means that the subject "estimates or appraises," i.e., "attaches a worth or value" to the object. This entails the inference that the "value" of the object cannot be intrinsic to it. This inference is entirely valid—with respect to the term "value." But this is not equivalent to saying that the object cannot be "good" in itself, i.e., "good" in an intrinsic sense. In the first place it should be noted that the subject attaches "a value" to the object. One could validly hold that this entails that thereby it attaches "value" to the object. But "value" here does not have an absolute sense; it means "some or other value"—i.e., "value" in a relative sense. Secondly, the word "value" here cannot be replaced by "good," saying that the subject attaches "a good," i.e., "some or other good," to the object. For "good" as a noun, especially in the statement "it (a person, a thing) is good" does not mean "some or other good." Here "good" has an absolute sense, which is absent from "value" and "worth"—when these words are used strictly, which is to say, not as surreptitious synonyms for

"good" in the absolute sense.[5] Therefore the conclusion of the
argument which we have been considering, that the object cannot
be "good" in an intrinsic sense, is invalid, and must be rejected.
The statement "it is good" has a meaning quite beyond what can
be expressed by the word "value."

The kind of theory with which we are concerned here is
that which can be generalized as the "subjective" theory of good.
That is, it is the theory which grounds "good" in the subject. In
the form of the theory which we have considered above, it grounds
"good" in the subject by conceiving "good" as meaning that the
subject has a certain "interest," "desire," "feeling," etc. with respect
to the object. In another form of this theory it grounds "good" in
the subject by conceiving "good" as dependent upon the "thought,"
"judgment," or "valuing" of some subject. In either form the theory
entails that the object cannot be "good" in independence of a
subject, and thus that the object cannot be "good in itself," i.e.,
"intrinsically good." This subjective theory must finally be rejected
as untenable because, by denying the possibility of an object being
"good in itself," it is admitting "good" only in an instrumental
sense, and is thereby involved in a *regressus ad infinitum.*

This could be taken as pointing to the acceptance of the
alternative theory, that the meaning of "good" is to be grounded
in the object. When we assert "it is good"—in the intrinsic, as
opposed to the instrumental sense—the "it" is an object, e.g., a
person or thing. This could be characterized as the "objective"
theory of good. In this theory good is referred to as being "objective"
in the sense of its being dependent upon an object—in contrast to
the subjective theory, in which good is dependent upon the subject.

The philosophical issue which arises with respect to this
theory is: what exactly is the status of "good" in this theory? If good
be dependent upon an object, this entails that good is not itself an
object in the sense of being an independently existing thing. We
have seen earlier that in the statement "it is good" or "x is good,"
"good" is a predicative noun, i.e., "good" is being ascribed to x.
This ascription of "good" to x entails that "good" has the status of
a "quality," i.e., it tells "what" x is—a "quality" answers to the
interrogative, of *what* kind or sort. This is in contrast to "good"
being a "quantity" (which does not entail "what" but "how much")

or a "relation"—a relation has to be excluded from the "what" since, if it be included, this would entail that "good" would be in part dependent upon that to which x stands in a relation, which would imply that x could not be "good in itself."

The issue has now to be raised whether good as a quality is to be conceived as on a par with all the other qualities ascribed to X as constituting "what" it is (i.e., its "essence"), with "good" thus being ascribed as a quality additional to the others? Or is "good" a distinct quality, different from the others in some fundamental respect—as is maintained for example in the doctrine of good as a "transcendental quality"? And also, is good as a quality to be conceived as "inhering in" the thing as do the other qualities?

This conception of qualities as simply inhering in a thing is one of long heritage in the Neoplatonic tradition and which has come to be widely accepted as an implicit presupposition. It needs critical scrutiny, in general, and in particular in respect of "good" as a quality. In the traditional doctrine, it needs to be observed, it is accepted that that in which a quality inheres must be a "substance," i.e., a self-subsistent existent. With regard to "good" as a quality, it needs to be considered, first, whether good necessarily inheres in a substance. And secondly, it needs to be examined whether good as a quality is indeed adequately conceived as "simply inhering."

Respecting the first, "good" is certainly ascribed, in some instances, to substances, e.g., to persons, and things. But is it *only* ascribed to substances? Consider the celebrated doctrine of Kant that "nothing in all the world—indeed nothing even beyond the world—can possibly be called good without qualification except a *good will*."[6] Will is clearly not a substance. Or consider Sir David Ross' conclusion from his examination of "what things are good": "Four things, then, seem to be intrinsically good—virtue, pleasure, the allocation of pleasure to the virtuous, and knowledge."[7] Again none of these "things" is a substance.

Are we to conclude from this that the conception of good as necessarily inhering in a substance is unacceptable? Will is not a substance, but is it not the case that it is the will of a person, i.e., of a substance? Does not the same hold with regard to "virtue," "pleasure," and "knowledge"? But if we agree that this is indeed

the case, does this entail that when, for example, Kant maintains
that only a "good will" can be accepted as intrinsically good, he
means strictly that it is the *person* who is intrinsically good? And
for Ross, that it is the *person* who is virtuous, or enjoying pleasure,
or possessed of knowledge, that is intrinsically good? It is clear, I
think, that this is *not* what Kant and Ross are maintaining. Of
course the "person" is involved, but not primarily in respect to
good; primarily for Kant it is *will* which is intrinsically good, and
the person is good in a derivative sense. Accordingly, it must be
concluded that the doctrine that good necessarily inheres in a
substance is indeed unacceptable.

III

But there is a further problem involved in this, the problem of how
precisely to understand the "inherence" of good in a thing. This is
an aspect of the still more general problem of how to conceive the
inherence of qualities in a thing.

There is a long tradition that this inherence is "simple,"
which is to say, not complex or analyzable into any further elements;
that is, the inherence of a quality is ultimate, beyond further
analysis. The inherence of a color is an instance of this: the color
is simply "in" a thing. Descartes exemplified this traditional conception in his doctrine of extension as the essence of physical
substance: extension was conceived by him as "simply inherent" in
matter. And it was this presupposition that Leibniz called into
question in his criticism of the Cartesian doctrine, Leibniz maintaining that the concept of extension is not "simple and primitive,"
that it is on the contrary "analyzable"—according to him into
"plurality, continuity, and coexistence."[8]

But this metaphysical presupposition involves, and indeed
rests upon, another, namely that of a "substance" or final self-
subsistent existent, as itself "simple." It is "one," and its "unity" is
"simple," i.e., not further analyzable. Leibniz shared this presupposition with Descartes. It is this metaphysical presupposition

which, it seems to me, has to be brought into question and critically examined. This is the conception of a "thing" or "substance" as with its inherent qualities, these constituting "what" the thing is, its "essence." The "substance" is the "subject" of the qualities, and does not exist apart from its qualities. Even when the substance is held to be "active"—as it is in the Neoplatonic tradition, this "activity" being that of "thinking"—the "activity" is conceived as a quality inhering in the substance. Descartes' *res cogitans* is an exemplification of this basic metaphysical conception; "thinking" is for him a quality constituting the "essence" of the substance, "what" it is. But the conception of "thinking" per se is an abstraction; there is no "thinking" apart from "thoughts," the "ideas." So it is the "thinking-ideas" that is the quality of this substance. A main point in respect to this philosophical position is that the substance with its qualities is self-contained, both in regard to its "conception"— it is completely understandable and conceived as a subject with its simply inhering qualities—and in regard to its "being"—as Descartes said, it "so exists that it needs no other thing in order to exist."[9]

I would argue that a crucial aspect of this metaphysical position is that of the conception of "acting" as a quality of a substance, and that especially this conception has to be critically examined.

The justification for my singling out "acting" is that since Plato, and certainly since Aristotle, and Plotinus, it has been seen that "acting" (ἐνέργεια) has to be admitted as a fundamental factor in what is accepted as τὸ παντελῶς ὄν, a complete or real being. It was the seventeenth century scholars, from Basso and Descartes, through Newton, who diverged from that insight in conceiving physical being as matter, which is inert, i.e., "inactive," in its essential nature. The physical science of the last hundred years has, however, had to abandon that doctrine, coming instead to conceive the physical as essentially active. It is the concept of "act," "acting," which today has to receive primary metaphysical attention.

This is not the occasion for an attempt at an extensive investigation of the concept; I can now only adumbrate the analysis of "acting" as fundamentally relational, as Leibniz in the modern period was the first to see and seek to develop, with his conception of the act of being of a monad as *perceptio*, that is, as essentially

relating it to another as object. Leibniz, however, remained entan-
gled in the Neoplatonic conception of the act of being as a "thinking,"
and consequently the object for him, as for Descartes, was primarily
"idea," rather than another being—i.e., it was the "idea of" another
being. This subjectivism has to be rejected; the object of acting
must be another being per se. If the object of acting is another
being per se, this means that acting is relational, i.e., an act of
relating a being to another.

In this conception, it must be appreciated, "a being" as
subject of acting is not complete in itself, with the "relation"
additional to it. In a final analysis of a being we find only "actings"—
the subject is not an entity distinct from the "acting"—and "actings"
are essentially relational. Now this means that what are to be
considered as "qualities," i.e., "what" the being is, inhere not in a
subject per se, apart from its acting—for there is no such subject—
but the qualities inhere in the "subject-acting." And since the acting
is relational, this means that the qualities "qualify" that relational
acting—"qualify" in the etymological sense of the medieval Latin
qualificare, "to make of a certain quality, to give a certain quality
to." That is to say, it is the "acting" which is qualified as of such
and such a kind, but since the "acting" per se is not apart from the
"relation," in a certain most significant sense the quality inheres in
the "relation,"—but not "relation" thought of as distinct or apart
from its terms, the acting subject and its object.

Further, this inherence is not to be conceived as a "simple
inherence," for "relational acting" is not "simple." In the first place,
a being as subject is not to be conceived as "simple," as having
only a single simple acting, i.e., one which is "ultimate," not further
analyzable. Rather, the acting of a being is highly complex, analyzable into an indefinite multiplicity of sub-acts. In the second place,
these actings are relational, which means that they relate to objects.
That is, the actings being relational, they have a multiplicity of
objects, which have to be distinguished into two kinds. The sub-
acts are necessarily related to each other, which means that they
have each other as objects, but with only one subject entailed in
these relations. These objects, and thus relations, are internal to
the acting being. The other kind of object is that constituted by
other beings. This multiplicity of relations, of both kinds, is in each

case defined by a "quality," itself not simple, but of degrees of complexity and thus analyzability.

IV

On the basis of this analysis we can now turn to a consideration of the nature and status of "good."

We must conclude as the outcome of the foregoing analysis that, first, "good" as a quality is not different from other qualities, in that it also must be conceived as involved in, and pertaining to, a being "in relation"; it inheres in the being in respect of its relations. Secondly, good is not any simple, i.e., not further analyzable, quality. Rather, good is a complex quality pertaining to and inherent in a complex of relations constituting some "whole."

One kind of "whole" is that which is the being itself, that which is the acting subject. In this, the complex of actings integrate into a unity, into a whole. Thus we have a kind of whole which is constituted by the internal interrelatedness of the actings of the being, in respect to their being an integral acting. Now this interrelatedness, as constituting a unity or whole, has, as such, a definiteness or character. That is, there is a particular complex character or quality which is that of the whole, and that character or definiteness qualifies the interrelatedness, the interactings.

Now, included in this complex character of definiteness of the whole is that quality or feature which we know as its "goodness." This feature, which we designate by the word "good," is one pertaining to the whole as constituted by an interrelatedness of actings. That is, "good" inheres in the interrelatedness constituting the whole. Further to be noted is that it is such a whole of interrelation which is "good in itself"—without regard to anything external. This is the primary instance of "good in itself," namely that pertaining to a being in respect to its own whole of interrelated actings.

However, a single being is not to be considered *only* in

the respect to which the internal interrelatedness of its actings constitutes it an integral whole, for its actings also necessarily involve other beings as objects. This means that there are also other wholes, constituted by the being in question and one or more other beings with which it is in interaction.

Let us consider the case of two beings in such interaction. We have here a whole constituted by the interrelatedness of the two, and this has a certain complex character or definiteness. This character or definiteness is partly determined by the particular characters of the two beings themselves, but the character of the interrelatedness itself also in part determines the individual characters of the two beings. This kind of whole of interrelatedness and its complex determinateness is instanced in a marriage, or a friendship. This whole of interrelatedness is that constituting a "society."[10] What is pertinent to us here is that the complex character of such a societal whole of interrelatedness includes also that feature which we designate by "good." Now when we consider that whole per se in respect to its goodness, it is "good in itself." But since the actings of each of the two beings also have other beings as objects, the societal whole can be considered also in respect to its interrelatedness with one or more other beings. In respect to this interrelatedness the societal whole could be considered as "useful" to the other beings, as e.g., furthering their purposes, etc. That is to say, this consideration of the societal whole would be of it as "good instrumentally."

It will not be necessary to go into an investigation of more complex wholes of interrelatedness; in principle the situation respecting the analysis of "good" will not be different: any whole of interrelatedness will in one consideration be "good in itself," and in another be "instrumentally good."

We can now, on the basis of the foregoing analysis, return to the issue examined in the second section, that between the "subjectivist" and the "objectivist" theories of good, and achieve a significant clarification of the issue. With the analysis of good as pertaining to the interrelatedness constituting a whole, we can conclude, in respect to that whole being "good in itself," that good is clearly to be accorded an objective status.

A problem arises, however, with regard to "instrumental

good," since the "instrumental good" would seem to imply someone for whom, and in respect to some purpose, the whole in question is "good." This would entail a relationship between that someone and the whole in question, a relationship in which that someone "judges" or "values" that whole as being "good for" some end. The crucial issue is whether that someone uniquely determines that whole in respect to its being "good for," so that without that someone judging or valuing, there simply would be no "good for" some end. The affirmative answer to this question is what constitutes the "subjectivist" theory of good.

But, I would argue, this analysis of "instrumental good" is not to be accepted as valid. For the whole in question is not dependent upon a judgment or valuation by another beyond it for it to be "instrumentally good," since the beings constituting that whole of interaction are, as we have seen, necessarily also in interactive relations with other beings. It is by virtue of, and in respect to, these relationships beyond itself that that whole with which we are concerned is "instrumentally good." These relationships, and the whole as in those relationships, are a "fact," and moreover, they are a fact antecedent to the judging or valuing. It is not the judging or valuing which bring that fact into being; rather it is the case that the judging, etc., presupposes that fact, and therefore is a judgment respecting that fact. This means that the instrumental goodness of the whole in question is "objective."

V

We have now to deal with another, and more difficult problem, with respect to the status of "good." Kant had maintained, as we noted earlier, that nothing is to be regarded as good without qualification except a "good will." This entails that "good in itself" pertains only to the moral. This conception, that good in the sense of "intrinsic good" is to be restricted to the "moral good," is a widely held doctrine. Another position, appreciably wider than this, in regard to what is to be conceived as "intrinsically good," is that maintained by Sir David Ross: "good is a characteristic belonging primarily only to states of mind, and belonging to them only in virtue of three characteristics—the moral virtue included in them, and intelligence included in them, and the pleasure included in them."[11] The issue is whether this kind of restriction in respect of what is "intrinsically good" is acceptable.

The issue here is ultimately a metaphysical one. What needs to be considered is the metaphysical foundation for that restriction in respect to what is validly to be regarded as "intrinsically good." The theories of this kind are, it seems to me, tenable on the basis only of either of two metaphysical positions. One is the metaphysical dualism so widely accepted since the seventeenth century, which would exclude "intrinsic good" from the entire realm of nature, confining it only to man. The other position, which is derived from a reaction to the dualistic one, holds that what is ultimately "real" is only the "mental" or "spiritual." The credibility of these two positions rests upon the acceptance of the seventeenth-century conception of physical or natural being as essentially "inert," with its corollary, the Neoplatonic doctrine that "act" pertains solely to mind. However, the situation has been fundamentally altered by the abandonment by twentieth-century physical science of the conception of the physical as inert, and by its de facto acceptance of the ultimate physical entities as essentially "active."

My analysis of "act" and "acting" above has been particularly concerned with human activity, but the concept of "act" can be generalized to all beings, i.e., to all which are acceptable as τὰ παντελῶς ὄντα, complete or real beings. Further, in respect to these, my foregoing analysis of "act" remains valid. I can here do no more than adumbrate this position.[12] In it a being, by its acting, affects another or others, thereby effecting some change in them. This was the view of "acting" which Kant, in his *Monadologia Physica* and other precritical writings, had advanced in place of Leibniz's subjectivistic *perceptio*, which entailed that only phenomenal relations were possible. Kant, however, correctly insisted on physical relations necessarily having to be "real."[13] In the position being maintained here, the acting of a being necessarily has to be relational.

This general metaphysical position now allows us to hold

that any whole of relational activity can be conceived as "good in itself." That is to say, there can be no metaphysical necessity to restrict "good in itself" or "intrinsic good" to human beings; it is to be extended to *all* beings. This means that any whole of relational activity constituting an integral being must be regarded as "good in itself." Further, as we have seen, relational wholes constituted by two or more beings can also be "good in themselves." The intrinsic goodness here is grounded in the relational acting of the constituent beings and pertains primarily to them in that interrelation.

Further, in terms of this metaphysical position, not only can there be no reason for restricting "good" to the human, but there can also be no reason for limiting "good" to the moral. The moral good must be regarded as a species of good in a generic sense.

VI

This brings us to the central and crucial issue involved in our topic. So far we have taken it for granted that there is a factor or quality which we term "good," and we have investigated its status, e.g., whether it is "subjective" or "objective." But central to the philosophical concern must be to seek to understand the nature of "good." This raises the issue of how that understanding is to be achieved. Of what does it consist? For the attainment of this understanding, I would maintain, it is necessary to go to first principles: this understanding is to be achieved only in terms of metaphysical categories and concepts.

One approach to this understanding is to seek the *cause* of people, things, etc., being "good." The classic instance of this approach, and one which has historically been of great influence, is the Platonic doctrine that the "cause" of things being good is to be found in the Form or Idea of Good. Another approach was that of Aristotle, who found the conception of a self-subsistent Form of Good quite untenable. His approach was to seek the understanding of "good" in terms of "end" (τέλος). He held that "good," in the most general sense, is "that at which all things aim."[14] It is true that for Aristotle *telos*, "end," is a cause, but it is a cause in the sense of "that for the sake of which" (τὸ οὖ ἕνεκα), by contrast with the Platonic cause as the "formal cause." These two approaches were combined in the medieval doctrine of God as the ultimate cause—the cause of "being," and also of "end," the *telos* of all creation.

But there are serious philosophical difficulties in these three positions. Let us start with the Aristotelian. In holding that "good" is "that at which all things aim," is Aristotle *defining* "good" in terms of "aim" or "end"? Is he maintaining that it is "aim" or "end" which *constitutes* "good"? Is it not, rather, that something is "aimed at" *because* it is "good"? Secondly, consistent with his criticism of Plato, Aristotle does not set out to find "the good"; rather he seeks to ascertain what is the highest, best, supreme (ἄριστον) good, or the complete, perfect (τέλειον) good. Thus he asks whether this good is to be identified with "pleasure" (ἐδονή), or with "happiness or well-being" (εὐδαιμονία), or with "virtue" (ἀρετή), or with "function" (ἔργον), or "activity" (ἐνέργεια), or "action" (πρᾶξις). We are, however, still left with the issue: what is "good"? Aristotle rejects that "the good itself" (αὐτὸ τὸ ἀγαθόν) could be the Platonic Idea or Form of Good;[15] that is, the "good" we are seeking cannot be a self-subsistent being. Nor, he argues, could it be a universal (τὸ κοινόν),[16] for a "universal goodness" could not be the "supreme good."[17] In contrast with these positions he puts forward that the "good" we are seeking is to be found in "that for the sake of which as an end" (τὸ οὖ ἕνεκα ὡς τέλος).[18] But it is still obscure how this gives us the meaning of "good."

The issue we have here, that as to the meaning of "good," is an extremely difficult one. It is difficult to see precisely what kind of answer is requisite, and the formulation of the problem is difficult. The issue has, however, been recognized, and thinkers down the ages have sought to deal with it in a variety of ways and in terms of various theories. One of these views, which has had a wide currency, even in recent times, has been to hold that in respect to "good" we have an ultimate and ineffable quality, which can only be "intuited." Most recent thinkers holding this view have not gone further and entered into the question of the metaphysical status of this quality. Some, however, have done so, and have given the answer in terms of objectively existing "essences"—e.g., by Nicolai Hartmann.[19] These "intuitionist" theories, it should be noted, involve some form of Platonism—whether or not this be recognized by their proponents.

At this point it is appropriate to turn to an examination of the Platonic position, one of the three approaches mentioned above in the understanding of "good." The Platonic doctrine is that the meaning of "good," in respect of the "things" which are regarded as "good," is to be found in the Form or Idea of Good. Now in this doctrine the Form of Good is itself "a being." Further, in many interpretations of the doctrine, this Form is taken to be the perfect exemplar of "good"—which is entirely consistent with the Form as "a good being." The question can, however, be raised as to the meaning of "good" in this "good being," the Form of Good. Doing so brings to light the difficulty, or fallacy, which in the Academy came to be referred to as that of the "third man." The difficulty is that in terms of this theory the meaning of "good" of a "good person" is grounded in the Form of Good. But since this Form is "a good being," the question must be raised as to the ground of that "good." Answer: another Form of Good—and so on *ad infinitum.* Aristotle urged this difficulty as fatal to the Platonic conception of Forms as "beings," and in particular to the Form of Good as a being.

Plato himself was well aware of this difficulty regarding the meaning of "good" inherent in his theory of Forms, and made one highly significant attempt to deal with it. He did so in the *Republic* in his celebrated simile of the sun. To see an object capable of being seen, there is required not only an eye capable of sight, but a third factor: the sun with its light; so analogously, to have knowledge and truth about things capable of being known, there is required not only a knowing mind (*nous*) with a capacity of knowing, but a third factor also is necessary: the Form of Good. But then Plato extends the analogy most significantly: "the sun not only gives the objects of sight their capacity of visibility, but also provides for their generation, growth, and nurture";[20] so analogously, the objects of knowledge not only receive from the presence of the Good their being known, but also their being or existence (τὸ εἶναι) and their essence (οὐσία) are provided by the Good.[21]

How is this argument, especially the latter part, to be understood? How are we to conceive the Good as providing things with their *ousia*, i.e., that whereby they are "what" they are? And not only that, but as providing also their very "being" (*to einai*), their existing? We get an answer to this question by considering this last passage together with ones in which Plato had earlier introduced the topic of the Good: "For you have often heard that the greatest thing to learn is the Form of the Good, that it is by this that just things and other such become useful and beneficial."[22] What Plato is getting at is missed if this passage be interpreted, as it so frequently is, as dealing with the merely utilitarian.[23] He is saying that, without the Form of Good, just actions, and pious, and brave actions, etc., would be simply pointless, without meaning or relevance, lacking entirely in worth. That is, unless just actions, etc., were "good," they would be completely meaningless and irrelevant. In that culminating passage of his argument (509B) given above, Plato extends his insight respecting justice, etc., also to knowledge, and to being and essence. Unless knowledge be "good," knowledge would be utterly pointless and irrelevant—it would simply not be worthwhile at all. And, *ousia*, "what" a thing is, equally would be entirely devoid of sense and meaning unless it were "good." Further, and most importantly, being or existing itself, unless it were "good" would simply be meaningless, without any point or purpose, devoid of anything whereby it would be worthwhile, and thus would be impossible.

In accord with the ontology which Plato maintained in his middle period, "the Good" is here stated to be the Form or Idea of Good. But in that culminating passage Plato proceeds to a most important statement, namely that "the good is not *ousia* (being, essence), but transcends *ousia* in dignity and power."[24] It is not surprising that he has been seen as, in this passage, going beyond the Form of Good—as one among the other Forms—and that many, such as Plotinus, have interpreted him as referring here to the Divine. This receives further credence from the scheme of the *Timaeus*, in which the *demiourgos* is spoken of as "good."[25]

My concern in the foregoing analysis of Plato's argument

in the analogy of the sun has been to bring out the following points. First, Plato himself had seen a most significant difficulty in his doctrine of Forms with respect to the meaning of "good". Namely, he saw that the problem of the meaning of "good" is not to be resolved in terms of a theory of Forms, for, contrary to the ontological position he then had been accepting, the Forms are not the final ontological ultimates he had supposed, since, in respect to "good," they are dependent, i.e., dependent on something as the principle, the source, of "good". In other words, the Forms are dependent upon this principle as that without which they themselves would be pointless and meaningless, and thus could not "be" in that final sense which he had earlier ascribed to them. Secondly, I have been concerned to bring out the implication that this difficulty consequently pertains equally to the modern theories of "essences" with respect to the meaning of "good." And thirdly, I wish to press the point that Plato's argument is entirely valid, and that we have consequently to recognize the metaphysical necessity of a *principle* of "good."

It was in Neoplatonism that the conception of a transcendent principle or source of "good"—i.e., of the "goodness" of things, and of *the very meaning of "good"*—was not only fully embraced, but was also identified with the Divine. This is the third of the approaches to the meaning of "good" mentioned above. This approach, like the other two, involves significant difficulties. In discussing these, a distinction has to be made in this Neoplatonic doctrine between the position of Plotinus and that accepted by most Christian Neoplatonism following Augustine. Both based the meaning of "good" in God, and in both positions God is the sole principle, source, or origin of all things. This means that for both positions God is the the *cause* of the "being" of things, and of their "good." The crucial difference between these two positions is that Augustine conceived God, the cause of "being," as "a being," in contrast to Plotinus who, mindful of Plato's argument in the *Republic* (which we treated above), held that God is "beyond being" (ἐπέκεινα της οὐσίας), in other words that God transcends "being."

Let us first examine the Christian Neoplatonist position respecting the grounding of the "good" of created things in God. What exactly does this position entail? The issue turns on the conception of the relation of God to "good." The position could be taken as expressed by the statement, "God is good," which could be interpreted, and usually has been, as meaning that God, as a being, has the attribute of "good," or "goodness"—of course in the superlative degree. God, then, is the cause of good in creatures by creating them with the attribute "good." This, however, leaves unresolved the problem of the meaning of "good," for this position runs into a vicious regress. The meaning of "good" in creatures has to be sought in God, but this raises the problem of the meaning of "good" in God. Evidently the argument is involved in the "third man" difficulty.

This difficulty is avoided by Plotinus, who clearly saw the validity of Plato's argument in the *Republic* as demonstrating the metaphysical necessity of a *principle* of "good." For Plotinus the One or God as the primary or ultimate principle of all and everything, including the "good" of all things, "cannot therefore itself be good" (ὥστε τῶ ἑνὶ οὐδὲν ἀγαθον ἐστιν).[26] Rather, "it is beyond good" (ἀλγ ἔστιν ὑπεράγαθον), which entails, as Plotinus says, that "it is the good, not for itself, but for other things, insofar as they are able to participate in it" (καὶ αὐτὸ οὐχ ἑαυτῶ, τοῖς δγ ἄλλοις ἀγαθόν, εἴ τι αὐτοῦ δύναται μεταλαμβάνειν).[27] This means that the principle of good transcends good—it is not itself a "good being." Accordingly, the meaning of "good" in good things has to be sought in that principle of good, but since that principle is not itself good, this position does not run into the "third man" difficulty.

Thomas Aquinas was the medieval Christian thinker who was most fully aware of this difficulty with respect to the conception of a one transcendent principle, or source and origin of all things, a difficulty which he sought to overcome with his doctrine of analogy and of transcendental categories. He maintained that "being" and "good" in respect of God are not to be understood univocally, i.e., in the sense in which they pertain to creatures; rather, they are to be understood *analogically*. This means that, as in regard to creatures we speak of their "being," i.e., their "having being," so with regard to God we can speak of God "being," not, however, in the sense of "*having* being," but as "being *per se*," *ipsum esse*. And, as in respect to creatures we predicate the attribute "good," so in respect to God we can predicate a "transcendental good." The problem with this doctrine is that the very notion of "transcendental predicates or principles" has itself to be understood analogically; that is, the "transcendentals" are not predicates or categories in a univocal sense, i.e., in the sense in which creatures have predicates; rather, they are "analogous to" predicates. However, to treat them consistently as thus analogous is exceedingly difficult, and all too readily the transcendentals are implicitly thought of as predicates which pertain to God, which means that God is thought of as having the attribute "good" (albeit in a superlative sense not pertaining to creatures). Thus God is implicity thought of as "a good being," with the consequence that the "third man" difficulty is not evaded.

What is requisite, I would submit, is to recognize explicitly, what Plato and Aristotle had effectually begun to appreciate,[28] and what Plotinus very clearly saw, that the primary or ultimate principle cannot validly be thought of in terms of categories at all, because categories cannot pertain to it, since such a principle is also the principle or source of the categories. That is, we need to recognize that what Aristotle had explicitly stated with respect to *hyle* as an ultimate principle, can validly be generalized to all ultimate principles, and thus that an *ultimate principle* "in itself is neither a particular thing nor a quantity nor designated by any of the categories by which being is determined."[29] In other words, an ultimate principle transcends all categories. Plotinus had concluded from this that accordingly the One must transcend knowledge, since knowledge is necessarily in terms of categories. Aristotle had, however, correctly argued that this conclusion does not necessarily hold in respect to primary principles, and that we can validly have knowledge (ἐπιστήμη) of a primary principle, one way being that of analogy,[30] as Thomas Aquinas also recognized.

VII

With this clarification of the concept of ultimate principles we can now turn specifically to the problem of the principle of "good," and attempt an approach different from those which we have reviewed and observed to have one or another serious defect. We can achieve such an approach, I would propose, from the standpoint of a metaphysics of "act."

In a metaphysical conception of all beings as "acting," every being stands in need of an "end," a *telos*, since "acting" entails an "end" toward which the acting is aimed or directed. Now the end of an agent is, logically, not generable by the agent in question, since to be an "agent acting" presupposes an "end."[31] Thus the end must be "given," i.e., it must be a datum for that agent. Can this end in question be derived as a datum from other agents? This cannot be because, (a) there can be no reason why any one agent among them all should be uniquely privileged as a donor; and (b) with a plurality of prospective donors, the agent in question is faced with the necessity of a choice, which presupposes an "end" as a criterion in terms of which to choose between them. This leaves as the only alternative that the requisite end for the agent in question must be "given" by, or derivable from, a transcendent principle or source of ends. That is to say, there is a metaphysical necessity for a transcendent teleological principle. This was clear to Aristotle.

It was equally clear to Aristotle that there is a necessary connection between "end" and "good." This is so because "end" entails τὸ οὗ ἕνεκα, "that for the sake of which." That is, the "end" entails "that on account of which," or "wherefore," or "the reason for which," the acting is done, and this "reason" must be that the end be in some respect "good." This "good," however, cannot be a purely "instrumental" one, and to escape an infinite regression we necessarily must come to a "good in itself" or "intrinsic good."[32] Thus we have Aristotle's general position that "the good is that at which all things aim,"[33] since "the good" is "that for the sake of which as an end."[34]

Now Aristotle, having rejected, as we have seen,[35] the conception of "the good itself" as self-subsistent or universal, held that it must be the supreme, complete, or perfect "good,"[36] and, he argued, it is to be identified with the divine unmoved mover as the teleological cause, i.e., as the teleological principle. This is a doctrine which has had a powerful influence on subsequent theological thought. Aristotle maintained the position that God is a thinker whose "thinking is a thinking on thinking,"[37] and argued that "the actuality of thought is life," thus that God's "self-dependent actuality is life most good and eternal,"[38] and therefore that "God is a living being, eternal, most good."[39]

The point in this argument which is of special relevance to us here is that it is because God is the highest or supreme good that God is the teleological principle, the principle of ends. In other words, God provides the end for all things by being that at which all things aim, and that he is this by his being the highest good. This Aristotelian position has been accepted by much subsequent theological thought.

It is most important, however, to appreciate that there is a crucial difficulty in this argument. The argument is that God is the transcendent principle, source, of ends by virtue of being the highest or principal good. The difficulty involved in this is that of the "third man." For we can validly raise the question, why or whereby is God "good"? To the answer that God is good by virtue of "thinking," a further question can be raised as to why "thinking" is the highest good, or indeed, "good" at all? The only way out of this difficulty, as Plato and Plotinus had seen, is to maintain, *not* that God is the *principal* good, but that God transcends good by being the *principle of* good.

The problem now is how the "principle of good" is to be comprehended. We can, I would suggest, most readily approach this problem from a consideration of "end." The "end" for a being means that at which its acting aims, and this entails some "order." What is implied is not merely any order, but an order which is "fitting," "suitable," "appropriate" for that being. Further, that end, the order, which is aimed at, is some form of definiteness as a possibility for its actualization. But every form of definiteness, considered simply as such, i.e., in complete abstraction from actuality or actualization, is a completely general possibility.

Now a form of definiteness as a general possibility entails that, since it is "general," it is without anything whereby it would be "better" or "worse" with respect to any given actual or acting being. That is to say, the realm of pure possibility, by virtue of its complete generality, is necessarily neutral with regard to its qualification of actuality. This means that the factor of "better" or "worse" is not inherent in, or derivable from, the realm of forms of definiteness per se. This factor must be derived from some other source. That source, I would contend, cannot be other than the transcendent principle of ends. For the "end," as we have seen, entails "fittingness," "suitability," i.e., that it be "best." That is to say, the "principle of end" entails that it be also the "principle of good."

But the "principle of good" cannot be, as Aristotle and much of the theological tradition have maintained, the "highest good." Rather, the "principle of good" must be that whereby, and from which, there is a distinction *at all* between "good" and "bad," "better" or "worse," "fitting" or "unfitting," "suitable" or "unsuitable," etc., *whereby, indeed, these words have any meaning at all.* This distinction is not inherent in actuality as such, nor in pure possibility as such. But it is a fundamental presupposition for any actuality, and a fundamental presupposition for possibility to have any relevance to actuality. Thus a transcendent "principle" of "good," which is also the "teleological principle," is an ultimate metaphysical necessity.[40]

NOTES

1 *Oxford English Dictionary,* "Good," A, adj.

2 Cf. *O.E.D.,* "Worth," arts. 1–2.

3 My italics; cf. *O.E.D.,* "Value," art. 1.1.

4 Liddell, Scott, Jones, *A Greek-English Lexicon.*

5 There has been a failure, in much recent philosophical literature, to recognize this highly significant difference in connotation between "good" on the one side and "value" and "worth" on the other, and the absolute sense, strictly pertaining only to "good," has been implicitly imported into "value" and "worth," with the consequence that spurious reasoning has passed undetected.

6 I. Kant, *Grundlegung zur Metaphysik der Sitten*, Erster Abschnitt, BA 1; trans. Lewis White Beck, *Foundations of the Metaphysics of Morals*, (New York: The Bobbs-Merrill Company, Inc., 1959), p. 9.

7 W.D. Ross, *The Right and the Good* (Oxford: At the Clarendon Press, 1930), p.140.

8 Cf. Letters to De Volder, 24 March 1699, 23 June 1699, April 1702, resp. pp. 516, 519, 527 in L.E. Loemker, *Gottfried Wilhelm Leibniz: Philosophical Papers and Letters* (Dordrecht, Holland: D. Reidel Publishing Company, 1969), and in G.W. *Leibniz: Philosophische Schriften*, ed. C.I. Gerhardt, (Berlin and Halle, 1849–55), 2: 169, 183, 241.

9 R. Descartes, *Principles of Philosophy*, Pt. 1, Princ. 51; E. Haldane and G.R.T. Ross, 2 Vols. (Cambridge: University Press, 1911), I: 239; Adam and Tannery, 8: 24.

10 I have dealt with this interrelatedness constituting a "society" in my papers "The Metaphysics of Social Relations" and "Community, the State, and the National Society," contributed to meetings of the International Society for Metaphysics (1980 and 1981), published forthcoming in the *Proceedings* of the Society.

11 W.D. Ross, *The Right and the Good*, p. 122.

12 For a fuller treatment see my "Matter, Action, and Physical Being" in *International Philosophical Quarterly* (March 1981).

13 See my *The Nature of Physical Existence* (London: Allen and Unwin; New York: Humanities Press, 1972), pp. 276–83.

14 Aristotle, *Nicomachean Ethics*, 1094a3: τἀγαθὸν οὐ πάνγ ἀφιεται.

15 Aristotle, *Eudemian Ethics*, 1217b8-1218a38.

16 Ibid., 1218a39-b2.

17 Ibid., 1218a39-b7.

18 Ibid., 1218b8-27.

19 Nicolai Hartmann, *Ethics*, trans. Stanton Coit, 3 vols. (London: Allen and Unwin; New York: Humanities Press, 1932).

20 Plato, *Republic*, 509B (my trans.).

21 Ibid., 509B.

22 Ibid., 505A (my trans.).

23 Cf. e.g., W.C.K. Guthrie, *A History of Greek Philosophy* (Cambridge: University Press, 1975) 5: 503–504.

24 Plato, *Republic*, 509B: οὐκ οὐσίας ὄντος τοῦ ἀγαθοῦ, ἀλỳ ἔτι ἐπέκεινα τῆς οὐσίας πρεσβείᾳ καὶ δυνάμει ὑπερέχοντος.

25 Plato, *Timaeus*, 29E.

26 Plotinus, *Enneads* 6. 9. 6.

27 Ibid.

28 This is why Plato, in the *Timaeus*, in his account of "the Gods and the generation of the all," (29C) had recourse to myth. Aristotle saw that the ἄρχαι, the principles, of things in becoming, viz., matter and the Forms, cannot be understood in terms of the categories.

29 Aristotle *Metaphysics*, 1029a 20–22.

30 Aristotle *Physics*, 191a 9–11.

31 The supposition that it is, is the basic fallacy of the subjectivist theory of good.

32 Cf. Aristotle, *Nicomachean Ethics*, 1094a 19–23.

33 Ibid., 1094a 3.

34 Aristotle, *Eudemian Ethics*, 1218b 10.

35 See p. 17.

36 Cf. *Nicomachean Ethics*, 1094a 22.

37 Aristotle, *Metaphysics*, 1074b 35: ἔστιν ἡ νόησις νοήσεως νόησις. (Tr. Ross.)

38 *Met.*, 1072b 28–29: ἐνέργεια δὲ ἡ καθ᾽αὑτὴν ἐκείνον ζωη ἀρίστη καί ἀΐδιος.

39 *Met.*, 1072b 29–30: τὸν θεὸν ειναι ζῷον ἀΐδιον ἄριστον.

40 Whitehead, I think, had a grasp of this in his doctrine of God as the "principle of concretion" having a "primordial valuation of pure potentials [whereby] each eternal object has a definite effective relevance to each concrescent process" (*Process and Reality*, Part 2, Chapter 1, Section 1).

5

THE KANTIAN CRITIQUE OF ARISTOTLE'S MORAL PHILOSOPHY

ROGER J. SULLIVAN

n the *Groundwork of the Metaphysic of Morals* and the *Critique of Practical Reason,* Immanuel Kant offers a cluster of criticisms against all previous moral philosophies. He implies that his significance as a moral philosopher rests mainly on his acuity in discerning and remedying the errors of earlier authors. Although he rarely mentions Aristotle by name, Kant does not exclude Aristotle's moral philosophy from his critique, and commentators on Aristotle have often used the Kantian arguments to claim that Aristotle does not offer us a moral theory at all. It is not clear that the Kantian arguments actually hold against Aristotle; yet they have been strangely exempted from careful examination. I will examine them in this paper.

I will conclude that the Kantian analyses of Aristotle's moral theory are historically inaccurate and the criticisms invalid. Further, those criticisms are focused in such a way that they tend to distract us from more fundamental issues, especially the different ontologies presupposed in each theory. If my arguments are sound, they show that much of Kant's moral philosophy is not as novel as he believed it to be nor as it generally has been taken to be.[1]

I

The core of the Kantian criticism consists in the contention that Aristotle's moral theory is fatally flawed by its failure to provide for the crucial moral significance of the notion of "duty," so that the line between prudence and morality is badly blurred. Consequently, as Robert Paul Wolff writes, Kant regarded "the philosophy of eudaimonism and all its variants. . .[as] the epitome of moral confusion."[2]

Among recent writers, the only detailed argument against Aristotle and in support of this contention has been constructed by Arthur W. H. Adkins in his *Merit and Responsibility: A Study in Greek Values*. He makes it clear that his study is conducted from a Kantian stance:

> For any man brought up in a western democratic society the related concepts of duty and responsibility are the central concepts of ethics. . .In this respect, at least, we are all Kantians now. Surely, we assume, in any society "What is my duty in these circumstances?" is the basic question which the agent must ask himself in any matter which requires a moral decision.[3]

After examining the role of moral responsibility in Greek thought before Aristotle and in Aristotle's theory, Adkins concludes that the Aristotelian theory amounts only to a prudential policy for attaining well-being.[4] Adkins' main arguments can be organized conveniently around the original Kantian critique, and they do what Kant himself did not do—apply those criticisms explicitly to the Aristotelian ethical theory.

Thesis I. Moral goodness (a morally good will) is the supreme practical good.[5] Aristotle does not and cannot appreciate this fundamental truth. The dominant value system of Greek society may allow him to take moral goodness to be a genuine excellence, but only as one among several; and he cannot, for example, assert the preeminence of moral goodness over the claims of individual merit based on ability to achieve military victory, by whatever means.[6]

Thesis II. Moral goodness is absolutely and always intrinsically good; its value does not depend on what it can accomplish.[7] But Aristotle reduces moral goodness to an instrumental good. Although "Aristotle never explicitly states that this is the case," his actual justification for the *aretē,* the excellence, of the whole man is not an appeal to a supreme moral ideal but a prudential reason: men with such excellences are necessary to the *eudaimonia,* the well-being, of the state.[8] Aristotle's appeals to ordinary language work so well because the ordinary language of Greece necessarily reflects the traditional Homeric values commending qualities vital to the survival and prosperity of the state.[9] Even for individuals, "what one 'ought' to do is what it is necessary to do in order to be *eudaimon.* . .the incentive to pursue the quiet [cooperative, moral] virtues has always been that to do so is a surer method of attaining prosperity—*eudaimonia* or some other word—than not to do so."[10]

Thesis III. There is always the possibility of a "natural dialectic" between the claims of morality and our desire for other, non-moral goods, and out of this dialectic emerge the principles of morality in the form of duty, that is, what we ought to do.[11] But Aristotle obscures moral conflict and so also the significance of the notion of duty by making morality a means to the nonmoral values constituent of the eudaimonic life. "There is no possibility of. . .setting 'duty' against *eudaimonia.* . .one 'ought' in one's own interest to pursue a course of action which is likely to lead to one's success."[12]

Thesis IV. "Ought" implies "can," for a man can be held responsible only for what is within his control. We always can, and therefore ought, to form our intentions rightly, but we do not have a strict duty to attain success in carrying out our intentions in the world, for there are too many factors over which we have little or no control and for which we cannot be held responsible. Consequently, moral action consists essentially in our adopting the *intention* to act dutifully.[13] Aristotle's "ought" is entirely different from the "ought" of duty, because the Greek view of the highest good for man includes all sorts of elements—personal qualities, power, health, wealth, position—not completely within a man's control, and because the emphasis in the Aristotelian view is on the need to succeed in order to gain that highest good. W. F. R. Hardie makes the point this way:

> The question of responsibility does not arise [in Aristotle's
> theory] in the same direct way. . .as in a Kantian theory. When
> the idea of duty is central, the idea of responsibility is also
> central, the idea that it is reasonable to praise people for doing
> their duty and blame or even punish them for not doing it.
> When the central ideas are happiness and virtue, as a condition
> or constituent of happiness, the topic of moral accountability is
> not in the foreground. For reflection soon shows that a man's
> possessing or not possessing admirable qualities. . .depends on
> many factors over which he has no control. [14]

Thesis V. Morality arises out of the nature of rational
agency, so that the fundamental truths of morality must apply to
all men. [15] Adkins admits that Aristotle's analysis of moral responsibility is very close to our own, both in terminology and point of
view. But, he argues, that analysis necessarily remains isolated
from the rest of Aristotle's moral theory: "Aristotle does not and
cannot furnish. . .a system of ethics which should enable the
application of this analysis in all cases in which we should consider
this relevant."[16] The reason is that Aristotle is forced to adopt a
Homeric conception of *aretē* and *eudaimonia*; both terms "commend
a whole leisured way of life," the life of the wealthy, who lavish
their prosperity on the state's interest and have only certain
respectable *technai*—farming and military skill but not merchan-
dising. [17]

Conclusion. "It should be evident," Adkins concludes,
"how far [Aristotle's] 'it is necessary' is removed from the 'Duty' of
a deontological ethic."[18] Aristotle offers us only a prudential policy
for attaining well-being. This is also true of any teleological ethical
theory, that is, one in which the notion of the "good"—the goal or
end of action—is taken to be fundamental and so definitive of what
is "right"—the rules or principles of practice. P. H. Nowell-Smith
puts the criticism this way: "It is characteristic of teleologists to
treat all 'oughts' as hypothetical and all rules as rules for attaining
a given end."[19] Hardie applies this criticism to Aristotle in several
passages:

> There are radical questions, connected with the difference be-
> tween prudent and moral conduct, on which Aristotle does not
> state a clear and consistent view. . . . Aristotle does not admit a

clear distinction between the rules of morality and the rules of
prudence. . . . [He] did not distinguish sharply, as Kant tried
to distinguish, between the rationality of the moral law and the
rationality of "enlightened self-interest" or, to use Aristotle's
word, "self-love."[20]

Aristotle does define the man of practical wisdom as a person who
desires above all what is best for himself.[21] This seems to be a
definitive indication that Aristotle's ethics, and any other teleological
ethic, confuse morality with prudence. Such a theory must try to
appeal to our desires, to enlighten us to our best good so that we
want it, and insofar as actions originate with desires rather than
from a sense of duty, they are done to satisfy inclinations, to achieve
pleasure or happiness. When we act out of desires, we necessarily
act out of self-interest—selfishly and prudentially, and we act either
amorally or immorally but not morally well. We do not achieve
moral goodness by merely seeking pleasure.[22]

Immanuel Kant claimed for himself a Copernican revolution, not only in epistemology and metaphysics but in ethics, too,[23]
and many thoughtful men have been convinced that his arguments
against Aristotle's analysis of morality (and any like it) are devastating.
D. J. Allan, for example, writes:

Even if we could overlook the refinement of our ethical notions
by Christianity, the whole social background of the *Ethics* is
vastly different from ours, and much re-thinking would be
necessary to make it palatable to the modern mind.[24]

II

The remainder of this paper will be devoted to an examination of
the Kantian critique. Since the structure of Kant's arguments tends
to obscure what is at stake, I shall focus my analysis through three
fundamental questions which any moral theory must try to answer.
The questions are: (1) What motives are morally good? (2) What

practical rules are ultimately right? (3) What end or system of ends is ultimately good? I shall begin by comparing the Aristotelian and the Kantian answers to the first question, for that is where the notion of duty arises most directly.

What motives are morally good? Aristotle and Kant are so frequently contrasted with each other that little attention has been given to the ways in which their theories do *not* differ. I will begin, then, by listing points of important and relevant agreement.

1. No case of fully human, and therefore morally assessable, action can occur without the agent's having an end in view; all genuinely human actions are purposive.[25]
2. We need to distinguish between ends and motives, for there are important differences between what a man aims at and his reasons for doing so.[26] This distinction, in turn, serves as the basis for distinguishing between morality and mere legality.[27]
3. Moral value is possible to man only because he is a rational agent, and the lack of proper moral value arises out of insufficiently rational grounds, in emotions inadequately permeated by reason; moral goodness requires appetition to be subservient to the rule of reason.[28]
4. Fully human action requires grounding in both reason and appetition, so that morally good practice cannot occur without the intellectual apprehension of the moral rightness of a particular action *and* a genuine caring about the accomplishment of that action.[29]
5. The mere performance of the right actions is not a sufficient condition for moral goodness; a man must act rightly because it is the right way to act.[30]

The major difference between the Aristotelian and the Kantian analyses of morally good motivation concerns the *necessity* of describing such motivation in terms of duty. Kant argues that, although the law of morality is of itself an objective principle, not an imperative, it *necessarily* appears to *us* in the form of an imperative because of the special nature of human practical reason. Our practical reason has two functions: one is empirical, based on desire, and aimed at securing pleasure and happiness; the other is pure, grounded in reason alone, and aimed at the moral good. These two uses of practical reason do not necessarily oppose each other (else the total final good would not be possible), but they always can. We have a will "exposed. . .to subjective conditions (certain impulsions)" constituting a morally negative aspect of our character, "either a hindrance, which we have to overcome, or an allurement which not be made into a motive."[31] Genuine moral motivation, then, consists always in the recognition that morality is our duty, and "the majesty of duty has nothing to do with the enjoyment of life;" even moral satisfaction is "merely negative with reference to everything which might make life pleasant."[32]

It is, Kant argues, moral fanaticism to believe we can ever bring our emotional life into such conformity with reason that we will pleasurably do what is right because what is right is, "noble, sublime, and magnanimous."[33] That kind of motivation can be of genuinely moral quality only for a being with the status of "holiness," which can be predicted accurately only of an agent like God, who has a nature so subjectively constituted that whatever he chooses will also necessarily be objectively good.[34] For men, the relationship between objectivity (the moral law) and subjectivity (a man's actual intentions) is always a contingent one. Because we "can never be wholly free from [pathological] desires and inclinations which. . .do not of themselves agree with the moral law," the best we can achieve is "virtue, i.e., moral disposition in conflict"—consciousness of being duty-bound under the dry and stern command of the moral law and dutifully submissive to it.[35] Nonetheless, holiness is, even for us, the practical ideal toward which we ought to strive, for it is the paradigm of how we ought always to choose; we are bound to make continual progress toward that ideal, even if we can never reach it.[36]

Aristotle has a radically different view of man. Despite the fact that we can experience internal conflict, the human psyche possesses an intrinsic tendency toward integrity and perfection, so that internal strife is not one of its essential qualities. Consequently, we find in Aristotle an isomorphic relation, rejected by Kant, between good men, right actions, and pleasure. Being a morally good man does not frustrate but rather actualizes a man's genuine self-fulfillment. Aristotle does not confuse morality with pleasure, but he also does not suspect for a moment that the immoral life is, by its very nature, more pleasurable than the moral life.[37]

For Aristotle the morally best man is the man of practical wisdom (*phronēsis*, sometimes translated as "prudence") and moral excellence (*sōphrosunē*, sometimes translated as "temperance"). As Aristotle defines these excellences (*aretai*) or characteristics (*hexeis*), they are but two aspects of the same ideal. Practical wisdom has both cognitive and imperative roles, sensitively discerning the morally right thing to do in each situation and effectively securing absolute cooperation from appetition in accomplishing what is right; and moral excellence is a disposition consisting in complete submission to the rule of reason and in affection only for what is morally good (the *kalon*).[38] The man of practical wisdom and moral excellence has achieved such integrity in his moral life that he does not experience excessive or deficient desires; he is, "as it were, a law unto himself."[39]

Hardie distorts Aristotle's doctrine based on his own Kantian perspective when he comments: "Aristotle has an un-Kantian appreciation of motives which are mixed and which *fall short of being the highest.*"[40] Since practical reason is a complex of reason and appetition, Aristotle sees no justification for thinking that a man's moral worth is diminished by his loving and enjoying what is morally right. Doing what is right is normally a pleasurable thing, but only the good man will consistently enjoy doing such actions for the right reason. What he apprehends as essentially good about right actions is their moral rightness; that they normally are also pleasurable is something "added on. . .like the bloom of youth in those who are in their prime."[41] The morally excellent person is not one who happens to find a happy congruence between what he experiences as pleasurable and what he recognizes as noble; he does not act as he does because his moral education has led him to like what he also recognizes as morally good. It is the other way around, and that is just what makes him morally good: he "finds no pleasure in anything that violates the dictates of reason."[42]

Hardie errs by taking moral excellence to be a nonmoral disposition. Aristotle's doctrine to the contrary is fairly summarized in this passage:

> Actions which conform to virtue [*kat' aretēn*] are naturally pleasant, and as a result, such actions are not only pleasant for

those who love the noble but also pleasant in themselves.[43]
The life of such men has no further need for pleasure as an
added attraction, but it contains pleasure within itself. We may
even go so far as to state that the man who does not enjoy
performing noble actions is not a good man at all. Nobody
would call a man just who does not enjoy acting justly, nor
generous who does not enjoy generous actions, and so on.[44]

Aristotle's point is clear. If a man has the kind of moral personality
which habitually leads him to choose right actions in the right way,
then he also will be the sort of person who appreciates and enjoys
doing them, and insofar as a man cannot enjoy doing such actions,
he shows he falls below the ideal of moral character. The essence
of moral motivation, according to Aristotle, is not dutifulness,
because, insofar as a man finds morally right actions *only* a duty,
he has not yet entered into the authentic spirit of morality.[45]

Aristotle's best man, then, has risen above the kind of
moral conflict within which the notion of duty arises. He is not
insensitive to the fact that other men may still experience such
struggles, but they are morally inferior men for doing so. Aristotle
discusses two kinds of moral personalities which experience internal
moral conflict: the morally strong person (*to enkratēs*, the "conti-
nent" man) and the morally weak person (*to akratēs*, the "inconti-
nent" man). Both know what it is to act rightly, but their desires
are not always subservient to the lead of reason. The morally strong
man, with effort, keeps his emotions under control, but the morally
weak man is not always successful in doing so. For such men the
relation between objectivity and subjectivity is often one of constraint, and then morality is experienced by them as their duty.[46]

The *kalon* is what we ought always to do, and this is clearly
a moral "ought," but it is not necessarily equivalent to Kant's notion
of "duty." Kant's claims on behalf of duty derive much of their
persuasive power from the fact that we cannot help but wonder
what we "ought" to do any time we are not sure what the right
action might be in our particular situation. But this "ought" does
not necessarily imply that we find the right action onerous, bur-
densome, dry, and unyielding. Often we are perfectly ready and
willing to do what is right; we want to do what is right, but we are
not sure what is right. Because Kant stresses moral conflict as our

paradigmatic moral condition, he tends to analyze moral epistemological confusion only as a special kind of moral conflict, and he
neglects the peculiar features of moral confusion in which moral
conflict plays no role.

R.-A. Gauthier claims that in the *Nichomachean Ethics* he
has found the word *dei*, "ought," used some 170 times "in a sense
which is uncontestably moral," and his estimate may be conserva-
tive.[47] But whether or not this moral "ought" should be understood
as equivalent to the "ought" of Kantian duty depends on the moral
personality involved. If a person is genuinely good, the "ought"
only reflects his rational wish, with no implication that there is also
a negative aspect to his character, consisting in potentially evil
desires. But if he is not morally secure, as most of us are not, then
the "ought" *may* involve what Kant described as "a good will,
exposed, however, to certain subjective limitations and obstacles."[48]
Even then, that need not be the case, for even morally imperfect
men do not find their inner moral lives a constant and unceasing
battleground; moral weakness is intermittent, and so too are the
temptations of the morally strong.

Hardie is right when he claims that the concept of duty
enters into Aristotle's theory differently than in Kant's and in a less
direct way, but he is mistaken in the way he construes this difference.
Each philosopher presents us with a different practical ideal: Kant's
holy agent is by nature so constituted that the relation between
objectivity and subjectivity is a necessary relation, while Aristotle's
man of practical wisdom and moral excellence enjoys only a
contingent integrity; he *will* naturally choose the objective good,
but this "naturally" is the result of practice; his character is his
"second nature," not his essential constitution as a man.[49] Kant
thought that holiness is unattainable by man, and Aristotle did not
believe that most men will—perhaps even can—achieve practical
excellence; they agree that most men are, at best, morally strong.[50]
But the practical consequences of their different ideals are enormous,
for they determine how we understand the role of appetition in our
moral life, and how, consequently, we conceive of the aims and
methods of moral education.[51] Likewise, the different ideals deeply
affect their respective moral epistemologies. Aristotle's theory of
action convinced him that there can be no ultimate moral norm,

but he was not dismayed by this, for he thought the really good man can trust his emotions to help him value rightly in each situation. Hence, his doctrine of *phronēsis aisthēsis*, the ability of the good man to have a sensitive *feel* for what is right. But Kant was left with no alternative but a purely rational ultimate norm for right action, that of consistency.

In effect, Kant's best moral man is Aristotle's second best, the morally strong person.[52] Hardie contrasts the two kinds of moral personality this way:

> If we ask ourselves which of these two kinds of goodness is the better, we find ourselves distracted by a difficulty. In one way we admire the man who behaves well in a battle without undue distress more than the man who has to overcome obvious terror. In one way a man naturally moderate in his appetites is better than a man who has to struggle to control them. On the other hand, the merit of moral victory seems to be enhanced when there have been obstacles to overcome. Is the saint, or the moral hero, the man who is not tempted or the man who struggles successfully with temptation. . . .Aristotle, I think, takes it for granted that "continence" is a second best to "temperance" or virtue: it is better not to have bad or excessive desires. He does not formulate and face the problem.[53]

Hardie's statement contains two errors. First, he again mistakes moral excellence or temperance for a nonmoral disposition instead of a state of moral accomplishment; and secondly, Aristotle did face the problem and he resolved it in favor of moral excellence.[54] To him it was transparently clear that the best person is the one who has so mastered himself that he does not have to struggle with opposition from within.[55] Opposition can always originate unexpectedly from without and frustrate any man, even the best, and then we ask of a man only the best that he can do. Surely we also admire the moral neophyte as he exerts great effort to control his recalcitrant emotions, but we do not think he is a morally better man because he is, as Aristotle describes him, "young in years or immature in character."[56] That is why, in 4.9, Aristotle argues that a sense of shame (*aidōs* or *aischunē*) is not a mark of moral accomplishment, and why he allows for but does not praise understanding (*sunesis*) in 6.10. Both are forms of conscience which occur only because a man has a moral personality inferior to the best. *Sunesis* is that form of moral conscience which occurs ahead of a possible action but which does not become practical and inform action, and shame is that form of conscience, equally inefficacious, which appears only after a man has performed badly. As R.-A. Gauthier puts it,

> If Aristotle's ethics is not an ethics of conscience, it is not for lack of having arrived at an elaboration of the idea of conscience and the related ideas of duty and moral obligation; it is on the contrary because [he] has thought it necessary to push on, to the notion of a practical wisdom which continues from the point at which conscience [*sunesis*] stops, at the threshold of free decision, and enters into decision and accompanies action up to its efficacious achievement, which it guides necessarily and infallibly to its conclusion.[57]

Why does Kant reject the possibility of at least some men attaining the moral status of practical excellence? In the *Groundwork* and the second *Critique*, at least part of the reason can be found in a misleading picture of motivation which Kant adopted, a philosophic rather than a psychological claim because it purports to state what is necessarily the case: insofar as an action is not done out of sense of duty, it must be done for the sake of pleasure, to satisfy pathological inclinations. There is an initial plausibility to this doctrine, because it seems to express nothing more than the claim that motivation divides into moral and nonmoral or immoral. But there is no logical necessity in the claim that if an action is not done from duty, it must be aimed at pleasure and so be amoral or immoral. Just as amorally motivated actions can have various ends, not all of which concern pleasure, so also moral motivation can take the shape of various dispositions, each having its own distinctive moral quality. In his *Religion within the Limits of Reason Alone* and his *Metaphysic of Morals*, Kant amended his theory to try to remedy its inadequacies.[58] In doing so, he moved closer to the Aristotelian view. To the end, however, Kant remained adamant in his claim that the law of morality always and necessarily appears to us in the form of duty, so that it is moral fanaticism to think that any of us can progress morally to the status where principles of morality need no longer be experienced as imperatives we place against ourselves.[59]

We might conclude that the reason for Kant's view is to be found in his Critical theoretical writings, and there is some justification for believing this. In the first *Critique* Kant had developed his famous doctrine of the two viewpoints: we find, he wrote, that we must regard man both as a natural thing like other things, inexorably bound by causal laws and amoral, and as a moral agent, radically free to live by his own principles. The natural and the moral realms, then, are mutually exclusive, though necessarily related, ways of viewing what it is to be a human being, and man also finds his agency torn between these two aspects, the natural and heteronomous on the one hand, and the noumenal and autonomous on the other. But this way of interpreting human agency breaks down, for it seduces Kant into a new version of the Socratic paradox: if heteronomy is defined deterministically, as it is in the first *Critique* and the *Groundwork*, then no man can be morally guilty; and if reason infallibly determines man as a noumenal agent, no man can be morally virtuous, either. In the second *Critique* Kant was forced to redefine heteronomy as a mode of freedom. Ignoring the fact that this revision was incompatible with his theoretical distinction between the noumenal and the phenomenal,[60] Kant also altered his view of the relation between appetition and reason, giving emotions an increasingly important role in moral motivation. Had he more carefully re-examined his theory of action and continued along this path, he would also have had to discard dutifulness as the highest human dispostion, and he would have been very nearly an Aristotelian on this point.

But Kant refused to allow the possibility of the integrity of Aristotle's man of practical wisdom, and his ultimate reason for doing so is to be found, I think, in the first book of his *Religion*. There he states his belief that all mankind suffers from a radical, innate, and inextirpable propensity toward evil. Like human freedom (of which moral evil is a heterogeneous mode) the origin of this propensity is inexplicable to human reason. However, experience shows that all men suffer from a will which tends to make pleasure the supreme incentive in practice. Because we are free, we are able to combat this propensity successfully, but we cannot radically alter our nature. That is why, finally, we should not hope to bring such integrity into our moral life that the condition of conflict between morality and pleasure and the notion of duty which arises out of that condition are no longer descriptive of our moral disposition.

What deserves particular attention in this doctrine in the *Religion* is the manner in which Kant derives knowledge of the nature of the human moral will, a noumenal reality, from empirical grounds, and then claims for that knowledge both necessity and universality! This is not the sort of procedure we would expect from the author of the *Critique of Pure Reason*. What led him to this extraordinary position, I think, was his concern to construct a moral theory consonant with Christian belief as he knew it, a belief stressing the reality and the pervasiveness of original sin. Kant takes pains to point out that his doctrine concerning the depravity of human nature "agrees well with that manner of presentation which the Scriptures use, whereby the origin of evil in the human race is depicted as having a [temporal] beginning."[61] If I am correct in my view, the main reason for the great emphasis Kant places on the notion of duty lies *outside* his moral philosophy, in his pre-philosophic Christian ontology. And if this is so, then criticisms directed against Aristotle's failure to properly stress duty in his moral theory should be understood as complaints, not that his moral philosophy is philosophically inadequate, but that it does not stand sufficiently within the Pauline-Augustinian-Lutheran tradition of Christian thought.

There is one last criticism to be considered under the heading of moral motivation: the charge that Aristotle's morally best man acts selfishly and amorally, for he seeks what is best for himself. Aristotle anticipated this criticism, and in the fourth and eighth chapters of "Book Nine" of *Nichomachean Ethics* he argues that selfishness does not consist in doing what one wants or even what one enjoys doing, but in placing so much value on material goods and sensual pleasures (emphasized in Kant's descriptions of happiness) that one becomes indifferent and even hostile to the needs and rights of others. Aristotle argues that moral goodness is both an individual *and* a political excellence, so that the morally good man is precisely the one who acts justly and benevolently toward others (and takes the greatest pleasure in doing so). It is clearly neither self-interest in a nonmoral sense nor selfishness in a morally derogatory sense to seek what is morally best. (Kant surely did not think so.) Aristotle's egoism—the proper valuing of one's self, of others, and of noble actions—turns out to be the ancestor of Kant's insistence on the absolute, unconditional value of morality. For the rationality of Aristotle's notion of self-interest *is* the rationality of the moral law. Consequently, the criticism does not hold.

Some remarks need to be made about Hardie's thoughts on this topic (see the conclusion in Section I preceding). They are confused, and that is why he alleges that Aristotle lacks a clear and consistent view about the relation between prudence and morality. In effect, Aristotle tells us that there is not a single right way in which to describe that relationship, for too much depends on the moral personalities involved. When a man achieves the integrity of practical excellence, then there is no distinction between what is morally good and what he sees to be in his own best interest. But with lesser men, there can be a conflict between morality and self-interest.[62] Once again, the difference between Aristotle and Kant shows itself most clearly in the different ideals they present to us: because Kant's virtuous man can never achieve integrity in Aristotle's sense, the distinction between morality and prudence must be kept and emphasized by Kant, and the tension between them cannot be resolved in this life.[63]

What practical rules are ultimately right? The second set of Kantian criticisms concerns the form of Aristotle's practical rules. Kant believed that all previous moral philosophers had not distinguished adequately between the rules of morality and the rules of prudence, and he implies that the classification of practical rules into hypothetical and categorical originated with him. The Kantian criticism holds only if Aristotle delineates morally right actions as only instrumentally good and all practical rules as hypothetical. But Aristotle is guilty on neither count.

Kant, of course, did not originate the distinction between instrumental and intrinsic goods. Aristotle, for example, *began* his book with a penetrating discussion of the difference between intrinsically and instrumentally good actions, and he then applied

that distinction, to contrast making (*poiēsis*) with doing or acting
(*praxis*). Poietic actions are only conditionally or hypothetically
good (*ex hypotheseōs*), for they are good only insofar as they are
effective in securing things or states of affairs distinct from, and
describable apart from, what is done to achieve them; and the
capacity to produce such products is a capacity for moral opposites.
Only "doings" have immediate moral value. They are intrinsically
good (*telos haplōs*), valuable for their own sakes, for their value is
not derived from something else but inheres in the activities
themselves (as forms of *energeia*), and the kind of character which
typically chooses them as intrinsic goods is itself unconditionally
good.[64] Aristotle, in fact, draws the line so clearly between poietic
and moral kinds of activity—"one does not include the other"—
that he has been taken to task for making the distinction too
harshly.[65]

Aristotle understood better than Kant that an adequate
moral theory needs a carefully constructed theory of human action,
and his distinction between poietic and properly practical activity
is derived partly from his theory of action: the end of an action and
its relation to that action define the nature of the action. In his
terms, the formal and final causes coalesce in morally exemplary
actions, and that is why we can call such actions both right (they
conform to the right rule) and good (they are themselves finalities
and also constituents of the morally good life as a whole). The fact
that they constitute the morally good life does not reduce them to
the status of instrumentalities, for that life is not something external
to and describably apart from them, just as good character is not a
separate end generated instrumentally by them.

We have already seen something of Aristotle's doctrine
concerning pleasure: pleasure is not a criterion of moral good, and
it is not something distinct from activity. Rather, pleasure accompanies intrinsically good activities so that they are naturally pleasurable; and instrumentally good activities are not. What makes
intrinsically good activities good is not the pleasure which normally
accompanies them but characteristics they possess by their very
nature. Moral motivation does not presuppose some other desire
for pleasure, for moral motivation is both the affective and effective
expression of an appreciative recognition of the absoluteness of
moral value.[66]

Although the morally good and the morally right are not distinct from one another in good actions done rightly, there is a sense in which Aristotle does think that the morally good is more fundamental than, and so legislative of, the morally right. His main reason for thinking this is to be found in his theory of action: practical matters involve so many variable contingencies that no practical rule can hold with genuine universality.[67] We can see the force of this doctrine by attending briefly to his notion of the "mean."[68]

Aristotle tries to use the notion of the mean as a way of clarifying the nature of the *kalon*, the morally good. But he is forced to admit that it does not hold with any precision: how it applies depends on the particularities of each situation, and it cannot be applied to every kind of action nor to every person in the same way. So the notion of the mean cannot function as an absolute norm for the morally good.[69] We need some other norm for determining when and how the mean holds, and that standard, Aristotle suggests, is right reason. But when is reason right? Aristotle concludes that we finally must look to "the man of high moral standards [*ho spoudaios*]. . .[for he is] the standard and measure. . .because of his ability to see the truth in each particular moral question."[70] He is also the man of practical wisdom, the person with the moral sensitivity (*aisthēsis*) to know exactly how to act rightly, and the good sense (*gnomē*) to recognize what is *kalon* here and how. Aristotle therefore gives the notion of the moral good precedence over moral rules, because moral rules do not include in themselves a standard for when and how they apply. But this is a far cry from taking such rules to be only instrumentally good.

J. Donald Monan adds a new criticism at this point. He writes:

> The *kalon*-concept receives no fully metaphysical elaboration in its derivation, for it is introduced as a category as though it were a primary intelligible needing no inquiry into its ancestry. . . .At this precise point, unfortunately, Aristotle's methodology reveals its limits, in the sense that it manifests no fully developed roots, nor indeed does it grow to maturity in any fully elaborated metaphysic of value.[71]

Since the *kalon* is the moral absolute, it is as impossible for Aristotle to derive it from something else as it is for Kant to provide a deduction of morality in the third chapter of the *Groundwork*.[72] The request is mistaken and should not have been made. What is possible is to explicate the *kalon* in terms of kinship, if not ancestry. Adkins is right in linking the moral *aretē* of the man of practical wisdom to the state, but he errs in taking it as a merely prudential relationship. Aristotle holds that the state has its own proper function (its *ergon*), to promote the best life for all its citizens: "the end of individuals and of the state is the same."[73] As we shall shortly see, that end is clearly moral in nature. Very early in the *Ethics* Aristotle points out the connection between practical and political wisdom, showing why he intends the *Ethics* to be read as a part of the *Politics*.[74] Although the notion of the *kalon* cannot be formally derived from anything else, its ontological foundations can be found throughout Aristotle's political and moral writings: in his doctrine concerning the nature of man as a rational agent and a political being, in his analyses of the nature of kinds of actions, the nature of the state as a moral entity, the special nature of the relations between citizens, between parents and children, between husband and wife, and so on. Monan would have been better advised to have criticized other moral philosophers who oversimplify the complexity of human moral life and attempt to explicate the fundamental nature of morality, as Kant did, only in terms of a single ontological doctrine, man's nature as a rational agent.

What end or system of ends is ultimately good? The last set of Kantian criticisms of Aristotle's ethical theory concerns the nature of the final, total good for man.[75] We can best assess these criticisms within the context of Kant's own doctrine on this matter, mentioned in passing in the *Groundwork* but elaborately presented in the second *Critique*. Briefly, Kant's doctrine is that because there are two heterogeneous but genuine kinds of good for man— morality and happiness—the final total good for man must consist in both.[76] Further, there must be a synthetic but noncontingent relation between the empirical and the a priori functions of practical reason: although they remain distinct, the very existence of reason itself demands that its two practical uses should not finally contradict each other. Kant concludes that man's "highest good" (*das höchste Gut*) consists in happiness proportionate to moral character. Virtue is still the "supreme good" (*das oberste Gut*), and that is why normative ethics is a doctrine not "of how to make ourselves happy but of how we are to be *worthy* of happiness."[77]

Kant defines happiness as "complete well-being and contentment with one's state" and as "a rational being's consciousness of the agreeableness of life which without interruption accompanies his whole existence."[78] On the basis of his observation that happiness, so defined, is not always commensurate in this life with virtue, he concludes that the highest good is possible only if there is a future life in which God sees to it that justice is done. Since the highest good is a demand of reason, we are justified in having a "rational faith" in the reality of the conditions necessary for the possibility of that good.[79]

Aristotle's conception of the ultimate practical good for man at first seems very much like Kant's: living a morally excellent life and possessing sufficient "gifts of fortune"—personal attributes and external goods—to live that life. But Kant thought of nonmoral good as a *final* good which must be an intrinsic component of the ultimate good for man, and Aristotle did not.[80] Aristotle concludes that nonmoral goods are at best instrumentalities, often necessary for attaining and living the ultimate good which, insofar as practice is concerned, is entirely and totally the effective expression of morally excellent character.[81]

Adkins' criticisms here ignore crucial texts and use arguments from outside the Aristotelian corpus to show that Aristotle could not possibly have done what he in fact did do, namely, eliminate the objectionable Homeric elements from his delineation of *eudaimonia*. Aristotle is always very careful, after considering the Homeric view, to insist that nonmoral goods are usually conditions for, or instruments in, the morally good life but *not* part of its essence.

One of Aristotle's reasons for opposing the inclusion of such good is just the objection which Adkins and Hardie make: if *eudaimonia* were the result only of fortune it would not be within the power of men to attain. Aristotle was much more deeply troubled than Kant by the role fortune does have in men's lives, and long sections of the *Politics* are devoted to discussions about how the state might be organized so as to minimize the vagaries of stepmotherly chance. Men can always be struck down by misfortune, but Aristotle contends that what is most important is not what happens to them but the manner in which they respond. Character has an inherent permanence immune to most outside pressures, and the good man will always engage in good and noble actions, making do with what he has, however little that may be.[82] Aristotle anticipates Kant by some twenty centuries with the observation that misfortunes can provide an opportunity in which the nobility of a man's character can shine in all its purity.[83]

Still, the fact that not all men have the same chance to develop and express their character fully according to the moral ideal is an enormous problem for Aristotle. Unlike Kant, Aristotle takes practice to *mean* acting in and on the world; without this external dimension, our thinking remains essentially theoretical.[84] Moreover, the ultimate good for man must be attained in this life if it is to be attained at all, and we are on our own, without the reassurance of divine assistance to compensate for our own ineptitude and failures of nature. The result is not the minimizing of moral responsibility, as Adkins and Hardie maintain, but far greater emphasis on responsibility, both personal and social. In the Kantian theory, the responsibilities for the attainment of the total final good are shared between God and men, but in the Aristotelian world, they are totally man's. It is small wonder that the notion of success looms larger in the Aristotelian theory than in Kant's. It is also understandable why Aristotle joined ethics to politics: what men cannot do alone, they can only do together, if at all.

The consequence of these differences is that, Adkins' and Allan's claims to the contrary, Aristotle does provide a moral *ideal* which can hold as an ideal for the entire community. They are right, of course, in saying that Aristotle did not extend his analysis of character and moral responsibility to everyone within the state. He could have, and he should have. His reasons for not doing so, however, are not to be found in his manner of depicting the nature of the final practical good nor in his delineation of moral character. Aristotle was able to restrict the extension of his analyses only by refusing to recognize their universal applicability.

III

Kant's criticisms of all previous moral philosophers are so sweeping and so severe that they invite careful examination. Yet the tendency has been to accept them at their face value, and the Kantian critique has appeared again and again in studies of, and references to, Aristotle's moral theory.

My examination has shown that the Kantian criticisms as a whole are not valid, for they rest on misconceptions about what Aristotle actually held. Yet reflection on those criticisms has suggested a number of extraordinary observations about Kant's moral theory and its relation to Aristotle's.[85] For example, there are large portions of Kant's theory which merely echo the Aristotelian view; this is rarely mentioned by Kantian scholars. Moreover, Kant gave nonmoral good a firmer ontological status than did Aristotle; this is the opposite of the usual interpretation. Finally, insofar as Kant retained his original view on the nature and role of duty in human moral life, he did so for religious rather than philosophic reasons; and, insofar as his views concerning the relation between morality and pleasure evolved closer to Aristotle's, his elucidation of moral practical reasoning is not as revolutionary as he, and many others after him, believed.

Adkins' long argument concludes with the statement that Aristotle could have had exactly the same views about morality as Kant only if Aristotle had had a Kantian "world-view." He is almost tautologically correct in this but mistaken in nearly all the arguments which preceded it. His Kantian focus skewed his reading of Aristotle, as it has for many others, and led him to attend more to contextual than to textual evidence. The concept of duty does enter Aristotle's moral theory differently than it does in Kant's and it does not achieve the prominence in Aristotle's theory that it has in Kant's, but not for the reasons Adkins gives. Kant's best man is Aristotle's second best man, because Aristotle affirms what Kant denies, that moral consciousness and appetition can achieve a state of rational harmony in this life. Moreover, the Aristotelian theory gives moral responsibility far greater emphasis than the Kantian theory, which includes a provident God to help achieve the highest good.

I will conclude by saying why I believe, that based on the matters examined here, Kant's view tends to hold the field today in what he called "ordinary moral consciousness." R.-A. Gauthier succinctly criticizes Aristotle this way:

> Aristotle's ethics is an ethics, not of conscience, but of practical wisdom, by the very feature which makes it a specifically pagan ethics and opposes it radically to Christian ethics: the optimistic humanism which made him believe that sin could be suppressed.[86]

Gauthier's statement is too sweeping, for many Christians think that, in the main, Aristotle, and not Kant, had the right view. But Gauthier is still right in pointing out that many Christians think Kant was right in seeing man as an irradicable sinner, yet with a mandate to strive for moral perfection. Men who are not Christian also tend to feel more at home with Kant, because most men in fact are *not* morally excellent. We are mostly either morally weak or morally strong, and, even though Aristotle also thought this was the case, Kant built this view of man into his moral theory in a way in which Aristotle did not.

Finally, many very important doctrines within Aristotle's theory depend on valuing accomplishment over striving. This was Aristotle's justification for thinking that completion is better than the process by which it is attained, for preferring mature adulthood to childhood, and for holding that *theōria* is superior to *praxis*, just as *praxis* is superior to *poiēsis*. But today men are skeptical of their ability to achieve truth, just as they are skeptical of anyone's ability to achieve moral goodness. When this is the prevalent view, striving tends to be valued as an accomplishment in its own right, whether it be theoretical striving, called research, or practical striving, called dutifulness. Kant valued striving as the highest moral achievement possible to us, hence his emphasis on trying to form intentions dutifully, intentions which cannot always be carried out successfully.

The result is that Kant's moral theory is far more compatible with the modern temper than Aristotle's, and this may be the reason Adkins seems more right than wrong in claiming we are all Kantians now.[87] But if I am correct in these speculations, Kant's significance today as a moral philosopher lies more in the view he had of man and the influence this had on his moral theory than in advances consisting in new clarity about the nature of moral responsibility and moral goodness.

NOTES

1 This examination will also show that the contrast between Aristotle and Kant should not be taken as a paradigm of the distinction between teleological and deontological types of moral theories. Some of Kant's criticisms in the second *Critique* are directed against the Stoics and Epicureans, and a new study of Kant's remarks concerning these two schools needs to be done.

2 Robert Paul Wolff, *The Autonomy of Reason, A Commentary on Kant's "Groundwork of the Metaphysic of Morals"* (N.Y.: Harper & Row, 1973), 46. Contemporary authors frequently repeat this criticism. For example, D. J. Allan tells us that Aristotle "takes little or no account of the motive of moral obligation;" see his *The Philosophy of Aristotle*, 2d ed. (Oxford: Oxford University Press, 1970), 140. G. E. M. Anscombe states flatly that none of the notions "of 'duty' and 'obligation', and what is now called the 'moral' sense of 'ought'. . .occur in Aristotle;" see her *Intention*, 2d ed. (Oxford: Basil Blackwell, 1963), 78n. P. H. Nowell-Smith is more cautious: "The notion of duty does not play the central role in traditional that it plays in modern ethics and the notion of doing one's duty for duty's sake hardly appears before Kant;" see his *Ethics* (Baltimore: Penguin Books, 1954), 13.

3 Arthur W. H. Adkins, *Merit and Responsibility: A Study in Greek Values* (Oxford: Oxford University Press, 1960), 2.

4 Ibid., 253, 329n5. In this section I have organized Adkins' arguments, as far as I could, to follow the argument in the first chapter of Kant's *Groundwork* (hereafter *Gr.*). Citations from *Gr.* are from the translation by H.J. Paton (N.Y.: Harper & Row, Publishers, 1964). All references to Kant's works use the Academy pagination. Adkins does not substantially alter his position in his later *From the Many to the One* (Ithaca: Cornell University Press, 1970).

5 See *Gr.* 1–2/393–94.

6 See Adkins, 6–9, 34–36, 49–52, 156–64, 339–40, 346–49. Adkins also repeats a common criticism relevant to this thesis: that Aristotle remains too much of a Platonist not to give *theōria* superiority over *praxis* (see *Eth. Nic.* 10. 7–8) so that Aristotle succeeds "no better than Plato in demonstrating why a man capable of philosophizing should at any moment choose rather to perform any individual moral or political action. . .why he should prefer any given moral claim. . .to his desire to philosophize" (Adkins, 346–47). Because this is not a peculiarly Kantian criticism, I will not attend to it in the text of this paper (and that is also my reason for not stating this thesis as "Moral goodness is the supreme good"). But because it supports the Kantian critique, I will need to indicate later why I think it does not stand up (see note 75 below).

7 See *Gr.* 3–8/394–96, 15–16/401.

8 Adkins, 75–76, 349–50.

9 Adkins, 336.

10 Adkins, 253.

11 See *Gr.* 8–13/397–99, 14–16/400–01.

12 Adkins, 253. Despite the length of his book, Adkins does not systematize his argument against Aristotle. The lines cited here occur within his discussion of Plato, but the criticism also applies to Aristotle, since, Adkins argues, the same Homeric values equally inhibit both Plato and Aristotle from developing an adequate (i.e., a Kantian) moral philosophy (see, e.g., 348–51).

13 See *Gr.* 3/394; *Critique of Practical Reason* 20–21 (hereafter *Pr.R.*).

14 W. F. R. Hardie, *Aristotle's Ethical Theory* (Oxford: Oxford University Press, 1968), 127–28; cf. Adkins, 2–3, 49–52.

15 See Gr. 28–29/408, 35–36/412.

16 Adkins, 8; cf. 7–9, 341–42.

17 Adkins, 339; cf. 334–35, 342–43, 353n15. D.J. Allan concurs: "[Aristotle] does not speak in terms of rules of conduct which apply equally to all men, and which all can understand" (Allan, 140).

18 Adkins, 329n5.

19 Nowell-Smith, 218.

20 Hardie, 231, 335; but cf. also 334–35.

21 See, e.g., *Eth. Nic.* 6.2.1139a36-b3; 6.5.1140a24-b11. Citations from this book are from the translation by Martin Ostwald (Indianapolis: The Bobbs-Merrill Company, Inc. 1962).

22 Kant presents this argument in the "Analytic" of the second *Critique* (see esp. 19–26, 62–65). The argument has been cogently restated by John R. Silber in "The Copernican Revolution in Ethics: The Good Reexamined" (*Kant-Studien* 51 [1959], pp. 85–101). Silber writes: "Kant has demonstrated that the classical tradition can never relate the good to the moral agent with the necessity of law and obligation. He has shown. . .that moralists who begin by defining the good prior to the moral law can never succeed in endowing their concept of the good with moral significance, and hence can never hope to offer a sound theory of ethics. . . .The classical tradition emerged with a homogeneous concept of the good, a concept in which no distinction was made between moral and non-moral good. . . .[As a consequence,] happiness and virtue cannot be distinguished. . .and the experience of obligation is impossible" (93).

23 See *Gr.* vii-ix/389–90; *Pr.R.* 39–41.

24 Allan, 140.

25 See, e.g., *Eth. Nic.* 1.1; *Pr.R.* 34; *Metaphysic of Morals* 383–84; *Theory and Practice* 279n. Kant's manner of describing moral action in the *Gr.* is misleading; he seems to say that morally good action is purposeless; cf., e.g., 40/414–43/416.

26 See *Eth. Nic.* 3.8.1116a17–1117a27; 7.9.1151b4–8; *Gr.* 38n/413n.

27 See *Eth. Nic.* 2.4.1105a27-b8; *Gr.* 10–11/398–99; *Pr.R.* 81, 85.

28 See, e.g., *Eth. Nic.* 1.13.1102b13–27; 3.12.1119b5–19; 9.8.1148b19ff; 10.9.1180a10–13; *Critique of Pure Reason* (hereafter, *Pu.R.*) A15/B29; *Gr.* 8/347, 14–15/400; *Pr.R.* 35, 73, 76, 84, 117–18, 156.

29 There is little need to show this is Aristotle's doctrine, but Kant's emphasis on moral affections is often neglected. Throughout his moral writings Kant insists that it is not possible for us to recognize moral value without respecting it and, further, our agency is such that we will not do the morally right action unless we take an interest in doing it, so that reverence for moral value is a necessary condition, as the subjective ground, for moral goodness. See, e.g., *Gr.* 14–15/400, 16n/401n, 20/403, 38n/413n, 79/436, 86/440, 102–04/499–500; *Pr.R.* 73ff. There are other moral emotions, including feelings of humility, guilt, pain, remorse, and the feeling of self-satisfaction which follows on the consciousness of one's own virtue (see *Pr.R.* 38, 73–75, 80–81, 87–88, 116–18). Insofar as they are emotions, they are "pathological," but they do not have a sensual origin. They are specifically moral emotions, possible only through a prior rational recognition of moral value. So important are they to the moral life that it is our "duty to establish and cultivate them" (*Pr.R.* 38).

30 See, e.g., *Eth. Nic.* 2.4.1105a17-b12; 3.7.1115b12–21, 1116a10–15; 3.8.1116a26–32, b3–31, 1117a1–9; 6.12.1144a13–37; 6.13.1144b17–30; *Gr.*

10–11/398–99; *Pr.R.* 45–46, 71, 72n, 81, 85, etc.

31 *Gr.* 37/412, *Pr.R.* 84; cf. 73, 76; *Pu.R.* A15/B29.

32 *Pr.R.* 89 and 88.

33 *Pr.R.* 157; cf. 32, 81–86, 122, 128, 155–57.

34 See *Gr.* 36/412, 39/414, 86/439; *Pr.R.* 32, 82.

35 *Pr.R.* 84; see 83–87.

36 *Pr.R.* 82, 83.

37 See *Eth. Nic.* 1.6.1096b23–25; 1.8.1099a11–22; 6.12.1144a1–3; 7.13.1153b7–18, 1154a1–6; 7.14.1154a7–21; 9.9.1170a18-b15; 10.3.11733–1174a10; 10.4.1174b14–1175a17; 10.5.1175b2–28, 1176a16–29.

38 See *Eth. Nic.* 1.13.1102b23–1103a3; 3.5.114b26–30; 3.12.119b3–18; 5.11.1138b5–14; 6.1.1138b19–20; 6.10.1143a8–9; 6.13.1145a9–11. On the word "kalon," see H. D. F. Kitto, *The Greeks* (Baltimore: Penguin Books, 1951), pp. 170–71.

39 *Eth. Nic.* 4.8.1128a33.

40 Hardie, 328 (italics mine).

41 *Eth. Nic.* 10.7.1174b33.

42 *Eth. Nic.* 7.9.1152a3; see 10.4.1174a4–8.

43 Aristotle adds this last phrase as part of his argument against Sophists who attempted to support moral relativism by discussing pleasure only in terms of sensations felt. Aristotle contends that, since men take pleasure in virtually everything imaginable, the discussion of pleasure must begin with a discussion of the objective nature of kinds of actions and of the pleasures naturally connected with or absent from actions of various kinds.

44 *Eth. Nic.* 1.8.1099a13–21.

45 See *Eth. Nic.* 2.3.1104b5–1105a12; 3.12.1119a21-b19, etc.

46 Despite his claim that "the classical tradition. . .was imperceptive in failing to see that the concept of the good is complex and that it has a moral as well as a natural usage" ("The Copernican Revolution," 96), John R. Silber's description of Kant's virtuous man applies with equal accuracy to either of Aristotle's morally inferior men. Such a man, Silber writes, "finds himself torn between that which he *desires* to do and that which he *ought* to desire to do. He frequently encounters the good as disastrously heterogeneous such that he is unable to fulfill the moral good apart from the sacrifice of the natural good, or vice versa." There is this important difference, however, between the Kantian and Aristotelian theories. Kant

thought there were two radically different but genuine practical goods—the natural and the moral, and that the natural good remains naturally good even when it is also morally evil. Aristotle, however, thought that, while nonmoral goods are rightly called "good" when discussed abstractly, this is only a tentative judgment; they are only "potentially good" for the individual, and in concrete situations of life, they can turn out to be not good at all when they are not good by the final criterion of morality (see, e.g., *Eth. Nic.* 1.3.1094b15–23; 1.12.1101b10–13; 5.1.1129b2–7; *Magna Moralia* 1.2.1183b20–30). Two important consequences follow. First, in Aristotle's view, only morally weak and morally strong men experience the practical good as "disastrously heterogeneous," and they do so because they are men having a "moral disposition in conflict." Secondly, and this is rather startling given a common construction to the contrary, Kant gave a firmer and more enduring ontological status to the non- moral good than did Aristotle!

47 See R.-A. Gauthier, *La Morale d'Aristote*, trans. by James J. Walsh and Henry L. Shapiro and included in their *Aristotle's Ethics: Issues and Interpretations* (Belmont: Wadsworth, 1967), 21.

48 *Gr.* 8/397.

49 See *Eth. Nic.* 2.1.1103a17–25; 2.5.1106a10.

50 See *Eth. Nic.* 1.5.1095b16–17, 19–22; 3.4.1113a35-b2; 7.7.1150a8–10; 9.8.1168b15–21; 10.8.1179a15–16; 10.9.1179b10–19. The Socrates of the *Republic* had pointed out that ideals do not have to be realized in order to operate as ideals; they can still give action right direction (see *Republic* 471c–72c). Interestingly, Aristotle is faulted as a moral aristocrat for his view, while Kant is praised for his sensitive insight into the limitations of human nature.

51 Since character "is concerned with pleasure and pain. . .as Plato says, men must be brought up from childhood to feel pleasure and pain at the proper things" (*Eth. Nic.* 2.3.1104b9–12). Kant's view was that children should be trained to ignore their desires so as to become obedient to the voice of pure reason.

52 "The relation of pleasure and desire to the will. . .was troubling to Kant. . . . He was. . .unsure regarding the role of pleasure in the moral determination of the will: he flatly contradicts himself by both affirming and denying that moral satisfaction can be a kind of pleasure and a determinant of the will as the faculty of desire" (John R. Silber, "The Ethical Significance of Kant's *Religion*," in *Religion within the Limits of Reason Alone*, trans. by Greene and Hudson [New York: Harper and Row, 1960], p. lxxxvi). Kant's overwhelming insistence on the notion of duty, however, supports the contrast I make here.

53 Hardie, 138–39.

54 The debate over this issue is still alive and arguments on one side or the other appear in unexpected places. B. F. Skinner, for example, criticizes those who tend to confer and withhold honors and dignities according to the presence or absence of internal and external opposition (*Beyond Freedom and Dignity* [New York: Alfred A. Knopf, 1971], 44ff). And the Anglican theological author, Dorothy Sayers, writes: "The Puritan assumption that all action disagreeable to the doer is *ipso facto* more meritorious than enjoyable action, is firmly rooted in this exaggerated valuation set on pride. I do not mean that there is no nobility in doing unpleasant things from a sense of duty, but only that there is more nobility in doing them gladly out of sheer love of the job. . . .The merit, of course, lies precisely in the enjoyment, and the nobility of So-and-so consists in the very fact that he is the kind of person to whom the doing of that piece of work is delightful." See *A Matter of Eternity: Selections from the Writings of Dorothy L. Sayers*, ed. Rosamond Kent Sprague (Grand Rapids: Wm. B. Eerdsmans Co., 1973), 62–63. The issue at stake tends to be confused by the belief, common to both sides, that "success is better when it is hard to achieve" (*Eth. Nic.* 2.4.1105a9–10).

55 See *Eth. Nic.* 9.4.1166a10–29.

56 See *Eth. Nic.* 1.3.1095b7; cf. 4.9.1128b29–35; 7.1–10.

57 Gauthier, 26–27.

58 In the *Metaphysics of Morals*, (trans. by Mary J. Gregor [New York: Harper and Row, 1964], 398.) for example, we find Kant going so far in the direction of Aristotle's view as to write: "In every determination of choice we go *from* the thought of the possible action by way of feeling pleasure or pain and taking an interest in the action or its effect. Now in this process our *emotional* state (the way in which our inner sense is affected) is either pathological or moral feeling. *Pathological* feeling precedes the thought of the law: *moral* feeling can only follow from the thought of the law." See also Silber, "The Ethical Significance of Kant's *Religion*," lxxx-lxxxii, cxiv-cxxviii.

59 I am not concerned here with that aspect of duty consisting in respect or reverence for moral value. Both Kant and Aristotle think that, since moral value is distinct from mere pleasure, we apprehend them differently, and moral emotions include reverence (see *Eth. Nic.* a. 12. 1101b10–1102a4). Kant's definition of duty as "the necessity to act out of reverence for the law" does not adequately convey his elucidation of moral struggle presupposed by the concept of duty (*Gr.* 14/400).

60 There are cogent reasons for arguing that even Kant's first exposition of moral agency is incompatible with the doctrine from the first *Critique*; see, e.g., Wolff, *The Autonomy of Reason*, 9–15, 118–23.

61 Greene and Hudson, 36–37. Lest it be doubted how Kant argues for his view of human nature on which he bases his claims for duty, I offer this citation: "[The proposition that man] is evil *by nature*, means but this, that evil can be predicated of man as a species; not that such a quality can be inferred from the concept of his species (that is, of man in general)— for then it would be necessary; but rather that from what we know of man through experience we cannot judge otherwise of him, or, that we may presuppose evil to be subjectively necessary to every man, even to the best. . . .That such a corrupt [*verderbter*] propensity must indeed be rooted in man need not be formally proved in view of the multitude of crying examples which experience *of the actions* of men puts before our eyes" (27–28, emphasis Kant's). So Kant admits that his view does not follow analytically either from the concept of rational agency or of human agency and therefore that his claim has no necessity about it (or universality, either). Yet this is the foundation for his claim that moral principles always and necessarily appear to us as imperatives and that, insofar as they do not, we cannot be recognizing them for what they are to agents like us.

62 Aristotle may well have been thinking of Socrates, as portrayed in the *Crito*, as his model for moral excellence, for Socrates feels no conflict between prudence and morality. But the lesser man, Crito, who has "a moral disposition in conflict," sees Socrates as losing everything that might make him content with his life, and he cannot understand Socrates' genuinely happy frame of mind.

63 The same comments apply to Silber's remarks in note 22 above.

64 On intrinsically good action as *energeia*, see *Eth. Nic.* 1.1.1094a4–6, 15–16; 1.6.1096b17–18; 1.7.1098a8–15; 6.2.1139b2–5; 10.4.1174a14-b13; *Pol.* 4.1.1288b10–24; 7.13.1332a8–16; *Metaph.* 9.6.1048b18–35; 9.8.1050a24. On morally good character, see *Eth. Nic.* 2.4.1105a26-b8; 2.6.1106a13–24; 4.9.1128b31; 5.1.1129a12–17; 6.9.1142b28–33; 7.2.1146a5–8. Since both making and acting are instances of rationally directed activity, both involve practical reasoning. Miss Anscombe remarks that "there is nothing necessarily ethical about the word 'should' occurring in the universal premise of a practical syllogism, at least so far as concerns the remarks made by Aristotle who invented the notion" (*Intention*, 65). Her remark is not illuminating. Both Aristotle and Kant take practical reasoning to be our ability to formulate and adopt general principles by which to direct our agency (see, e.g., *Eth. Nic.* 1.7. 1098a3–4; *Gr.* 36/412; *Pr.R.* 19–20). Neither Aristotle nor Kant tried to claim that all practical thinking must be moral in character. Aristotle holds that the artist, the merely clever man, and the moral man each has occasion to deliberate about how to act.

65 *Eth. Nic.* 6.4.1140a5; cf. also 24–32 and 7.2.1153a25–26.

66 "There are many things for which we would exert our efforts even if they would not entail any pleasure, for example, sight, memory, knowledge,

and the possession of the virtues [*aretai*]. It makes no difference whether
pleasures necessarily accompany these things, for we would choose them
even if we were to get no pleasure from them" *Eth. Nic.* 10.4.1174a4–8;
cf. 4.1.1120a23–1121b10).

67 See *Eth. Nic.* 1.3.1094b12–27; 2.2.1104a1–11, 27-b2; 2.7.1107a29–32;
7.12.1152b27–32; 9.2.1164b23ff; *Metaph.* 6.2.1026a33–1027a27;
11.8.1064b30–1065a6. To hold otherwise, Aristotle argues, leads us into
immoral legality; see *Eth. Nic.* 5.9.1137a9–12; 9. 2. 1165a2–13.

68 See *Eth. Nic.* 1.7.1098a26–32; 2.2.1103b34–1104a10; 2.6.1106a26–
1107a27; 2.7.1107b4–6; 4.1.1120b7–19; 4.2.1122a25–28; 4.5.1125b27ff;
6.1.1138b19–32.

69 See *Eth. Nic.* 1.7.1098a26–32; 2.2.1103b34–1104a10; 2.6.1106a26–
1107a27; 2.7.1107b4–6; 4.1.1120b7–19; 4.2.1122a25–28; 4.5.1125b27ff;
6.1.1138b19–32.

70 *Eth. Nic.* 3.4.1113a33–34; cf. 2.6.1106b36–1107a1; 6.5.1140b8–10;
6.12.1144a23–32; 6.13.1144b21–25.

71 J. Donald Monan, *Moral Knowledge and its Methodology in Aristotle*
(Oxford: Oxford University Press, 1968), 101–02.

72 See also *Pr.R.* 44–47. Kant's epistemology causes him to structure his
reasoning here differently than Aristotle, but the two men agree that,
insofar as moral value is unconditionally good, it is not derivable from
anything else.

73 See *Eth. Nic.* 1.2.1094b7–10; 1.10.1099b29–32; 1.13.1102a5–13; *Pol.*
7.5.1334a12–13.

74 See *Eth. Nic.* 1.2.1094b4–12; 1.7.1097b8–11; 1.13.1102a14–25;
6.1.1129b27–1130a3.

75 I need to indicate briefly how I think the passages in *Eth. Nic.* 10.7–8
giving primacy to *theōria* need to be understood (see note 6 above).
Throughout the rest of the *Ethics* Aristotle portrays *praxis* as intrinsically
and absolutely good, and as an essential part of the good life (see, e.g.,
6.1.1138b35–1139a17; 6.12.1144a1–6). But he also consistently argues that
theōria is a still more perfect form of life, the kind proper to God, to be
sought by men insofar as they can attain it. *Praxis* also provides conditions
necessary for its possibility. However, even if we engage in intrinsically
good activities "for the sake of something else, one would still classify them
among things intrinsically good" (1096b18–19). Both forms of life, then,
are intrinsically good, and because of this each has its own functions and
rights. Despite the fact that *theōria* is the more perfect activity, the
decision about which takes precedence in any particular life or situation
belongs to *political* wisdom. As "the most sovereign and most comprehensive
master science," it has both the function and the right to regulate the

contemplative activity of individuals (see *Eth. Nic.* 1.2.1094a26-b7; 1.9.1099b30; 6.7.1141b21–23). As a consequence, Aristotle gives superiority to *theōria* in the abstract but still allows practical reason to legislate why, in Adkins' words, "a man should prefer any given moral claim. . .to his desire to philosophize." The theoretician is not immune to the ontological claims of his own nature as an agent and a citizen nor to the claims of special roles he may have.

76 See, e.g., *Gr.* 1/393, 7/396; *Pr.R.* 4, 108, 110–13, 124–40.

77 *Pr.R.* 130 (emphasis Kant's).

78 *Gr.* 1/393 and *Pr.R.* 22.

79 See *Pr.R.* 124–25.

80 Although Kant repeatedly emphasizes the genuine goodness of natural goods and of man's sensible nature which seeks them, the claim and its great importance to his theory are sometimes not adequately appreciated.

81 See *Eth. Nic.* 1.5.1095a15–1096a10; 1.8.1098b13–19; 1099a31-b8; 1.9.1099b25–28; 1.13.1102a14–16; 4.1.1120a4–14; 4.3.1123b27–1124a4, 20-b3; 9.8.1168b15–24, 1169a3–17; *Eth. Eud.* 1.2.1214b11–28. It should now be evident how meaningless is Adkins' charge that there is "no possibility. . .of setting 'duty' against *eudaimonia*" (75). One might as well complain that Kant cannot oppose "duty" to the "supreme good." It is also relevant here to mention that because Kant does not completely internalize morality, his doctrine also is not completely different from Aristotle's; in many passages Kant recognizes how important natural goods are a "means to the fulfillment of one's duty" (*Pr.R.* 93; cf. also, e.g., 88; *Gr.* 2/393, 12/399).

82 See *Eth. Nic.* 1.9.1099b8–24; 1.10.1101a1–6; 4.1.1120a4–11, b7–19; 4.3.1124a20-b4; *Eth. Eud.* 1.3.1215a8–19.

83 See *Eth. Nic.* 1.10.1100b12–33; 7.3.1146b11–24; *Pol.* 8.13.1332a18ff.

84 Aristotle emphasizes that *both* intentions *and* results are morally significant. Ineffectiveness is never a moral virtue but often a moral defect. Moreover, intentions (*bouleseis*) "by themselves are inscrutable, and unjust men also make a pretense of wishing to act justly. . . .If a man cannot perform any actions which display his moral excellence,. . .how else can he show his character?" (*Eth. Nic.* 10.8.1178a30–34; translation mine; cf. 34–1178b1).

85 My aim in this paper has been a limited one: to attend only to those doctrines, or aspects of doctrines, in Aristotle and Kant which are immediately relevant to the issues Kant raises. Other contrasts, of course, can be drawn, and all of the implications of my claims cannot be discussed in this paper.

86 Gauthier, 27.

87 But most liberal arts educators tend to be Aristotelians in the sense that they aim to produce students who are so "into" a particular activity that they sense its intrinsic value and love what they are doing.

PART TWO

DETERMINING MORAL NORMS

6

EMOTIONS AND CHOICE

ROBERT C. SOLOMON

I

Do we choose our emotions? Can we be held responsible for our anger? for feeling jealous? for falling in love or succumbing to resentment or hatred? The suggestion sounds odd because emotions are typically considered occurrences that happen to (or "in") us: emotions are taken to be the hallmark of the irrational and the disruptive. Controlling one's emotions is supposed to be like the caging and taming of a wild beast, the suppression and sublimation of a Freudian "it."

Traditionally, emotions have been taken to be feelings or sensations. More recently, but also traditionally, emotions have been taken to be physiological disturbances. Accordingly, much of this century's literature on emotions is dedicated to mapping out the relationship between sensations and correlative occurrences. William James, for example, takes consciousness of emotions to be consciousness of physiological occurrences. Other philosophers and psychologists, for one reason or another, have tried to reduce the emotion to a physiological occurrence, or, alternatively, have focused on the feeling of emotion and denied any conceptual role to the physiological occurrence. But these traditional worries should be quite irrelevant to any analysis of the emotions, for an emotion is neither a sensation nor a physiological occurrence, nor an occurrence of any other kind. "Struck by jealousy," "driven by anger," "plagued by remorse," "paralyzed by fear," "felled by shame," like "the prick of Cupid's arrow," are all symptomatic metaphors betraying a faulty philosophical analysis. Emotions are not occurrences and do not happen to us. I would like to suggest that emotions are rational and purposive rather than irrational and disruptive, that they are very much like actions, and that we choose an emotion much as we choose a course of action.[1]

Emotions are intentional; that is, emotions are "about" something. For instance, "I am angry *at John for stealing my car.*" It is not necessary to press the claim that *all* emotions are "about" something. Kierkegaard's dread may be an emotion which is not "about" anything, or, conversely, may be "about" everything. Similarly, *moods*, which are much like emotions, do not have a specific object. Euphoria, melancholy, and depression are not "about" anything in particular, though they may be caused by some particular incident. We might wish to say that such emotions and moods are "about" the world rather than anything in particular. In fact, Heidegger has suggested that *all* emotions are ultimately "about" the world and never simply "about" something in particular. But we will avoid debating these issues by simply focusing our attention on emotions that clearly seem to be "about" something specifiable.

Let us use the statement, "I am angry at John for stealing my car." It is true that I am angry. And it is also true that John stole my car. Thus we are tempted to distinguish two components of my being angry; my feeling of anger and what I am angry about. But this is a double mistake. It requires that a feeling (of anger) be (contingently) directed at something (at John's having stolen my car). But feelings are occurrences and cannot have a "direction." They can be caused, but to say that I am angry "about" John's having stolen my car is very different from saying his stealing my car caused me to be angry. John's act might cause me to be angry "about" something else, for example, my failure to renew my

insurance. It might be false that John stole my car, though I believe
that he did. Then it is false that John's stealing my car caused me
to be angry, but still true that what I am angry "about" is John's
stealing my car. One might suggest that it is not the alleged *fact*
of John's stealing my car that is in question, but rather my *belief*
that he did. But what I am angry "about" is clearly not that I
believe that John stole my car, but rather *that John stole my car.*

Feelings do not have "directions."[2] But I am angry "about"
something. The relationship between my being angry and what I
am angry about is not the contingent relation between a feeling
and an object. (Though it is surely contingent that I am angry at
John for stealing my car.) An emotion cannot be identified apart
from its object; "I am angry" is incomplete—not only in the weak
sense that there is more information which may be available ("Are
you angry about anything?") but "I am angry" requires that there
must be more information available ("*What* are you angry about?").
But feelings have no such requirements. Anger is not a feeling;
neither is anger a feeling plus anything else (for example, what it
is "about").

Neither can "what I am angry about" be separated from
my being angry. Of course, it makes sense to say that John's having
stolen my car is something different from my being angry at him
for doing so. But it is not simply the *fact* that John stole my car
that is what I am angry about; nor is it, as I said above, my *belief*
that John stole my car about which I am angry. I am angry about
the intentional object "that John stole my car." Unlike the *fact* that
John stole my car, this intentional object is opaque; I am not angry
that John stole a vehicle assembled in Youngstown, Ohio, with 287
horsepower though that is a true description of the fact that John
stole my car. I am not angry that someone 5'7" tall got his fingerprints
on my steering column, yet that is a true description of the fact
that John stole my car. Sartre attempts to point out this feature of
what emotions are "about" by saying that their object is "transformed;" D. F. Pears points to this same feature by noting that it
is always an "aspect" of the object that is the object of an emotion.
What emotions are "about," as in beliefs, can only be identified
under certain descriptions, and those descriptions are determined
by the emotion itself. This does not mean that emotions are about

beliefs—only that emotions share an important conceptual property of beliefs. "Being angry about. . ." is very much like "believing that. . . ." To be angry is to be angry "about" a peculiar sort of object, one that is distinguished by the fact that it is what I am angry "about." Husserl describes this peculiarity of mental acts in general by insisting that an intentional act and an intentional object are *"essentially* correlated." For our purposes, the point to be seen is that emotions cannot be discussed in terms of "components," by distinguishing feeling angry and what I am angry about. (Pears, for example, begins by making this distinction.) In Heideggerian phrase, I am never simply angry, but there is always "my-being-angry-about-. . . ."

If there is no legitimate distinction between feeling angry and what I am angry "about," or, to put it in a different way, if the connection between my being angry and what I am angry "about" is a conceptual and not a causal connection, then it is easy to explain a feature of emotions that has been pointed out by many analysts. A change in what I am angry "about" demands a change in my anger; if I no longer feel wronged by John, who only bought a car that looks like mine, I cannot be angry at John (for stealing my car) any longer. One cannot be angry if he is not angry "about" having been wronged. Similarly, one cannot be ashamed if he does not accept some responsibility for an awkward situation, nor can he be embarrassed if he does not find the situation awkward. If emotions were feelings, it would be a peculiar coincidence that the feelings were so faithful to our views of our situation, that they did not hold onto us with a momentum of their own after opinions had passed, that they were not so "irrational" as to pay no attention to our opinions at all. But emotions are not feelings, nor feelings plus what they are "about;" the format of an emotion is ". . .-about-. . . ." And so it is no surprise that emotions change with our opinions, and so are "rational" in a very important sense.

Emotions typically involve feelings. Perhaps they essentially involve feelings. But feelings are never sufficient to differentiate and identify emotions, and an emotion is never simply a feeling, not even a feeling plus anything. Moreover, it is clear that one can have an emotion without feeling anything. One can be angry without feeling angry: one can be angry for three days or five

years and not feel anything identifiable as a feeling of anger
continuously through that prolonged period. One might add that
one must have a disposition to feel angry, and to this, there is no
objection, so long as being angry is not thought to *mean* "having a
disposition to feel angry." I do not know whether it makes sense
to suppose that one can be angry without ever feeling angry. But
I do know that it does not even make sense to say that one feels
angry if one is not angry. This might seem mysterious, if we accept
the traditional view that anger has an identifiable feeling attached
to it (for then, why could one not have the feeling without whatever
else is involved in anger?). And this might seem obvious in the
traditional view that anger *is* a feeling (for then being angry is
nothing but having the feeling of anger). But in our approach, anger
is not a feeling, nor does it involve any identifiable feeling (which
is not to deny that one does feel angry that is, flushed, excited,
and so on, when one is angry). One can identify one's feeling as
feeling angry only if one is angry. It is true that I often feel something
when I become angry. It is also true that I feel something after I
cease to be angry. I am angry at John for stealing my car. Then I
discover that John did not steal my car; I immediately cease being
angry. Yet the feeling remains: it is the same feeling I had while I
was angry (flushed and so on). The feeling subsides more slowly
than the anger. But the feeling, even if it is the same feeling that
I had while I was angry, is not a feeling of anger. Now it is just a
feeling. Sometimes one claims to feel angry but not to be angry.
But here, I would argue that the correct description is rather that
one does not know exactly what one is angry "about" (though one
is surely angry "about" something); or perhaps one is angry but
does not believe he ought to be. One cannot feel angry without
being angry.

   A familiar move in the analysis of emotions subsequent to
the discovery that emotions are not feelings or occurrences, is the
thesis that emotions are conceptually tied to behavior; that is, the
ascription of an emotion to a person is the ascription to him of
various sorts of behavior. Thus, to be angry is necessarily to "anger-
behave." Of course, it is evident that one can *pretend* to be angry,
that is, anger-behave without being angry, and so pretending has
become a major topic in the analysis of emotions. (More on this in

Part II). What is generally agreed is that a single piece of behavior
is never conceptually sufficient to identify an emotion, or to
distinguish emotions from pretense. E. Bedford, for example,
suggests that what is always needed is at least "more of the same."
Since Ryle's *Concept of Mind*, this "more of the same" is provided
by the suggestion that ascribing an emotion to a person is not to
simply describe one or more episodes of behavior but rather to
ascribe to him a disposition to behave. But there is considerable
confusion about the nature of such disposition-ascriptions, and the
suggestion is clearly unsatisfactory as an analysis of *my* having an
emotion. The behavioral analysis does maintain one important
feature of emotions, their intentionality, though authors (such as,
Ryle, and Armstrong) who favor this analysis are often intent on
rejecting "intentionality" as well. But for our purposes, we can
remain uninvolved in these issues which have become virtually
definitive of "philosophy of mind." We can agree that it is undeniably
true that if a person is angry he has a disposition to anger-behave
and leave entirely open whether this connection between emotions
and behavior is conceptual, or causal or something else. The purpose
of this essay is to show that emotions are very much like actions,
and if it should turn out that emotions are actions in any such
straightforward sense, this can only make our task easier. And so,
we can simply say of the behavioral analysis: insofar as it is true, it
supports our thesis.

"Emotions are caused." The idea that emotions are occurrences naturally gave rise to the idea that emotions are caused.
Many philosophers would argue that, if emotions are occurrences,
then they must be caused, and conversely, that if emotions are
caused they must be occurrences. But if, as I am arguing, emotions
are not occurrences, then they cannot be caused.

Many people would say I am wrong. We do speak of the
cause of anger, the cause for sadness, a cause for fear. And surely
emotions, as intentional, are typically if not necessarily *reactions*
to something that happens to us. Sometimes this cause is manifest
in what the emotion is "about;" for example, I am angry about your
hitting me; your hitting me is the event which caused me to become
angry. But sometimes the cause for an emotion is *not* what the
emotion is "about." The cause of my anger might be too little sleep

and too much coffee. The cause of my love might be sexual deprivation. But I am not angry "about" lack of sleep and hyperstimulation, and I am not in love with my sexual deprivation (nor is my love "about" a cure for my sexual deprivation).

The cause of an emotion is a function in a certain kind of explanation. The cause must in every case be distinguished from what my emotion is "about" (its "object"). The cause is always an actual event (or state of affairs). The object of my emotion is always an intentional object. The cause is subject to certain law-like generalizations in a way that objects of emotions are not. If I claim to be angry because of a harsh review of my book, pointing out that I have not become angry at previous harsh reviews of my book is sufficient to show that the cause of my becoming angry is not (my reading of) the review of my book, but it is not sufficient to show that I am not angry "about" the harsh review. I am not in any special position to know the cause of my emotion (though only I know, as a matter of fact, that I did not sleep last night, that I have had four cups of coffee); I am always in a privileged position to identify the intentional object of my emotion. This is *not* to say that my knowledge of the object of my emotion is "immediate" or "direct," nor is it to claim that my identification of the object of my emotion is "incorrigible." It is possible and not unusual that I should misidentify—sometimes in a gross way—what I am angry about, or whom I love, or why I am sad. I may identify the object of my anger as John's having stolen my car, but I am really angry at John for writing a harsh review of my book. I may think that I love Mary, when I really love my mother. And I may think that I love Mary when I am really angry about the harsh review of my book. The problem of "unconscious emotions" would take us far beyond our current argument. For now, it should suffice for us to insist that the difference between identification of the cause of an emotion and its object is not a difference between direct and indirect knowledge—as traditionally conceived—or a difference between corrigible and incorrigible identification. The cause of an emotion is an occurrence (state of affairs, etc.) of a type that stands in a law-like connection with emotions of that type. The object of an emotion is simply "what the emotion is about," whether or not it is also the cause, whether or not it is even the case, and whether or not the subject himself knows it to be the object of his emotion.[3]

We have noted that emotions are interestingly similar to beliefs. We can now explain this similarity by claiming that emotions are judgments—normative and often moral judgments. "I am angry at John for taking ("stealing" begs the question) my car" *entails* that I believe that John has somehow wronged me. (This must be true even if, *all things considered,* I also believe that John was justified in taking my car.) The (moral) judgment entailed by my anger is not a judgment *about* my anger (although someone else might make such judgments to the effect that my anger is justified or unjustified, rational, prudent, foolish, self-indulgent, therapeutic, beneficial, unfortunate, pathological or amusing). My anger *is* that judgment. If I do not believe that I have somehow been wronged, I cannot be angry (though I might be upset, or sad). Similarly, if I cannot praise my lover, I cannot be in love (though I might want her or need her, which, traditional wisdom aside, is entirely different). If I do not find my situation awkward, I cannot be ashamed or embarrassed. If I do not judge that I have suffered a loss, I cannot be sad or jealous. I am not sure whether all emotions entail such judgments; moods (depression and euphoria) surely present special problems. But emotions in general do appear to require this feature: to have an emotion is to hold a normative judgment about one's situation.

The idea that an emotion is a normative judgment, perhaps even a moral judgment, wreaks havoc with several long cherished philosophical theses. Against those romantics and contemporary bourgeois therapists who would argue that emotions simply *are* and must be accepted without judgment, it appears that emotions themselves are already judgments. And against several generations of moral philosophers who would distinguish between morality based upon principle and morality based upon emotion or "sentiment," it appears that every "sentiment," every emotion is already a matter of judgment, often moral judgment. An ethics of sentiment differs from ethics of principle only in the fact that its judgments are allowed to go unchallenged: it is an ethics of prejudice while the latter is typically an ethics of dogma.

We can now see why "what an emotion is about" is not simply a fact; nor is it even a fact under certain descriptions. The object of an emotion is itself "affective" or normative. It is not an object *about* which one makes a judgment but is rather defined, in part, by that normative judgment. The peculiar emotional object, *that John stole my car*, can only be fully characterized as the object of my anger. "That John stole my car" is also the name of the object of my belief, of course, and perhaps of any number of other propositional attitudes I hold. But the object of my anger, that John stole my car, is an inseparable piece of my being angry. This sounds strange, no doubt, if the intentional object of the emotion is thought to be a fact or a proposition. But my anger-at-John-for-stealing-my-car is inseparable from my judgment that John in so doing wronged me, while it is clear that the *fact* that John stole my car is very different from my anger or my judgment. My anger *is* my judgment that John has wronged me.

It has always been recognized that there is some difference between our ascriptions of emotions to ourselves and our ascriptions of emotions to others. I know that I am angry and what I am angry about very differently than I know that John is angry and what he is angry about. (This first person privilege remains the presupposition of, and is not undermined by, either the Freudian concept of "unconscious emotions" or by recent philosophical attacks on "incorrigibility.") In the traditional view, in which emotions are feelings, this difference has been explained by appeal to the peculiar "privacy" of sensation-like occurrences. But emotions are not feelings and not occurrences, we have argued, but rather judgments. Yet the difference between first-and other-person cases can still be made out, and in a far more convincing way than on the feeling-analysis of emotions. *You* can say of me, "he is angry about the review, which actually was favorable, but only because of his lack of sleep and his having drunk too much coffee." *You* can say of me, "he doesn't really love Mary, but rather a mother-surrogate." But *I* cannot say these things of *myself*. "I am angry at John because I think that he stole my car, which he didn't" is nonsense. If emotions are judgments, then the sorts of "pragmatic" paradoxes that have long been celebrated regarding judgments in general will apply to emotions also. "I am angry about x, but not x" raises the same problems as "P, but I do not believe P." No feeling-account of emotions can account for such paradoxes. But, if emotions are intentional, emotions must partake in conceptual relationships in a way that mere occurrences, feelings or facts do not. If I am angry about John's stealing my car, there are certain beliefs which I logically cannot hold, for example, the belief that John did not steal my car.

The difference between first- and other-person ascriptions of emotions lies in the realm of the "pragmatic paradoxes." Given that I have a certain emotion, there are certain beliefs which you can have (including beliefs about me) but which *I* cannot have. The most interesting set of beliefs in this regard are those which pertain to the *cause* of an emotion. Earlier, we argued that the cause of an emotion is a fact (or state of affairs) which can be variously ("transparently") described and occupies a role in law-like generalizations. The *object* of an emotion, however, is limited by certain judgments (is "opaque") which are determined by the subject's having that emotion. But this distinction, we can now add, breaks down in the first-person case. If I am angry *about* John's stealing my car (the object of my anger), then I cannot believe that the sufficient *cause* of my anger is anything other than John's stealing my car. *You* can attribute my unjust anger to my lack of sleep. *I* cannot. If I attribute my anger to lack of sleep, I cannot be angry at all. And this is not simply to say that my anger is "not reasonable." (I cannot say that of myself either, except perhaps in extremely peculiar circumstances, for example, following extensive psychoanalytic treatment, which here, as elsewhere, confuses all distinctions, as well as the patient, regarding first- vs. other-person ascriptions of emotions, motives, intentions). I can only be angry as long as I believe that what has caused me to be angry is what I am angry about. Where the cause is different from what I am angry about, I cannot know that it is.

One can argue that the person who is angry (or in love, or sad) is in the worst position to pick out the cause for his anger (or love or sadness) *as opposed to* its object.[4] We can only add that this thesis marks out a conceptual necessity. We earlier pointed out the familiar phenomenon that our emotions change with our opinions and argued that this was not a causal matter and not a coincidence, but a consequence of the thesis that emotions are themselves judgments. We can now add that our emotions change with our knowledge of the causes of those emotions. If I can discover the sufficient cause of my anger, in those cases in which the cause and the object are different (and in which the newly discovered cause is not itself a new object for anger, as often happens), I can undermine and abandon my anger.

It is here that Freud's often debated notion that emotions are "defused" by bringing them to consciousness contains an important conceptual truth too often and too easily dismissed by philosophers. Once one becomes aware of the cause of his emotions as opposed to its intended object, he can indeed "defuse" his emotion. And in those familiar Freudian cases in which one mistakenly identifies the object of his emotion (he thinks he is angry at his teacher: he is "really" angry at his father), correcting this identification can, in those cases where the correctly identified object is also the cause of the emotion, also "defuse" it. Where Freud opened himself to unnecessary criticism, I believe, was in his construing this as a *causal* relationship, a "catharsis" of repressed emotional air bubbles in the mental digestive system. But it is not as if my recognition of the true cause of my anger *causes* the easing of my emotion. Rather, my recognition of the true cause of my emotion amounts to a denial of the judgment which is my emotion. When I see that my anger is wholly a result of my lack of sleep and overdose of coffee, I thereby abandon my anger. Of course, the flushing, pulsing, irritable *feelings* of anger may thus be *caused* to diminish by the disappearance of my anger, but these are, as we have argued, in no case my anger.

If emotions are judgments and can be "defused" (and also instigated) by considerations of other judgments, it is clear how our emotions are in a sense *our doing*, and how we are responsible for them. Normative judgments can themselves be criticized, argued against, and refuted. Now if *you* criticize my anger at John by maintaining that he has not wronged me, you may conclude that my anger is unreasonable, unfair, and perhaps unbecoming. But if you should convince *me* that John has not wronged me, I do not simply conclude that my anger is unreasonable, unfair, or unbecoming. *I cease to be angry.* Similarly, I can make myself angry at John by allowing myself to be convinced that he has wronged me. I can dwell on minor behavioral misdemeanors on John's part, building them into a pattern of overall deceit and abuse, and then become angry at any one or any number of these incidents.

Since normative judgments can be changed through influence, argument, and evidence, and since I can go about on my own seeking influence, provoking argument, and looking for evidence, I am as responsible for my emotions as I am for the judgments I make. My emotions *are* judgments I make. Now one might argue that all we have shown is that one can take steps to *cause* changes in his emotions, much as one can take steps to diminish a pain by pulling out a splinter or take steps to prevent being hit by a bus by crossing only on the proper signals. And it is true, of course, that one cannot *simply* choose to be angry or not to be angry, but can make himself angry or cease being angry only by performing other activities. But this is true of judgments in general: I cannot simply choose to judge a situation fortunate, awkward, or dangerous.[5] It is worth noting that I cannot *simply* perform most actions either: I cannot simply assassinate a dictator. I must do something else (pull the trigger of a rifle, let slip the string of the bow, push the button activating the detonator). Yet, although it is also true that I can cause the death of the dictator (I do not cause the killing of him), I kill the dictator. Similarly, making judgments is something *I do*, not something that happens to me and not something I simply cause, even though I cannot *simply* make a judgment in many cases. (Legal judgments by an appropriately empowered judge or judiciary should *not* be taken as paradigms.)

I must be in appropriate circumstances to pass judgment, have some evidence, know something of what the judgment is about. Of course, one can make judgments rashly, with minimal evidence and with superficial knowledge of what the judgment is about. Emotions, we can now see, are rash judgments, something I do, but in haste. Accordingly, the evidence upon which I become emotional is typically (but not necessarily) incomplete, and my knowledge of what I am emotional about is often (but again not necessarily) superficial. I can take any number of positive steps to change what I believe and what judgments I hold and tend to make. By forcing myself to be scrupulous in the search for evidence and knowledge of circumstance, and by training myself in self-understanding regarding my prejudices and influences, and by placing myself in appropriate circumstances, I can determine the kinds of judgments I will tend to make. I can do the same for my emotions.

II

We argue that emotions are rational in opposition to the near-platitude. This is not only to say that they fit into one's overall behavior in a significant way, that they follow a regular pattern (one's "personality"), and that they can be explained in terms of a coherent set of causes. No doubt this is all true. But emotions, we have argued, are judgments, and so emotions can be rational in the same sense in which judgments can be rational. (Of course, judgments can be irrational, but only within the context of a rational activity.) Judgments are actions. Like all actions, they are aimed at changing the world. But, although the expression of a judgment may actually produce such a change, the judgment itself is more like the winding of the mainspring of an intention to change the world rather than the overt activity which will do so. But if emotions are judgments, and judgments are actions, though covert, emotions too are actions, aimed at changing the world (whether or not their expression actually does succeed in changing the world). In other words, emotions are purposive, serve the ends of the subject, and consequently can be explained by *reasons* or "in-order-to" explanations.

Because emotions are usually thought to be occurrences that we suffer, the idea that emotions are purposive actions has not been given sufficient attention. But consider the following very familiar sort of case:

Joanie wants to go to a party: her husband does not. She begins to act bored and frustrated; he watches television. She resigns herself to reading, sighing occasionally. He asks if she has picked up some shirts from the laundry; she has not. He flies into a rage. He needs shirts (he has hundreds). He needs one of the shirts she was to pick up (they are all the same). He claims that she is negligent (she was busy), and that she takes advantage of him (she stays with him). Naturally, she rebels, but she is upset, both guilty and angry. She thinks him unreasonable, impossible, and slightly neurotic. Their encounter is short-lived. She goes off to read; he settles back before the television. The party is out of the question.

What are we to say of this familiar case? It appears that the husband's anger is inappropriate. His being angry about his wife's failure to pick up his shirts seems unreasonable, and the *intensity* of his anger is most surely unwarranted. The standard interpretation of a case of this type, since well before Freud, has been to suppose that the husband is really angry about something else; perhaps he is redirecting anger from his day at his office— anger which could not be expressed as safely towards his superiors as it could to his wife. Or perhaps the anger is accumulated anger from weeks or months of minor marital frictions. Or perhaps, it might be suggested, the anger is caused by the fact that the husband is tired.

But, in this case—and many other cases—there is an alternative sort of explanation that is available and persuasive. The anger can be explained, not in terms of what it is "about" or what causes it, but in terms of its *purpose*. The husband, in this case, has *used* his anger to manipulate his wife. He has become angry "about" the shirts *in order to* get his wife's mind off the party and in order to stop her irritating reminders. His anger is not a disruption of his activities (watching television, refusing to go to the party) but a part of it, its winning strategy. The best explanation of his anger is not that it was caused by anything (although that is not precluded) and not that it was "about" anything in particular (although that is surely true), but that he got angry at his wife *in order to* continue watching television and in order to insure that his refusal to go to the party would be successful.

But if emotions are rational and purposive, why is it that emotions are so often counter-productive and embarrassing to us, detour away from our aspirations and obstacles blocking our ambitions? Why do emotions so often appear as disruptions in our lives, threats to our successes, aberrations in our rational behavior?

We can outline three distinct accounts of the apparent "irrationality" of emotions.

First, it is the situation in which one becomes emotional that is disruptive, a detour, an obstacle, a threat, and not the emotional response. Emotions are urgent judgments; emotional responses are emergency behavior. An emotional response occurs in a situation in which usual intentions are perverted or frustrated; an unusual response is necessary. The normative judgments involved in having an emotion are inseparable from the overall network of our motives, beliefs and intentions. The fact that emotions typically lead to apparently "pointless" behavior is not a consequence of emotions being irrational, but a natural consequence of the fact that emotions are responses to unusual situations in which usual behavior patterns seem inappropriate. The intentions of an emotional reaction are not infrequently impossible. The angry or sad man may wish to undo the past; the lover may want to possess, and be possessed by, his loved one. This is why Sartre calls the emotions "magical transformations of the world." One can always reduce the range of his emotional behavior by developing stereotyped responses, by avoiding all unusual situations or by treating every situation as "usual." These are common but perhaps pathological ways of choosing our emotions. But such common "control" is not the avoidance or the suppression of a wild psychic beast; it is simply the avoidance of situations (or recognition of situations) where one's usual behavior patterns will not suffice. Emotions are rational responses to unusual situations. They differ from "cool" judgments and normal rational deliberate action in that they are prompted by urgency and in contexts in which one's usual repertoire of actions and considered judgments will not suffice. An emotion is a necessarily hasty judgment in response to a difficult situation.

It must be added that the "hastiness" of a judgment does not entail that it is made quickly. For example, one can make a hasty judgment after weeks of half-hearted deliberation. Similarly, although emotions are typically urgent and immediate responses, one can become increasingly angry over a period of time, or one finds that an emotion which is formed in urgency is then maintained in full force for weeks or even years. But what distinguishes emotions from ordinary judgments is their lack of "cool," their seeming urgency, even after weeks of simmering and stewing. There is no cold emotion, no cool anger, no deliberate love. Emotions are always urgent, even desperate, responses to situations in which one finds oneself unprepared, helpless, frustrated, impotent, "caught." It is the situation, not the emotion, that is disruptive and "irrational."

Second, and consequently, emotions are short-term responses. Emotions are rational in that they fit into a person's overall purposive behavior. But this is not to say that a person's various purposes are always consistent or coherent. Short-term purposes are often in conflict with, rather than a means toward, the fulfillment of long-term purposes. My desire to drink at the reception may lead to a disastrous meeting with a celebrity even though meeting him was my reason for going to the reception. My desire to visit Peking may undermine my ambition to become an FBI agent. Similarly, emotions often serve short-term purposes that are in conflict with longer-term purposes. I may be angry with John because I feel I have been wronged, but this may be inconsistent with my desire to keep a close, unblemished friendship with John. I may love Mary, but this might be totally inconsistent with my intention to preserve my marriage, to remain celibate, or to concentrate on my writing. Thus, the husband in our example might succeed in staying home from the party by becoming angry, but break up his marriage in so doing. It is this sense that emotions are "blind"; more accurately, they are *myopic*. Emotions serve purposes and are rational; but because the purposes emotions serve are often shortsighted, they appear to be non-purposive and irrational on a larger view. For the sake of a passion, we destroy careers, marriages, lives. Emotions are not irrational; people are irrational.

Third, there is an anthropological response to the idea that emotions are irrational. In a society that places taboos on emotional behavior—condemns it in men and belittles it in women—it is only to be expected that emotions will be counter to ambitions. A society which applauds "cool" behavior will naturally require strategies which are similarly "cool." In such a society, emotional behavior appears as "irrational" because it is bad strategy, not because it is not purposive. Perhaps it is not at all difficult to envision a society in which *only* emotional behavior would appear rational—where only short-term emotional responses had any meaning at all. But it is surely not Anglo-American society in which "reason is and ought to be the slave of the passions."

Against our view that emotions, as actions, are purposive and that a person chooses his emotions rather than being victimized by them, there is a uniquely powerful objection. A person cannot identify the purpose of his emotion when the emotion occurs. The husband who uses his anger to manipulate his wife cannot identify the purpose as opposed to the object-cause of his anger. If he were to identify the manipulative function of his anger, the effect would be the destruction of his anger. One cannot be angry and know that his anger has a purpose.

This is much more, of course, than a mere pragmatic claim. It is certainly true that the husband cannot tell his wife that his anger is purposive, for the very purpose of the anger is to distract his wife from that purpose. But the claim here is that the husband cannot even think to himself, "I am being angry in order to. . . ." If the husband is unusually self-aware, he may know that he, in general, uses his anger to manipulate people; but he still cannot entertain that thought at the time of his anger and remain angry. If he does, he ceases to be angry and continues, at most, only to act angry—to feign anger.

One's inability to see the purpose of one's emotion is a conceptual matter, just as previously it was pointed out that one cannot (conceptually) make certain judgments, such as the judgment that what one is angry about is not the case, or that the cause of one's anger, where this is different from the object of this anger, is a sufficient explanation of the anger. We can now add to this list of conceptual inabilities the inability of one to suspect the *purpose* of his emotion. Now many philosophers would argue that, regarding intentional actions in general, one cannot fail to be aware of his motives and intentions at the time of acting. It would take us too far astray to argue against this view here, but notice that this inability to notice one's purpose is not limited to emotions. Consider, for example, Nietzsche's account of belief in God as a belief whose function is to serve certain purposes (achievement of salvation; a basis for "slave-morality" and self-righteousness; to seek power). Yet, even if a purposive analysis of belief in God is true, this neither denies that people do in fact believe in God nor need it suggest that believers could state these purposes. To the contrary, we can add, if they were to think seriously that their belief was held to serve a purpose rather than because it was true, we would have to conclude that they did not believe at all. (A conclusion that Nietzsche too easily comes to on the basis of an argument from the third-person to the first-person case.) To believe is not to believe for a purpose; yet beliefs can still be purposive.

Judgments in general, not only emotions, can be purposive but cannot be recognized (by the person who makes them at the time that he makes them) as purposive. If I judge, calmly and deliberately, without a hint of that urgency and intensity that characterizes anger, that John has wronged me by stealing my car again (he does it all the time), I may be rationalizing an opportunity to take out John's wife. In fact, I may even say to myself, "since he has wronged me so, I feel justified in taking out his wife." But I cannot believe that my judgment that John has wronged me has been made for this purpose. I can at most believe that since he has wronged me, my behavior is justified. Similarly, I may judge, calmly and deliberately, without the slightest hint of that urgency and intensity that characterizes love, that Mary is a magnificent woman, attractive and intelligent, strong-willed and sensitive. But, knowing that Mary is John's wife, I may be so judging as a way of rationalizing an opportunity to run off with John's mistress. Now I may openly judge that John does not need his mistress, since his wife is so magnificent, and so I can feel justified in running off with his mistress. But I cannot believe that I judged Mary magnificent for this purpose. In other words, judgments, no matter how calm and deliberate, when they are made for some purpose (leaving open the question whether all are so made), cannot be recognized as having been made for a purpose. In this sense, all judgments are "blind." To recognize the purpose for which a judgment is made is to undermine the judgment. One cannot judge that he has been wronged and at the same time recognize that he has judged that he has been wronged only in order to justify an act.

One must also consider apparently "unintentional" actions, to which emotions bear a striking resemblance. Some act-types allow for only intentional acts, for example, murder, fishing. Others allow for only unintentional acts, for example, forgetting, slipping, stumbling, tripping, losing, in short, most of those actions that make up the subject matter of what Freud calls the "psychopathology of everyday life." Yet Freud demonstrated that such "unintentional" actions function in a remarkable accordance with a subject's overall purposes and intentions. Freud surely does not want to say that these simply *appear* to be intentional (as some authors have argued, for example, R. S. Peters, A. MacIntyre), but rather that they truly are intentional, the difference being, in his terms, the "inaccessibility" of the intention to the subject. The status of such actions remains a matter of controversy, but we feel reasonably confident that most philosophers and most everybody else would agree that such "actions" are indeed actions and can be demonstrated, at least in some cases, to be done for a purpose; yet the subject cannot state that purpose. And once again, the "cannot" is a *logical* "cannot," since a man who knows that he is losing his wedding ring in order to show his opinion of his marriage is making a gesture, not losing his ring. And a man who knows he is forgetting to call his office in order to avoid extra work is not forgetting but refusing to call his office. Thus we can see in what senses such actions may appear to be both intentional and "unintentional." They are intentional insofar as they clearly fit into the purposes and intentions of the subject; they appear to be unintentional insofar as they cannot be stated as purposive or intentional by the subject. Similarly, anger is purposive and intentional insofar as it can be clearly shown to fit into the structure of the subjects purposes and intentions; it appears to be "unintentional" and thus differs from many straightforward actions, in that these purposes and intentions cannot be known by the subject at the time. Emotions, when they are purposive and intentional, are essentially devious.

Can one feign anger? One might think, "Of course; act angry when you are not angry." But what is it that constitutes the anger apart from acting angry? The traditional answer to this is simple enough: a feeling. To feign anger is to act angry but not feel angry. To feign love is to act lovingly but not feel love. To feign an emotion would be, in general, to pretend one has a feeling which one does not have, as a child pretends—usually badly—to have a cramp in order to stay away from school. But we have seen that an emotion is not a feeling. This traditional analysis does lend support to our contention that to have an emotion to achieve an end is not to have that emotion. But, in our argument, the difference is not due to the presence or lack of a feeling. Rather, to have an emotion is to make certain judgments; to feign an emotion, then, is to pretend that one holds certain judgments which one does not hold.

But this makes the notion of feigning emotion much more difficult than has been supposed in the simple "feeling" analysis. Andrē Gide has written that feigned emotion and "vital" emotion are indistinguishable, and in this there is an often unseen giant of a truth, one that would appear absurd on the thesis that emotions are feelings. Miss Anscombe, replying to J. L. Austin, has distinguished between mock performances and real pretences. The most obvious difference between the two is that one is intended to mislead others, the other not. Accordingly, the one should be more cautiously consistent and prolonged than the other: a successful mock performance may be announced as lasting only thirty five seconds, a real pretense must go on as long as it must go on.

But the most important difference between mock performances and real pretenses is the *context* (what we have been calling "the situation"). A mock performance may be performed on a stage, in any context in which it can be announced or in which it is evident that this is a *mere* pretense. A real pretense, however, requires that the context of performance be appropriate; anger can only be feigned in real pretense if the situation is one in which anger is appropriate. One can only pretend to be in love with someone whom it is plausible that he should love. But the appropriateness of the situation is not a causal determinant of a feeling of love or anger. Rather it is the context in which judgments of the requisite kinds make sense and are plausible. But if the real pretense of anger is acting angry in a context in which the anger-related judgments are plausible, it is easy to see how one could, upon prolonged pretense, come to accept those very judgments. If, over a protracted period of time, I pretend to love a woman whom I have married for her father's wealth, it is more than likely that I shall grow to love her (if I do not first come to openly despise her). And if I pretend to be angry about a political issue in order to be accepted by my friends, it is not at all unlikely that I shall come to be really angry about that same issue. Perhaps there is no better way to choose to have an emotion than to decide to pretend that one has it. As Sartre has said, the best way to fall asleep is to pretend that you are asleep. And here, I think we may say that Gide's theory has a plausibility which cannot be explained on the idea that what one pretends to have is a feeling.

Emotions are intentional and rational, not disruptive and "irrational." Emotions are judgments and actions, not occurrences or happenings that we suffer. Accordingly, emotions are choices and our responsibility. Yet I am never aware of making such choices. Emotions, we argued, are hasty and typically dogmatic judgments. Therefore, they cannot be made together with the recognition that they are dogmatic and not absolutely correct. What distinguishes emotions from other judgments is the fact that the former can never be deliberately chosen and carefully considered. Emotions are essentially non-deliberate choices. Emotions, in this sense, are indeed "blind" as well as myopic; an emotion cannot see itself. Few things are more disconcerting than suddenly watching one's angry reflection in the mirror, or reflecting on one's anger to see its absurdity *in media res*.

If emotions are judgments or actions, we can be held responsible for them. We cannot simply have an emotion or stop having an emotion, but we can open ourselves to argument, persuasion and evidence. We can force ourselves to be self-reflective, to make just those judgments regarding the causes and purposes of our emotions, and also to make the judgment that we are all the while *choosing* our emotions, which will "defuse" our emotions. This is not to opt for a life without emotions: it is to argue for a conception of emotions which will make clear that emotions are our choice. In a sense, our thesis here is self-confirming: to think of our emotions as chosen is to *make* them our choices. Emotional control is not learning to employ rational techniques to force into submission a brutal "it" which has victimized us, but rather it is the willingness to become self-aware, to search out, and challenge the normative judgments embedded in every emotional response. To come to believe that one has this power *is* to have this power.

In response to our argument, one might conclude that we have only argued that one can choose and is responsible for his *interpretation* of his situation and his emotions. But then I simply want to end by once again drawing Nietzsche to my side and quipping, with regard to emotions, "there are only interpretations. . . ."

NOTES

1 Perhaps we should distinguish getting into an emotional state and being in one (for example, getting angry vs. being angry). But nothing turns on this, for being in a state as well as getting into a state, like God's maintenance of the Universe as well as his creation of it, requires devoted activity. Accordingly, I shall be arguing both that we choose an emotion and that we continuously choose our emotions. There is no need to separate these arguments.

2 I take this to be definitive of the difference between "emotion" and "feeling" as I am using those terms here. Emotions are intentional; feelings are not. I do not deny that the everyday use of "feeling" is broader than this and includes both of these concepts. I find this ambiguity less objectionable than others surrounding "sensation" and like terms.

3 There is nothing in our analysis which is not compatible with an all-embracing causal theory. We might agree with writers like A. I. Goldman, who argues that intentional characterizations of actions (in terms of "reasons") also function in causal explanations of a Hempelian variety. I do not wish to argue a similar thesis regarding emotions here, but I want to be careful not to preclude any such theory. Similarly, nothing I have said here bears on the so-called "free will problem"; I want to show that emotions should be viewed in the same categories as actions, whether or not there are further arguments that might lead us to conclude that not even actions are chosen freely.

4 Freud has a curious way of defending this thesis, which is surely central to much of his theory. Because he attempted to maintain a thesis of the intentionality of the "affects" within a strictly causal model, he obscured the distinction between object and cause. Without crucifying Freud on this point, as Peters, MacIntyre and others have attempted to do, it is important to see that Freud typically confuses first-person and third-person accounts, and the concept of the "unconscious" as an "assumption" (e.g., see the essay "The Unconscious," Collected Papers, Vol. VI) often depends upon the failure of the subject to be capable of applying third-person ascriptions—notably, ascriptions of the cause as opposed to the object of an emotion—to himself. Without in the least detracting from Freud's overall conception of the unconscious, we must insist that the subject is never logically privileged with respect to the causes of his emotions, but that he does have some such authority (without infallible authority) with respect to what he is "affected about."

5 Though perhaps I can simply *express* such a judgment.

7

HUMAN NATURE AND ABSOLUTE VALUES

JOHN L. RUSSELL

The term 'value' has been used by philosophers in many different senses. I shall not attempt to define my own use too precisely at this stage; it will, I hope, emerge more clearly during the course of this paper. I merely presuppose that a system or scale of values provides us with a criterion for choosing between different alternative courses of action when these are open to us in a given situation. And since actions are normally directed towards goals, it is the goal of our actual or possible striving to which value will normally be ascribed or denied. A goal has value for us in so far as we regard it as worth striving for. One must, however, distinguish between real and apparent value. We may sometimes be misled into thinking that a goal has value whereas in fact it has not, in which case the value will only be apparent. Similarly, one can distinguish between relative and absolute value. A goal may have value for a particular person in a particular situation, or it may be unconditionally valuable for everyone, whether or not it is actually being sought or attained. In this case it will have absolute value. Whether there is such a goal or goals has been much debated. The purpose of this paper will be to enquire whether a consideration of human nature can help us towards an answer.

Man's nature has much in common with other animals and much that is unique. Common to all is the characteristic that their processes and activities are goal-directed. This is true, in the first place, of processes which are unconscious such as growth, maintenance of bodily integrity and repair of injury. It is true of the conscious drives or activities which man shares with the animals, such as satisfaction of hunger, sexual drives and desire for self-preservation. It is true also of those more specifically human activities which are self-conscious and deliberate.

In order to bring out more clearly the differences between human activities and those of the lower animals, I shall begin by considering some general features of the latter. It is characteristic of all members of the animal kingdom that they can be classified into well-defined groups or species. (There may sometimes be a doubt whether a given group should be considered as one species or several, but this is irrelevant for present purposes). The members of each species have a characteristic physical structure and characteristic patterns of activity which are conditioned by the fact that each species is adapted to a particular way of life, occupying one particular niche in a complex and generally balanced ecological community. There will be a close correlation between the physical structure of an animal, the sort of goals which it seeks to achieve, and the patterns of activity, whether innate or learned, which are directed towards their achievement. The tiger has sharp claws and teeth, powerful jaws and leg muscles; the corresponding goal-directed activity is to stalk other animals, leap upon them and eat them. The antelope, with its teeth adapted for browsing, its acute senses and long legs adapted for speed, lives on vegetation and seeks to escape by flight when threatened.

For each species there will be, broadly speaking, a more or less standard type which will have the optimum adaptation to the particular ecological niche which it occupies. Any significant deviation from the norm, either in structure or behavior, is likely to put it at a disadvantage. Over the course of millennia the standard type may gradually change but in the short term it is effectively fixed. And such is the competitive nature of existence that structure and way of life must be closely coadapted to each other. The goals which an animal seeks are prescribed for it—"written in" to its nature by its heredity and the environment to which its genetic inheritance is adapted. There is, and must be, a close correlation between its specific nature and the sort of goals which are available to it.

Man, in his specific physical structure and teleology, resembles the other animals in some respects but also differs profoundly from them. His infra-conscious teleology resembles theirs. There are similar processes of maintenance and repair, and the same tendency to grow towards a fairly standard physical type, although his degree of physical variability is greater than most. He shares certain basic conscious drives with them, such as those towards satisfaction of hunger and sexual needs. But in one very important respect he is unique. He is not committed by virtue of his physical form or instinctive endowment to any particular way of life. He is unique in that he can choose from an immense variety of different goals or ways of life, any one of which can be regarded as worthwhile by particular individuals in particular circumstances. Some can spend their lives, fruitfully and satisfyingly, in densely populated cities, others as pioneers in the wide open spaces of North West Canada. One may live by cultivating a patch of land in tropical Africa; another by hunting seals in the Arctic. Others will choose to be carpenters, doctors, artists, metal workers, soldiers or criminals. Heredity and environment may incline an individual to one way of life rather than another; they do not prescribe it.

Man's unique position is made possible, in the first place, by his capacity to invent and use implements. Animals, with a few relatively unimportant exceptions, do not use them. Instead, they evolve bodily specializations in order to cope with the problem of surviving in a competitive world. Each species becomes adapted to exploit some particular, relatively restricted ecological niche. A mole lives by tunneling underground, thus escaping from most of its natural enemies and at the same time tapping a food source which is not available to other species. In order to do this it must be able to dig efficiently. It does not have the intelligence to design a tool for the job; instead, its paws become adapted, by a process of evolution, into efficient instruments for digging. One might say that evolution by natural selection is a technique which enables living organisms to grow the implements which they need to survive. But, although it is an efficient method, it imposes severe constraints. Once a mole has become specialized for digging, there is not much else it can do except dig. It is finally and irreversibly committed to one particular way of life and to the corresponding types of goal-seeking activity. Not all animals are as highly specialized as the mole but all are more or less circumscribed in their activities by the bodily specializations which are their means of survival.

Man alone has been able to free himself from the constraints of specialization. His own peculiar endowment is a highly developed brain and central nervous system, together with hands and fingers adapted for precision manipulations. He thus becomes capable of making tools which enable him to reap the benefits of a wide variety of different ways of life. If he wishes to dig down into the earth he does not have to grow spade-like paws; he invents a spade and, later, a mechanical excavator. If he wishes to exploit the resources of the sea he does not grow fins; he builds boats. The advantages which other animals gain through wings, claws, hard integuments, high running speeds, etc., he can achieve through his artifacts. The result, as we have seen, is that his goals are not prescribed by his physical structure. An unlimited number of ways of life are open to him. He can exercise his skills on land, sea or air. He can compete with every other species, even to the extent of depriving them completely of their means of livelihood. Anything they can do he can do; if not always better than they can, then at least more powerfully and ruthlessly.

Man, therefore, inevitably has a disruptive effect on any ecosystem which he invades. A natural system is relatively stable because each species has its prescribed way of life and, as a result of a long evolutionary process, these dovetail into each other to produce an integrated whole. Man has no such innate prescription. It is not that he has somehow forgotten or renounced his natural place; there simply is no specific way of life laid down for him. As soon as he gets beyond the most primitive hunting and food-gathering stage he must modify any ecosystem which he invades. He must mold it into a new form which will enable him to live in a worthwhile human way.

If we look at the world today we might be tempted to conclude that the situation is alarming, if not hopeless. Man is the one species with no prescribed way of life: no set of built-in goals which will harmonize with those of other natural species. He seems to be an outcast and an alien, competing with all other species and wrecking any ecosystem which he invades. Some of the more extreme prophets of doom have indeed taken this view. Man, they would say, is simply an animal who, by his discovery of tools, acquired a power incomparably greater than any other species but who still retains the animal instincts of his pre-human days. In particular, he retains an instinct for aggression which served him well in his old way of life but which has now got out of control and will inevitably prevent him from living at peace either with his own kind or with his environment.

If man were merely a very powerful animal driven by instincts which are no longer ordered towards any natural goal, for whom no appropriate ecological niche exists in any balanced ecosystem, then the outlook for him would indeed be grim. This, however, is far too narrow a view. Man is not a creature who has lost his natural goals but one who must create them for himself. He can find satisfaction and fulfillment in many different ways. He can select his own goals, choosing deliberately between one and another. He does not have to wreck his environment; he can mold it in such a way as to create a new ecological harmony in which he himself participates.

The multiformity of his possible goals is both a danger to him and an opportunity. Instead of having his way of life built into him as the other animals do, he must make a deliberate choice. If he fails to do so, then his life will be meaningless and frustrating. It will be neither truly animal nor truly human. On the other hand, if he recognizes that he has a choice of goals (even though this choice may be restricted unduly by external circumstances), then he can accept his human vocation and commit himself to one rather than another. To do this he needs values.

The problem of choice tends to become obscured because so often our freedom is limited. This is particularly the case in primitive societies or in those where environmental conditions are severe. Until recently Eskimos in the Arctic or Negroes in Central Africa had little opportunity for choosing one sort of life rather than another. But where environmental constraints are less severe or have been overcome by human inventiveness, the problem must arise. It may be an agonizing problem. It may lead some to hanker after a return to a simpler, more primitive society where environment and custom give to each his appointed place; or to opt for a dictatorship where the goals of all are imposed by a higher authority; or to welcome a permissive society where every goal and every way of life is given equal value.

None of these alternatives can be permanently satisfactory. History shows that neither artificially reconstructed primitivism nor dictatorship will permanently resolve the problem of choice. And a completely neutral, anarchic attitude to values breeds selfishness, frustration and despair.

We cannot, therefore, shelve the problem or shift the burden entirely onto other shoulders. We must face the question: how do we evaluate the goals which are open to us? Traditionally, of course, it has been a primary function of religion to give guidance on this point. As a Christian and a Catholic, I believe that Christ has revealed to mankind both the supreme goal to which all human endeavor should be directed, and the sort of values which should motivate our conduct if we are to reach it. But I am not now appealing to Divine Revelation. Instead, I wish to enquire whether human nature, as we experience it for ourselves, can give us any guidance. Is there, in fact, some ultimate goal which human beings can, in principle, recognize as supremely valuable? Can we, correspondingly, discern in our nature intrinsic tendencies or drives which positively orient us towards this goal? If there is such a goal it is clearly not one which is imposed on us of necessity by our heredity and environment. In this it will differ essentially from any purely animal goal. For animals the goals are immediate; the ways of attaining them are narrowly prescribed; there is no previous reflection or deliberate choice. Man's natural goal, if it exists, must be consciously recognized and deliberately chosen. It need not be immediate but may be in the remote future. The means for attaining it must be thought out. Many people evidently do not recognize this natural goal nor consciously strive towards it.

What then can we say about human nature? First, that it is dynamic and restless, never satisfied, always trying to go a bit further, do more, acquire more, learn more. Although this is not necessarily true of every individual or even of every society, it is true of human history as a whole. Human societies do not remain for long in a state of balanced equilibrium with each other or with their environment. New discoveries and inventions alter our relation to the environment. Desire for wealth or power, desire to convert others to our way of thinking, alter the relations of one society with another. However much has been achieved in the way of knowledge, invention, standard of living, etc., still leaves us asking for more. Saint Augustine expressed this vividly in his well-known saying: "Thou hast made us for thyself, O Lord, and our hearts are restless till they rest in thee." Even those who do not believe in God may agree with the negative part of this: that we shall never be entirely satisfied with the things of this world. This same restlessness found expression on another occasion which is worth recalling. During the Middle Ages the national motto of Spain was *Ne plus ultra*, "No more, no further", which expressed the current belief that the Iberian peninsula was the furthest limit of the inhabitable world. But when new worlds were opened up by the discovery of the Americas the *Ne* was struck out and the motto became *Plus ultra*, "More, further." And *plus, ultra* might well be the motto of the human race as a whole.

I believe that this *plus ultra* is a basic characteristic of human nature. Our dynamism is open-ended and will not permit a stable equilibrium in any foreseeable future. I do not mean by this that we must be constantly trying to advance in every direction indiscriminately, constantly making bigger or more powerful machines, covering more and more of the earth's surface with steel and concrete. There are many different ways in which we can go forward and these will vary from one epoch to another.

The idea that human nature is open-ended, in the sense already discussed, is implicit in the Christian view of man but has not always been sufficiently recognized. Teilhard de Chardin, to whose views I am very much indebted, has perhaps done more than anyone to develop it. Previously it had tended to be obscured through the influence of Greek philosophy, especially of Plato and Aristotle. Both of these great philosophers do seem to have thought of human nature as something complete: something which could in principle be actualized in all its perfection in a single individual.

For Plato there was an ideal human type subsisting in a realm of ideas which was more truly real than the transitory, changeable world in which we live. All actual men are more or less imperfect exemplars of, or participations in the ideal man; we can approach the ideal more or less closely even if we can never actually reach it. Aristotle rejected the Platonic subsistent ideas but nevertheless seems to have accepted the principle of a perfect human type into which every man would grow if not impeded by accidental circumstances arising from the general intractability of matter.

If we look at the animal world, this theory of ideal types has a certain purely empirical validity. It could quite reasonably be postulated that there is, for instance, an "ideal" type of tiger, optimally adapted to its particular way of life in the jungle, taking its place with other animals and plants in a perfectly balanced ecosystem, and that all tigers with a normal genetic endowment would, barring accidents, conform reasonably closely to this type. In the nature of things such an equilibrium could not be permanent but it might endure for quite a long time. But can we even conceive of an ideal human type, towards which all normal individuals tend to grow or ought to try to grow? What is the ideal human temperament and would the world be a better place if all men had it? What is the ideal human way of life: artist, craftsman, farmer, scientist, doctor? The answer is immediately obvious: there is no one ideal type. Human society becomes more valuable and more truly human in proportion to how it can unite within itself individuals of widely different temperaments and ways of life, living in harmony with each other. This is one of the basic functions of society. No one man can realize within himself all human perfections. But men and women living together in society can, in some degree, begin to explore the full range of human potentialities—can begin to realize what it is to be human.

We should therefore aim at a complex society. And by complex I do not mean merely complicated. It is not a case of many different people brought together and doing different things haphazardly but of different types of people living together in a community, interacting with each other, depending on each other in such a way that each may fulfill himself in his own fashion and at the same time may make it possible for others to do so in theirs. I believe that throughout human history the dynamism of our nature has been urging mankind, more or less blindly and gropingly, towards complex societies of this sort. There have been setbacks, as in the early Middle Ages, and no doubt there will be more, but the overall picture is one of increasing complexity as we pass from primitive hunting groups in the Old Stone Age to the first settled agricultural communities, the founding of the first cities, the more elaborate civilizations of Classical times and now the immensely involved interrelationships of the modern world.

There is no doubt about the pressure towards increasing complexity at the present time. The different communities of the world are far more interdependent than ever before; they interact much more; there is more mutual concern. To a large extent this is an inevitable result of advancing technology, which is itself an expression of the "plus ultra" in man: of his urge to know more, to invent more, to overcome the environmental constraints which limited our ancestors and to open up new fields for human endeavor. A modern car may contain iron from Sweden, nickel from Canada, copper from Zambia, tin from Malaya, running on oil from Arabia brought to this country by tankers built in Japan and so on. The whole world, one might say, converges upon it. Modern communications enable us to converse with friends in Australia as if they were in the same room, or to witness events in any part of the world while they are actually happening. For the first time in history, science and technology have provided the material and mechanical substructure for a truly world society.

At the moment the ideal world society is clearly beyond our powers. For one thing, the process of industrialization has gotten out of control. Besides threatening universal destruction by nuclear weapons, it is in danger of wrecking the environment, squandering limited resources, making the rich richer but leaving the poor as they were or even worse off. Improved communications can generate hostility as easily as friendship between distant peoples. It is no longer sufficient to stumble along blindly. If our civilization is not to collapse into chaos we need a clearer consciousness of the goal we are aiming at.

So, to come at last more explicitly to the question of absolute values. If the human race is to go forward without disaster, we need some common unifying purpose. We must agree that there is a goal which has absolute unconditional value. And the only goal that corresponds fully to the needs and tendencies of our nature in a world society in which the greatest possible unity of love and mutual support is combined with the greatest possible opportunity for each individual to develop in his own unique way, so that the possibilities of human nature may be more fully and richly actualized.

Is this just a Utopian dream like so many which have been put forward in the past? I think it differs in several important respects. The conventional Utopia has always been given too narrow a base. It has not taken into account the infinite variety of ways in which to be human; it has sought to impose a single well-defined social system and that system has been closed. Once achieved, there would be nothing more to do except keep it in being. The dynamism of our nature would be frustrated until the system was once again broken open. The great danger, always, is that we fail to distinguish between unity and uniformity. There is a constant temptation to suppose that true unity is attained when we all think the same thing, act the same way, have the same culture and the same institutions. Too much uniformity always must unduly constrict the human spirit. The sort of goal we ought to envisage is a unity which can incorporate the greatest possible variety of social structures, cultural traditions and ways of life not, of course, precisely as they are today but mutually adapted so that each is compatible with the others, contributes to the common stock of human achievement, and enables each member of the human family to help and to be helped by every other member.

I am not suggesting that the goal could ever be completely achieved in this world. We cannot conceive at all clearly what such a society would be like. It is, indeed, impossible in principle to foresee it clearly since we cannot know what are the capacities of our nature until we see them realized and we can never know when or if they have been realized. However far we go, there will probably be a "plus ultra." This means, also, that we can never hope to have universal agreement as to the means by which the end can best be approached. There must be disagreements, conflicts, tensions, even among those who are genuinely seeking the same goal. But so long as there is a common goal, the conflicts can be fruitful and constructive; they should never be simply divisive and destructive.

For the Christian, the goal I have been discussing is expressed in the two commandments which Jesus gave to his followers: "Love the Lord your God with all your heart, with all your soul, with all your strength, and with all your mind;" and "your neighbor as yourself." To love God involves an absolute commitment to the "plus ultra"—a recognition that the ultimate goal of our endeavor lies beyond anything that we can achieve here and now, nothing we could ever accomplish in this world would be enough. To love our neighbor is to recognize that our lives are bound up with those of our fellow men; we find our fulfillment in mutual dependence and mutual help. Only in this way can we and all others find the conditions in which we can expand and diversify in a truly human way. In Christ's teaching the two commandments are ultimately one. Love of God must express itself in love of others.

The goal is in accordance with Christian teaching but there is no reason why it should be confined to Christians, though others will see it in a different perspective and will have different ideas for reaching it. These will generate conflicts, but as long as we recognize that we have a common goal there is no reason why the conflicts should not be constructive rather than destructive. A forward-looking society must be in a state of creative tension. Just as arguments are sterile unless there is some common ground or premise from which the disputants can start, so conflicting policies are mutually obstructive and frustrating unless there is some basis of agreement on goals.

The question remains: Is not this goal too remote and shadowy? If it can never be attained, how can it be a genuine motive for action?

Admittedly, the goal of perfect unity with maximum variety may be unattainable this side of heaven, but it is one towards which we can always be striving. It has immediate practical applications. It excludes, here and now, both the imposed uniformity of totalitarianism and the selfish individualism of laissez faire. It can suggest guidelines for action though it cannot give cut and dried solutions. For instance, Great Britain is likely to be confronted, in the near future, with formidable nationalist upsurges in Scotland and Wales. These are healthy insofar as there are authentically English, Scottish and Welsh cultural traditions and ways of life which help to enrich the total human experience and should be fostered. On the other hand, if these movements merely resulted in the fragmentation of Great Britian into three mutually competing and inward looking little nations, each of the cultures would be impoverished. In the long run a culture is only viable if it is sufficiently adaptable and outward looking to be able to integrate with others in a more comprehensive unity. Similar problems are arising within the European Economic Community; many of us who strongly support it in principle fear that it may try to impose a degree of uniformity on its member states which would be inimical to true unity. How are we to reconcile the conflicting tendencies?

There are no easy solutions to these or innumerable other problems which confront societies and individuals in the modern world. We cannot expect agreement about present policies. But if we can agree about ends—about the sort of human society we want and why it is valuable, at least we shall have a sense of common purpose.

I conclude, then, by repeating that our ultimate goal should be a society comprising the whole human race united by a common bond of mutual love and respect, in which each individual has the maximum possible opportunity to realize his human potentialities in his own unique way, while a part of a union with all others. It is a remote goal; one which we ourselves can never hope to see in our lifetimes; one which probably never will be perfectly realized in this world. Nevertheless, even if strictly unattainable, it remains within the sphere of practical endeavor. It can suggest the broad lines along which our particular societies should try to evolve. It can be recognized as having absolute value by all those who are genuinely concerned with the well-being of the human race. It should therefore be capable of giving all men of good will a basic sense of common purpose even when they disagree strongly about immediate policies. Finally, I have tried to show that human nature itself has a dynamic orientation towards this end. We have an urge to go forward to it. It is an urge which is, for us, confused and obscure; it has led, in the past, to innumerable blind alleys and fruitless conflicts. When misdirected it can find expression in mindless violence or uncontrolled aggression. We need to recognize its true nature and to direct it towards its true goal. We must accept that nothing less than this almost unattainable goal will ever satisfy our restless nature.

8

INDIVIDUAL RESPONSIBILITY IN ADVANCED SOCIETIES

ADRIAN PEPERZAK

This paper has three parts. The first part is a sketch of the conception which modern, "advanced" society has of itself, its main problems and the way it tries to solve them. The second part concentrates on the moral responsibility of the individual who sees himself confronted with the problems exposed in the first part. What can be done with regard to the universal urge for material satisfaction and cultural fulfillment? Is democracy the ideal framework within which individuals can realize a better world? Totalitarianism and anarchism have attacked the idea of modern democracy. Can it be saved or are certain assumptions on which it is based open to criticism? In the third and last part I try to show that the attitude of a universal planner who would rule in order to remake the world overrates man's possibilities and has to be transcended by a more modest, still painful but less moralistic attitude of participation, dialogue and peace.

The fact that we call modern industrialized societies "advanced" manifests a global vision of society according to which the true meaning of social history consists of the development of a sort of life and of certain structures and forms of production and well-being prevalent in modern, "advanced" societies. A nation or state which has not yet reached this stage of development is not advanced but underdeveloped, or on the way to the level of developed nations. If it is true that today's "advanced" societies are passing through a serious and perhaps fundamental crisis concerning their basic assumptions and values, an analysis of our ideas and attitudes with regard to the sort of advancement involved here may throw some light on the nature of our crisis and give us some clues for overcoming it. I will therefore begin by sketching briefly the idea of advancement or progress, which dominates most of our thinking about "man, society and the state." At the same time I shall trace some other ideas closely related to the idea of progress which are equally responsible for certain characteristics and problems of contemporary society.

Modern Society

The notion of advancement or progress includes a representation of a future state of affairs towards which the advancing subject is moving. From the perspective of societies calling themselves "advanced" the situation towards which they move, and of which they have already realized certain aspects, is seen not only as something which can be real, but also as a goal that *ought* to be realized. The progressive realization of this special sort of future is part of the *meaning* and of the *value* of today's social life. We work for the society of tomorrow. The image of a better state in the future animates our present life and constitutes at least part of its worth.

All periods of western history have known forms of "progressive" thought and a longing for more or less Utopian golden ages in the future. Since the 18th century, however, the idea of progress has also been accompanied by the idea that progress itself and the ideal future towards which it is directed should be the results of man's own efforts, and that they cannot be expected from any superhuman power. Whereas in former times it was thought obvious and natural that history was not totally in the hands of mankind but depended on "higher" powers—gods, spirits, stars, fate or one almighty God—the Enlightenment exiled the Divine to an unearthly heaven and trusted the destiny of world and society to human autonomy. The horizon of human history was transformed into a sort of *practical* atheism (although it took a longer time to abolish *all* of the functions of God because of the general conviction that morality would perish if there were no God to judge the immortal soul after death). Progress towards an ideal future thus became the task of man. Mankind has to produce its own wealth, peace, safety, happiness and life. Social well-being is no longer a question of fate or grace but is a human product. Divine Providence has been abolished or restricted to questions of "life after death"; human history has been conquered as the domain where humanity itself is at home as master of its destiny. Human society and human history have become the greatest and most enthralling material of human creation. The good life is a question of self-realization: man has to reveal and realize his essence by humanizing everything else *and* himself. He is the creator of a humanity that is truly human and created "in his image."

True, many thinkers of the 19th century, like Marx and Comte, saw history itself as a sort of providence transcending human individuals and groups in power and wisdom. But the ambiguity of their notion of history, according to which history is simultaneously identical and not identical with real mankind, illustrates that they also adhered to the overall scheme of self-realization and saw humanity as a "cause of himself" (*causa sui*).

The means which would enable man to perform his task and to guarantee his success were to be found in *science* and scientific *technology*. The objectifying character of modern science makes it especially apt for that goal. The style of scientific observation and verification through experiments fits the great project of the modern demiurge mastering and re-creating the world in accordance with his wishes. The new clockmaker needs a certain distance from his material so that he can handle it autonomously, not being involved himself in the objects and structures on which he concentrates. The subject-object scheme is an ideal frame for this attitude:

everything appears as an object for the only subject: not only nature, but man's behavior and social life as well. Only insofar as he objectifies and plans everything else, the human subject escapes from objectification himself.

Scientific objectification and the technological application of it are, of course, much easier to achieve with regard to non-human things than in relation to human behavior, social life and cultural performances like written texts, works of art, moral codes and religions. This seems to be the reason why modern science, after several centuries, has not yet been able to do justice to the typical human features of those human, social, cultural and historical realities. Its successes are most impressive in those fields in which it either makes abstractions of those features (e.g. in the "psychology" of rats) or weakens the claims of scientific methodology. Therefore it should not surprise us that the faith man formerly had in science has considerably faded away. On the level of natural sciences, the expectations have become more realistic than a century ago. But the attitude of the great clockmaker and master of the universe has not altogether disappeared. In psychology, sociology and economy, modesty has won over the boastful announcements of a near solution to all major problems, and the sciences which concentrate on literature, art, religion, morality and philosophy are even less trustful about their possible results. But even there, some people persevere in the hope that technology and research one day will put an end to our disagreements.

These problems are intimately connected with the crisis of modern society. Modern man would wish to create a more human world by the application of solid, objective and exact knowledge. Symbols of this hope are for instance the great *"Encylopédie"* and its successors, the idea of a *university* of sciences as a theoretical center providing the state with the insights necessary for organizing and ruling society's practical life, and the whole system of *education* seen as the upbringing of good citizens through integration of modern science in more or less popularized forms. If, however, modern science is incapable of telling us what the nature, the possibilities and the meaning of human life are, how human well-being should be defined, and how it can be realized, then we are altogether committed to pre-scientific, naive, philosophic or religious opinions and testimonies.

Modern society does, however, not rely on any spontaneous consensus concerning those basic questions. Notwithstanding its material, scientific and technological wealth, the "advanced" societies are rather poor as far as common wisdom and patterns for a good and noble life are concerned. In fact modern society is marked by an extreme diversity of vision, codes and values to which its participants adhere and by the prevailing relativism of its cultural policy. Modern veneration for science is the reverse of a typical distrust towards any authority. Religious commands and dogmas, as well as "metaphysical" doctrines and secular wisdom, excite more suspicion than adherence. Heroes of thought and examples of holiness are not welcome because they contradict a general conviction that "everything is relative." On the basis of individual autonomy—the great discovery of modern times—modern man has emancipated himself from church, state and all cultural authorities. The result of this emancipation is a complete relativism with regard to esthetic, moral and religious norms and questions. Democracy is the political expression of the fundamental demand that everybody should be treated as every other's equal. On the cultural level the same demand takes the form of a complete freedom for every individual to independently make up his mind with regard to all goals and values to be realized. The principle of individual autonomy has led to a general privatization of cultural standards. But how can such private persons still unite, if they have no way to point out authoritatively or scientifically what sort of minimal culture should set the standards and the rules for social life? In fact, we have still some convictions in common, but has it not become impossible to justify them? Do we base our society on pure contingency?

From the principle of individual autonomy only one moral standard follows: if every individual has the right to do what he wants, we must all behave in a way which does not destroy another's right to do the same. Everybody has the same right; we are all equal as subjects of the same human rights. This norm is, however, purely formal. It does not give any indication about the *content* of what every individual and society as a whole should try to realize, or about the meaning of "well-being", "happiness", "a good life", or a "satisfactory" or "advanced" society.

Lacking any general agreement on the goals to be realized within a human society, modern societies have restricted themselves

more and more to the satisfaction of those needs which fulfill a
necessary condition for the existence of individual subjects of human
rights. Not even an extreme form of relativism can deny that human
rights imply at least a demand for the satisfaction of those primary
needs. Here, then, we have a minimal consensus on which modern
society and the state can concentrate their efforts. But even on this
very important although low-level, modern techniques and political
economy have not yet attained control of reality. We do not exactly
know what the best methods would be for putting an end to hunger
and poverty, and science cannot answer the ethical question of
what proportion of the goods of the earth should be owned by and
distributed among different nations, classes, enterprises or private
persons.

Others will enter into the great economic problems of our
time and give their views on the scientific and technical aspects of
those problems. The struggle between capitalism and socialism, the
scandalous disproportion between oversatisfied and hungry people,
the forms of pollution destroying the victories of technology, and
many other scandals, can be thematized scientifically—perhaps
even solved—by thorough planning and the development of new
techniques, or by putting an end to old ways of production. But all
of these problems also have moral aspects. They urge us to look for
an ethically legitimate answer to the question of whether the way
which modern society has advanced until now is good and whether
it should be changed. In the following comments I want to stress
one aspect of this question. Although it would be very important if
we could agree in this time of moral relativism on certain moral
norms or standards, it seems to me even more important to
determine a basic standpoint and attitude from which our considerations and evaluations are to be given.

Responsibility of the Individual

Faced with the unsolved problems of today's "advanced" societies, a consciously living individual will ask himself how he should evaluate his situation and what he can and should do about it.

One initial answer can be sought in the direction of a better form of theory and practice than those developed until now. Faced with a world full of hunger, pollution, war, discrimination and injustice, we should make plans and develop new techniques to master the natural, social, economic and political structures which determine the well-being of mankind. But the development of technical skills and brilliant management are in themselves not enough to solve these problems. These skills and techniques must *serve* mankind and must therefore receive their orientation from moral standards. The available resources, money, scientific knowledge, technical means and skills, should be mobilized for fairer, cleaner and better production and distribution of all those goods which are essential for a really human life.

This orientation presupposes a moral attitude on the side of those who have power concerning the use of resources. They should regard the public good not only of their nation but of all mankind, including successive generations. Their interest in the public or universal good is not necessarily at odds with well-understood self-interest, as Adam Smith and other theoreticians of the 18th century said. But we no longer believe that everybody's pursuing his own interest results necessarily in a happy life for all. The coincidence of self-interest and public interest is perhaps true on a very deep and fundamental level, but the way in which individuals often regard primarily their own happiness is not pure enough to be the main source of the public good. It is simply not true, as Kant would own, that devils, too, can constitute a good state. Although morality is not enough (questions of structures and social techniques needing also to be solved), the public-regarding attitude should prevail in those who are powerful enough to have some or much influence on the mechanisms of world economy, politics and social life. Moral attitudes without structural enforcement are too weak to change the world, but structural reform without morality becomes prey to the cynical.

A society is lucky when it has an undisputed moral code demanding that every member take heed of the public good and work for it. The world would be fortunate if it had such a worldwide moral code. The only code it seems to possess nowadays consists of the idea that every human being is a subject of basic rights and a rather abstract enumeration of these human rights. But nobody knows exactly how the world should be organized or how peoples and nations would have to think and act in order to substantiate those rights.

The individual person is, however, able to anticipate, in a way, the realization of a fair and good world by accepting the idea of universal human rights as the norm of his behavior every time he has to deal with some other human individual or group. His attitude with regard to them will be the test of his willingness to limit his own demands by his interest in a better world-order. This may sound trivial, but it may demand almost heroic efforts, for example, in a situation of generalized corruption, where one has to choose between participation in the "normal" game and honesty.

The morality of human rights, however important and indispensable it is, cannot completely answer the question of the moral standards for a better planning of contemporary society, because these rights (just as their basis, man's autonomy) are too formal and abstract. We do now know exactly what we have a right to, and although we can determine a minimal content of our rights (e.g., a human being should not die by exhaustion), that content alone would not constitute a really human life.

Man does not live by bread alone. Music, poetry, dance, religion, philosophy, meditation, etc., also belong to life and are perhaps indispensable to its full meaning. Artists sometimes risk their lives for art; boredom results from complete satisfaction on the level of wealth and material consumption; philosophy and religion venerate another sort of life than that which consists in the contentment of the well-fed gentleman.

Is it possible to satisfy the universal urge for less material consumption by planning culture and education on a world scale? Should UNESCO try to follow the example of organizations like the World Bank and the World Health Organization and treat the cultural wants of mankind as another class of needs to be satisfied by cultural consumption? Can and must art, religion, literature, philosophy, information and conversation be programmed, planned, produced and distributed in ways analogous to those used in material consumption? Should scientific theories and research, philosophy, and theology be organized in accordance with the same scheme?

The organization of our world on the level of culture meets with an enormous diversity of cultural patterns, codes, beliefs, ideologies. . .and lacks a perspective or standard by which it could unify that diversity. The modern western discovery of the world through exploration and colonialization together with historical, social and anthropological research, has resulted in cultural relativism. This has deprived man of the highest perspective and an absolute standard, so that he can no longer order the chaos of the huge museum into which the world has transformed itself. Modern man no longer occupies the absolute standpoint from which he could sovereignly oversee the world and its history. Insofar as one still has profound personal convictions, one is apt to relativize them in public and fear imposing them on other people.

The lack of universally accepted cultural standards makes it difficult, or rather, impossible, to plan world culture as a harmony of so many traditions and beliefs. How is it possible to combine our skepticism with the making of a world-wide plan which itself will be oriented by a particular belief or ideology? How could we escape from dogmatic imperialism, if we would have the power and the money to start such a plan?

There are ways to organize the encounter of different cultures and ideologies: the idea of our congress, for example, is to organize such a dialogue. The organizers do not interfere and try to be as neutral as possible, offering a common space within which the diversity of different ways of thought and life can converse and struggle. In this case the scheme of a highest subject who plans the world has, however, been replaced by a subject who invites other subjects to discuss with him the issues at stake. The plan master has then abdicated in favor of an encounter and interpenetration of cultures. Nobody is the master and everybody is involved. Instead of planning we participate then in an adventurous history, for which all the participants are equally responsible.

Modern democracy is meant to maintain the idea of planning

without losing the benefits of dialogue. The only dogma of democracy is that the freedom of each participant has to be respected by all participants. But concrete freedom implies the possibility of projecting a whole way of life for oneself. The conflicts which result from the general realization of this possibility are to be overcome by a universally accepted limitation of everyone's freedom. Because of the principle of individual autonomy, the decision by which that limitation is determined and imposed is to be made by all. As long as all members of a democratically organized country share one general moral code or ideology this will, perhaps, be possible, but as soon as important disagreements manifest themselves, one general rule will have to be determined by some group which will then have to impose it on the rest. While most of the pre-modern political philosophers opted for an enlightened or aristocratic elite to make and enforce the rules, typical modern theorists like Locke and Rousseau claimed that right for the majority, thinking that the majority of votes would represent the authentic "will" of the whole people. We need not get into their arguments; it may suffice to state that the decision of the majority can only then be considered as the expression of a *general* will if *all* the members of such a people *beforehand* have decided and expressed their decision that the decisions of the majority should prevail. That first and fundamental decision of *all* cannot be expressed by a *majority* of votes (e.g., in a referendum in which 90 percent of the voters say "yes"), but only by an explicit or implicit consent of *100 percent* of the voters saying, "yes." If this is not the case, the majority imposes its *particular* will on the rest and becomes dictatorial.

In fact, we see in our time several symptoms of a diminished belief in democracy and perhaps the beginning of its agony. The first symptom is that politicians and pressure groups are almost obliged to use modern forms of demagogy. The political, economical and social problems of contemporary society are much too complicated to be judged by the large majority of people, most intellectuals and scholars included. The fiction that we all have a part in the general discussion and decision on these problems is maintained by asking our opinions, votes and sometimes signatures. In order to obtain our votes, politicians try to seduce us to have opinions which we cannot really justify rationally. We let ourselves be seduced by the sympathetic image of a "great leader," by the fine declarations of a party or by flaming protests against established authorities we hate or against the rich of whom we are jealous. Very often *passion*, instead of reason, rules our contributions to democracy.

A second symptom of the crisis of democracy is the widely spread feeling that the parliamentary majority is not representative of the actual majority of the people they represent, and that even if both majorities would more or less coincide, they take or support decisions which go against the public good. Here we reach the point where the democratic idea and the whole framework of contemporary planning can break down and be replaced by one of two alternatives. One possibility is an extremist interpretation of individual autonomy: every individual and every group of like-minded individuals takes the responsibility for its own way of life and isolates itself from the state and the larger group of those who do not want to follow them. Of course such anarchistic groups can only survive if they go back to a small scale of production and to a very simple life. But are they not any more interested in the poverty and needs of other groups and countries? If they would try to get hold of the resources of the state and to rule the state or even mankind as a whole, they would realize another alternative: the way of an elite who believes that it knows what good is for everyone and thinks that this knowledge justified its taking over the central powers of state, economy, science and technology.

Democracy, anarchy and totalitarianism are the three major political alternatives to which the modern conception of freedom has led. Are all three dead ends? Are we able to save democracy if we do not have any wisdom about the meaning and the true standards of a truly human life? Or is there some hidden truth in the aversion many young people felt for the modern democratic state and in their flight from politics and prosperity to exotic religions and the inner world of meditation? Does the idea of modern democracy and the whole project of a man-made world, as sketched above, rely on some basic assumption or attitude which has to be criticized or changed?

Mastership and Acceptance

The perspective of modern praxis is the planning and production of a future world ruled by an enlightened mankind enjoying happiness and doing justice to its members—a secularized paradise of which man is the only master.

This description is, of course, a caricature, due to its neglect of certain moral and religious traditions which also belong to the modern history of Western society. However, one cannot deny that modern Western culture distinguished itself from older and Eastern cultures mainly by a conception of itself in which man figures as a great technician and constructor of his universe. The preceding pages attempt to describe some consequences of this basic perspective without giving much attention to other, more traditional features, which counterbalance the tendency to see man as the absolute.

One of the moral consequences of the modern perspective is a vivid consciousness of man's responsibility for the well-being of the whole of mankind living now and in the future. This terrible burden was formerly left to Divine Providence, but is now imposed on everyone who adheres to the perspective indicated above, and especially on those people who through scientific knowledge, technical skills, and economic or political power have the most influence on the course of events. Because the burden of this responsibility is so heavy, many people are tempted to escape from it by putting it on the state or on human society as a whole, trying to forget that they are constitutive parts of that society and their state. If they realize the latter, they see themselves confronted with an overwhelming task. Sharing their responsibility through democratic procedures does not solve the difficult technical and moral problems included in that task, because those procedures do not answer the question of the standards by which we can judge the value of our performances. In a climate of ethical relativism the standard one chooses is either arbitrary or the result of some private emotions. There is still a sort of general assumption that egoism is not the best attitude and that the making of a better world demands a public-regarding mentality, but what conditions have to be fulfilled for the realization of the public good and more radically what the content and the meaning of the true public good are, are questions which demand more wisdom than is available in today's market of information, opinions, slogans and political rhetoric.

In fact, without having rationally justified their emotional preferences, for example, with regard to the use of nuclear energy, some groups feel obliged to agitate for their vision by making others out to be morally deprived. With great enthusiasm they fight a sort of crusade against the powers of evil, considering themselves to be representatives of the true public good. To many others the obligation of determining, in the name of mankind, the content of the true good and choosing the best methods for its realization seems a superhuman task, so that they may consider themselves as dispensed from it and excused in advance if they do not choose the right goals or means. Both attitudes are dead ends; to refuse the moral responsibility for a better world is immoral, but to identify the good itself with a subjective emotion is arrogant and degenerates into violence. Indifference or exaggerated pretensions seems the dilemma to which the idea of a man-made future inevitably leads. The claim of a self-elected elite that it knows what is good for all meets with the claims of the state and other powers of the establishment which defend, hypocritically or not, the right of another conception of the good life and public well-being, whereas the great majority of mankind follows its humble paths without pretending to have an answer to all of those terribly big problems of all humanity.

But is not the whole idea of that universal and absolute responsibility a huge exaggeration of moral responsibility? Has modern secularism not resulted in an unrealistic and unbearable moralism? Is it conceivable that the great history of emancipation and autonomy comes to an end with the recognition that we are not capable of accomplishing the task we took on from the moment we considered ourselves as autonomous constructors of a truly human world?

The recognition of universal *human rights*, the definition of well-being as complete *satisfaction of needs*, and *universal planning* are the three key concepts of modern praxis. Without denying in the least their importance and necessity, I want to suggest that they are not the most fundamental concepts of social life and practice and that they have to be rooted in a more profound perspective, from which they should receive their ultimate meaning and proportion.

Respect for *the basic right of every human individual to a truly human life* is the great moral discovery of modern times which we should practice more consistently and never lose. But the perspective of rights, claims and demands is not the highest possible perspective on life. This truth manifests itself, for instance, in the weariness and the bitterness in which the endless and never totally successful repetition of such demands result. In a world full of injustice it is fair to claim the fulfillment of one's own rights, and highly moral to fight for the rights of others, but full justice will remain far away. Can we accept this outcome of our struggle for a better world? We *must*, because there is no alternative. But if we can accept injustice (without any approval and with pain), rights and justice, although they are absolute claims, cannot be the highest perspective on life and history.

The perspective of human rights has been exaggerated in the idea that a human being possesses a basic right not only to develop his own life according to his own preferences and decisions, but also to decide whether he will live or not. A right to live (and consequently a right to die) seem to me an inner contradiction. How could a non-existing subject possess any right? If a right is not conceivable without a human subject having that right, how could we conceive of a right to decide whether we shall live or die?

The impossibility of talking about a right to life, that is, to receive or to refuse life, together with the very real right to organize for oneself the life one has got, shows that human life contains some element of *passivity* or receptivity. Life cannot be chosen, but one can assent to it and realize the given possibilities it includes. All planning is preceded by a start, which has characteristics of its own, and by a concrete history in which we are engaged without having been asked if we wanted to take part. The idea of a subject overlooking the world and human history, his own life and that of mankind, makes abstraction from the only real standpoint on which all our science and construction rests.

The second key concept, *a particular definition of human well-being*, is closely connected with the concept of human rights, because it is meant to substantiate the content of those rights. The model of consumption has led us to define well-being as a complete satisfaction of needs. Now many philosophers, such as Plato, Thomas, Kant and Hegel have pointed out that since our needs are finite and opposed to one another, they cannot compose a totality, so that the idea of a *complete* or *total* satisfaction of needs is impossible and nonsensical. If the happiness all human beings long for cannot consist of a total satisfaction of needs, and yet is not an absurd idea itself, another sort of desire and appeasement should be looked for, transcending the level of needs and consumption. The message of great religions and philosophies holds that the human heart is essentially moved by a radical desire for peace with the universe, to be attained by accepting the universe and assenting to it as it is, notwithstanding its misery and terrors and the suffering it causes us. Such an acceptance implies that the satisfaction of vital needs is not the most important thing in the world (although it should never be denied that it follows as a strict obligation from the principle of human rights); that is, that questions of life and death are not the ultimate ones. To die is not the greatest enemy and to live is not yet the highest joy. More important than the construction of a comfortable world is an attitude of fundamental receptivity or—if we do not identify this word with the contrary of activity— a sort of *"passivity"* capable of accepting and bearing existence and history as they are given and to continue gratefully, although painfully, the moral tasks which they include.

It becomes clear from this that the third and most fundamental key concept of modern times, *the idea of universal planning*, will undergo a transformation as soon as it is integrated and embedded into a more modest attitude of humanity—an attitude in which human beings realize that they cannot completely objectify their own lives and history, but must carry on their risky task with serious dedication and without the exaggerations of an extreme moralism as sketched above. If such an attitude of acceptance, and even of serious gratitude, cannot be assumed, the attempt to master human life will result in general discouragement. The moral responsibility of the individual proves then to be an impossible claim, so that most people will confine themselves to their own interests and those of their immediate neighbors. The future of our own and other societies is then left to irrational powers and the spiritual climate becomes very dark. Without a certain trust in something like a fundamental "Logos," "Substance," "Spirit," or "God" hiding as well as revealing itself in world history, it seems impossible that moral responsibility could be accompanied by joy.

By way of conclusion I would like to sum up the main theses and viewpoints I have defended in this paper.

1. My general presupposition is that to state something meaningful about "man, society and the state," we first should diagnose the situation of contemporary "advanced society." All sorts of epistemological difficulties threaten the attempt to write such a diagnosis, but notwithstanding despite the uncertainties and probable mistakes involved, we cannot do without an insight, however provisional, into the main perspectives and beliefs guiding our thought and action.

The description given in this paper is based upon the assumption that we find ourselves in a situation of crisis and passage between the period of "modernity," which is coming to an end, and a period of which we do not yet have a clear idea, although we may discover some of its traits by looking for new phenomena not fitting the patterns of modernity.

2. Modernity can be characterized by an ideal image which modern man has of himself. His ideal self-image could be called the "myth" of modernity. The core of this myth seems to consist in the idea of human autonomy: *(a)* mankind has become "the highest being" for himself, a ruler of the world and history; *(b)* every individual is a free subject having the same basic rights as any other individual; and *(c)* the sovereign state is considered to be the collective will of equally free individuals who realize their own will by choosing simultaneously the same common good.

3. The main elements of the modern myth of human autonomy can be understood as diversifications of form and content.

Form is the idea of autonomous man ruling nature, society and history by science and technology. Man wants to preserve the autonomy of all individuals and their equal rights by the foundation and the philosophical justification of a democratic state.

The *content* of public and private life consists, according to this conception, in ends which are not imposed but freely chosen by individuals or at least consented to freely by all who are involved in the common enterprise of humanization and self-realization. As a totality of ends on which *all* individuals agree this total end can only consist in an obvious and inevitable goal which nobody can reject, that is, in the satisfaction of basic needs. This basic satisfaction is therefore the primary meaning of human *happiness*. In the name of the doctrine of equal rights, *justice* has to be realized as actualization of material well-being and as participation in the collective production and consumption of this sort of happiness.

4. As far as other human values are concerned, like literature, music, philosophy, faith, theology, etc., the old traditions, which were imposed by sacred and profane authorities, have lost their force, because the axiom of freedom urges every individual to decide for himself which values and ends he wants to pursue. The only standard of solid truth is scientific precision; everything else is a question of private feeling or choice.

5. Notwithstanding his relativistic convictions about esthetic, moral and religious values, modern man has burdened himself with a great and noble moral task: as ruler of the world and of himself, he recognizes and claims an absolute responsibility for a reconstruction of nature and society in accordance with the demands of freedom and equality. Justice must be established. Production and distribution, development and progress are deduced from the high moral task as means to a more just society.

6. The myth of modernity contains certain exaggerations which are being demystified practically and theoretically.

The *practice* of modern self-realization has led to serious questions concerning the possibility of a man-made world of general comfort without self-destructive pollution and of a consequent realization of the democratic ideal of universal equality.

Theoretically the concept of happiness as total satisfaction of vital needs can be proved to be an impossible notion, because our needs cannot be fully nor definitively satisfied. The sort of happiness resulting from their satisfaction disappears as soon as we reach it, because we cannot prevent time from destroying it. Even if we could, the dimension of material well-being does not interest us enough to fulfill our fundamental desire.

The democratic ideal cannot be realized, because it would be a wonder if all individuals would choose by their own initiative exactly the same values and norms to rule their common life.

Whenever a less than unanimous majority imposes its ideals and laws on a minority having other preferences, it sins against the basic idea of equal rights based upon the infinite worth of individual will.

7. The dead end into which modernity has moved may be overcome in two directions simultaneously:

a) The doctrine of equality, which presupposes a sovereign subject overlooking the whole of humanity, itself included, should be subordinate to, and integrated into, an ethics of dedication to the *other* person. On a higher level than the true and absolute level of human rights we are not equal, but unequal: the appearance of another puts obligations on me. The infinite task of development made possible by science and technology continues, but the perspective has changed: the primary meaning of the world does not lie in our satisfaction, but in the world being a possible gift to others. In achieving whatever we can in order to ameliorate human existence, we live for another generation, for people who will be alive when we are dead. This way of transcending our death defines a morality which seems to me an essential feature of Israel's prophetic message, but also of Buddhist sympathy, Confucian respect, Islamic generosity and Christian love.

b) The second direction into which the self-image of modernity, as I have sketched it, can transform itself is indicated not only by all the great metaphysicians like Plato, the Stoics, Plotinus, Spinoza and Leibniz, but perhaps even by Marx. The experience of human freedom reveals its lack of self-sufficiency: man cannot choose his own existence, but finds himself as given to his own awakening consciousness; his existence precedes his ability to choose. Instead of a cause of himself (*causa sui*) man discovers himself as a given reality which cannot be refused but may be accepted willingly. This acceptance or gratitude includes hope, but is certainly not an alibi for the heavy burden of humanization and self-realization which has to proceed on the basis of a sort of fundamental trust in reality.

9

PROGRESS AND EVOLUTION: A REAPPRAISAL FROM THE TRADITIONAL PERSPECTIVE

SEYYED HOSSEIN NASR

There is little doubt that the idea of human progress, as it has come to be understood since the eighteenth century in Europe, is one that is confined to Western philosophy, especially in the wedding of the idea of progress with material evolution. Moreover, this idea came late to Western civilization, although some have tried to find its roots among the Greeks.[1] Traditional Western man, like his fellow human beings in various Eastern civilizations, saw the flow of time in a downward rather than upward direction, whether this was conceived of as cycles, as among the ancient Greeks and Romans, or in a linear fashion, as in the Judeo-Christian traditions. Nor was the moving force of history seen in purely materialistic terms except in rare instances, such as in ancient antiquity. But even in such cases the concepts involved were very different from those held today: the ancients did not have the concept of, or even the word for, matter as this term is used today. For most pre-modern peoples of the West, the moving forces which governed human existence and its history were, in any case, non-material, whether these forces were seen as *moira* or *dyké*[2] by the Greeks or the Will of God and various angelic hierarchies in Judaism and Christianity.

As for the non-Western world, among all of the civilizations which this world embraces, the perfection of the human state has always been seen as being at the beginning or the origin of time and reflected perpetually in the ever-present now. The perfect state of things, for both individual and collective man, has been envisaged as being at the time of the first Emperor in the Far East, or at the beginning of the last Golden Age or Krita Yuga in Hinduism and the like. Likewise in Islam, which is closer to the Judeo-Christian tradition, perfection is associated with the Origin. The most perfect man is the Prophet of Islam and the most perfect society that of Medina. Even in cases where perfection has been described as belonging to the future it has always been associated with another Divine intervention in human history: with the coming of the Saoshyant in Zoroastrianism, or the Kali Avatara in Hinduism or the Mahdi in Islam. The traditional East joined the traditional West in distinguishing clearly between a messianic vision based on Divine Agencies and a messianism which is reduced to purely human proportions.

To discuss the idea of human progress through material evolution in Western philosophy is, therefore, to deal with a recent phenomenon in Western intellectual history. It is also to deal with an idea which is confined to modern civilization as it developed in the West, although it has spread during the past century beyond this geographical area. The ideas and concepts which served as the background for the rise of the typically modern idea of human progress through material evolution are, however, somewhat older. Some reach back to the origins of the Western tradition although these ideas were in every case distorted, and even subverted, to make it possible for the idea of progress based on material factors to be created from them.

Perhaps the most basic factor which gave rise to the modern idea of human progress through material evolution was that reduction of man to the purely human which took place in the Renaissance. Traditional Christianity saw man as a being born for immortality, born to go beyond himself for, as St. Augustine had stated, to be human is to be more than merely human. This also means that to seek to be purely human is to fall below the human level, to the subhuman level as the history of the modern world has demonstrated so clearly. Renaissance humanism, which is still spoken of in glowing terms in certain quarters, bound man to the earthly level and in doing so imprisoned his aspirations for perfection by limiting them to this world.[3]

Until that time, and for a short period afterwards, since no major change of this order can come about so abruptly, progress had been associated with the perfection of the human soul, and perfection of society with the kingdom of God to be established on earth with the coming of the Messiah and the new Jerusalem. Renaissance and post-Renaissance humanism and secularism made the traditional idea of the progress of the human soul towards its perfection, which resulted in its ultimate wedding with the Spirit, and the actual reality of the eschatological events associated with the descent of the celestial Jerusalem and the coming of the Messiah even more "far-fetched" and inaccessible until both were reduced to the category of illusion, superstition or some form of psychological subjectivism. But the imprint of the idea of progress and perfection in human nature was too profound to be obliterated so easily. Man still lived and breathed with these ideas in his heart and soul.

Meanwhile, the conquest of the New World, Africa and Asia was bringing great wealth into Europe and creating a new mercantile society which saw in its power to manipulate the world, the possibility of perfecting it in a material and economic sense. Certain forms of Protestant theology, in fact, saw moral virtue in economic activity and were associated with the rise of capitalism and its well-known link, until very recent times, with the idea of material progress.[4]

With this new confidence gained by European man in his ability to conquer the world and to mold it, the human background was prepared for the transfer of the idea of perfection and the progress of the soul from its upward, vertical dimension towards God to a purely this-worldly and temporal one. These ideas, thus suppressed, had to find an outlet in the world view of modern man since they were so deeply ingrained in the human soul. The natural outlet was provided by this exceptional chapter of European history, during which, despite incessant wars between Catholics and Protestants, Spain and England, England and France, etc., European man found himself mastering the earth rapidly and being able to mold the destiny of humanity. It took but a single step to see in this very process of the expansion of European civilization and the amassing of wealth which accrued from it, the road to human progress and the confirmation of the secularized conception of man which had made such domination possible in the first place.[5] This success was due to the secularization of man and in turn hastened the process of secularization and this-worldliness by encouraging human beings to devote all their energies to worldly activities as the hereafter became a more and more distant concept or belief, rather than an immediate reality. Moreover, the belief in human progress in history provided a goal which aroused men's fervor and faith and even sought to satisfy their religious needs. Perhaps there is no modern ideology which has played as great a role in replacing religion and, as a pseudo-religion, attracting the ultimate adherence of human beings, as the idea of progress which later became wed to evolutionism.[6]

Another element of great importance whose secularization and distortion contributed a great deal to the rise of the idea of human progress through material evolution, was the Christian doctrine of incarnation and the linear conception of history associated with it and, especially, with the Christology adopted by the Western Church. For Christianity, Truth entered into history, into the stream of time, and, through this event, time and change gained significance beyond the domain of time itself. In other religions time is also significant. What human beings do affects their immortal souls and the state of their beings in the worlds which lie beyond time. Whether the world is seen as *māyā*, as in Hinduism, or as mirrors reflecting God's Names and Qualities, as in Islam, there is not the concern in these religions with the "historicity" of the incarnation of Truth in the way that one finds it in Christianity. This statement would also include Zoroastrianism, although it sees time itself as an angel, and would hold true even in later developments of the religion in the form of Zurvanism, where Zurvan or "boundless time" is seen as the principle of the Universe itself.

As long as the integral Christian tradition was alive in which Christ was seen as the eternally present Logos and not only as an "historical personality," the doctrine of incarnation was preserved from desecration, distortion and perversion, but as suprasensible levels of being began to lose their reality for Western man and Christianity became bound solely to an historic event, history itself became impregnated with ultimate significance affecting Truth as such. From this position there was but a single step to take to arrive at nineteenth century European philosophy, with which Hegel converted the philosophy of history practically into theology itself. The secularization of the Christian concept of incarnation removed Christ, to one degree or another, from the center of the arena of the historical and cosmic drama but preserved the idea of the ultimate significance of temporal change in human existence. To a large extent, belief in human progress through temporal and historical change replaced the central role occupied by the doctrine of incarnation in traditional Christian theology. One cannot imagine a philosophy which makes changes in human history the ultimate determining factor of human destiny, and even of Truth itself, arising anywhere but in a world in which the historical flux had been impregnated to an extraordinary degree with theological significance. In a way, Hegelianism and Marxism could have arisen only in a world whose background was Christian, and Marxism could only be a Christian heresy as far as its philosophical aspect is concerned. However, its concern with every aspect of life makes it, in a sense, a parody of Judaism which has an all-embracing notion of Divine Law incorporated in the Talmud.

As for the linear conception of time which is to be found in traditional Christian sources such as St. Augustine; history is viewed as a single line or movement punctuated by that one great event which was the descent of the Logos, or the Son, into time. Time had three points of reference: the creation of Adam, the coming of Christ, and the end of the world associated with his second coming. History had a direction and moved like an arrow towards that target which is described so powerfully in the *Revelations of John*. There was no cyclic conception of growth, gradual decay, and decomposition, followed by a new period of rejuvenation resulting from new interventions by Heaven upon the human plane such as one finds in so many Oriental religions. Nor was there an emphasis upon the cycles of prophecy as we see in Islam, although the more metaphysical and esoteric forms of Christianity were certainly aware of the ever-lasting and ever-present nature of the

Logos. But as these more profound teachings became less accessible and theology more rationalistic, it became easier for the secularistic thinkers to take the one step needed to convert the Christian conception of linear time into the idea of continuous and linear human progress and the popular idea that things simply *must* become better every day simply because time moves on. As the celestial Jerusalem became replaced by a vaguely defined perfect society in the future, the Christian conception of linear time became replaced by the secular one, which kept the idea of the linear character of time moving towards the goal of perfection in some undefined future, but rejected the trans-historical significance of historical events as envisaged by Christianity. In a sense, historicism, and the idea of progress associated with it in many philosophical schools, is the result of the secularization and perversion of a particular type of Christology adopted by the mainstream of Western Christianity.

It is in this context that one must understand the rise of the idea of utopianism, another important element among the array of factors and forces that gave rise to the idea of progress in the modern West. Traditional teachings had always been aware of the ideal and perfect society, whether it was the *Civitas dei* of St. Augustine or the *al-madīnat al-fāḍilah* of al-Fārābī not to speak of Plato's well-known description of the perfect state described in *Republic*, which antedates both. But in a profound sense these "cities" were not of this world, at least not in the ordinary sense of the term "world." The word *utopia* itself, used by Sir Thomas More as the title of his famous work, reveals the metaphysical origin of this concept. Utopia means literally no-where (*u* which implies negation and *topos* which means space in Greek). It is the land that is beyond physical space, in the eighth clime as the Muslim philosophers would say. It belonged to the spiritual world and was not realizable on earth unless this celestial city itself descended.

The secularization which took place in the West after the Middle Ages gradually transformed the idea of utopia, creating utopianism in its modern sense.[7] In this transformation, messianic ideas emanating from Judaism, and to a certain extent Christianity, were also to play an important role. The already secularized notion of utopianism gained much momentum from this religious zeal to establish a perfect order on earth and became a major force in Western society. It is not accidental that the most dogmatic Western ideology based on the idea of inevitable human progress, namely Marxism, was to combine a pseudo-religious fervor, derived in many ways from a subversion of messianic ideas, with utopianism. The role of the messiah in establishing the kingdom of God on earth became converted into that of the revolutionary bringing about the perfect social order through revolutionary and violent means. In this way eschatology was also converted, or rather perverted, into the secular vision of the perfect order established by means of human progress through material evolution or revolution, for both views existed among the Western philosophers of the eighteenth and nineteenth centuries.

As far as material evolution is concerned, it too is the result of transformations which began during the Renaissance and reached their peak in the seventeenth century scientific revolution, although the evolutionary idea itself was not to appear until two centuries later. The science of the Renaissance was still medieval science, based on symbolism, correspondence between various levels of being, and concern with the totality and the whole rather than parts and other features associated with the traditional sciences.[8] The scientists of the age were concerned with Hermeticism and Kabbalistic sciences and the sciences associated with names of such men as Marciglio Ficino, Pico della Mirandola, Nicola Flamel, and even Leonardo da Vinci and Giordano Bruno, recall more holistic sciences of nature than the mechanism which came to the fore in the seventeenth century.

Yet, it was during this period that the cosmos was becoming gradually decentralized following the nominalistic perspective of the late Middle Ages which has depleted the cosmos of its sacred presence. This was also the period of the eclipse of a serious philosophy based on certainty and the vision of Being.[9] The result was the quest after a new science and a new philosophy, the science based on a mechanistic conception of the universe as developed by Galileo, Kepler and Newton, and the philosophy upon the certainty of one's individual consciousness divorced from the world of extension or "matter" as developed by Descartes. The two went hand in hand in creating a view of things in which the knowing subject, or "mind", was totally other than the known object, or "matter", which then became reduced to a pure "it" or "thing" in a mechanistic world where quantitative laws were to explain the functioning of all things. [10]

This new transformation of the European mentality was itself responsible for the birth of the very concept of "matter" as it is known to modern man today. Neither ancient nor medieval people had the conception of matter which is taken for granted today, nor do those sections of the human race who, even today, are not affected by the influence of modernism. Neither the Greek *hylé*, the Sanskirt *prakriti*, the Arabic *māddah*, nor even the Latin *materia* means matter in the modern sense. It was the seventeenth century scientific revolution, combined with the philosophical changes associated with Cartesianism, which made possible the very idea of something being "material" and materialism in its current sense. Even the so-called materialistic philosophers of the Hellenistic period or the Hindu atomists cannot be considered, strictly speaking, as materialists since the modern concept of matter had no meaning for them.

Although the birth of mechanistic science and a purely material conception of the world is associated with the seventeenth century, the world view of this period was still a static one. Even radically materialistic philosophers such as La Mettrie envisaged the material world as a static order with change occurring within it, but not with the directed movement which would be associated later with the idea of evolution. This latter idea was to come not from the domain of physics but from the temporalization of the ancient philosophical idea of the "great chain of being" which was applied to the world of living things and was the paradigm through which natural historians since Aristotle had explained the chain of life relating the creatures of the three kingdoms to each other and to the whole of creation.

Traditional man saw a scale of perfection in existence ranging from the angels to the dust beneath the feet of earthly creatures. As long as the intuition of the world of Platonic Ideas, on the one hand, and living faith in a Divine Being who created and ordained all things, on the other, were alive, man had no problem in envisaging this "chain of being" in a "spatial" manner so that the hierarchy of the planes of being was a living reality for him. This static vision of the cosmos did not of course preclude the possibility of cosmic rhythms stated explicitly by the Greek philosophers and alluded to by certain Jewish and Christian sages, but such a vision did definitely preclude the possibility of a gradual growth in time from one state of being to another. Such growth was possible inwardly in the life of man but not for the species as a whole.

The eclipse of faith, the spread of secularism, the loss of intellectual intuition, and the mechanization of the cosmos, combined to make the hierarchy of universal existence appear as unreal. Having lost the vision of the immutable, Western man could not but turn to the parody of the concept of the chain of being in time. The vertical "great chain of being" was made horizontal and temporal, resulting in the birth of the idea of evolution.[11] Wallace and Darwin did not induce the theory of evolution from their observations. Rather, in a world in which the divinity had been either denied or relegated to the role of the maker of the clock, which the seventeenth century conceived the universe to be, and where sapiential wisdom based on the contemplation of the higher states of being had become practically inaccessible, the theory of evolution seemed the best way of providing a background for the study of the amazing diversity of life forms without having to turn to the creative power of God. The theory of evolution soon turned into dogma precisely because it rapidly replaced religious faith and provided what appeared to be a "scientific" crutch for the soul, enabling it to forget God. It has, therefore, survived to this day not as theory but as dogma held by many scientists whose worldviews would crumble if they were but to take evolution for what it is: a convenient philosophical and rationalistic scheme enabling man to create the illusion of a purely closed universe around himself. That is also why logical and scientific arguments against evolution have been treated not rationally and scientifically, but with a violence and passion that reveals the pseudo-religious role played by the theory of evolution among its exponents.

This loss of the vision of the immutable was to generalize the idea of evolution and extend it far beyond the domain of biology. At the same time Hegelian dialectic was introducing change and becoming the heart of reality as it was conceived by nineteenth century European man. It did not take much to transform Hegel's idealism into materialism, considering the prevalence of the various materialistic schools of thought at that time. The new form of materialism announced by Marx, however, differed from its pre-decessors in its insistence upon the dialectical process upon which was grafted the idea of progress, a development already mentioned. In the crucible of nineteenth century European thought the strands of the ideas of human progress, materialism and evolution became welded together under the general banner of human progress through material evolution. Of course, there were major differences among the Marxists, the French exponents of progress, the English evolutionists—not all of whom were "materialists" strictly speak-ing—and others. But these were all variations upon the same themes of central concern which had grown out of the experience and thought of post-medieval European civilization and which had reached a point of view that was totally different from that of other civilizations in either East or West.

During the nineteenth century, Christian theology re-mained, in general, opposed to the amalgamation of ideas and forces outlined above, especially the theory of evolution and materialism. But as it was not able to marshal evidence of a truly intellectual—rather than simply rational or sentimental—order, it fought a continuously defensive battle. The opposition to these forces and ideas usually remained on the emotional level, often associated with various fundamentalist positions bereft of intellectual substance. Nevertheless, evolutionary concepts remained for the most part outside the citadel of Christianity.

One had to wait for the twentieth century to witness a fusion—which can also be called a perversion—of these ideas within Christian theology itself; the most radical and far-fetched example of this is perhaps Teilhardism. This fusion phenomenon is partic-ularly strange because the idea of progress itself has not attracted the attention of the most perceptive of Western thinkers for several decades and many people in the West are seeking to rediscover the nature of man beyond the image of the mammal evolving to higher states of consciousness or to a more perfect society as presented in the nineteenth century. It is a paradox that at the moment when the idea of progress through material evolution is itself becoming a victim of historic change and going out of vogue, the force of religion which had for so long resisted this idea is becoming influenced by its theses. Contemporary man's direction in life will be determined by the degree to which he is able to distinguish once again between the immutable and the changing, the permanent and the transient, and the apparent in contrast to the real progress available and possible for him. For man is a being who, no matter how much he changes, remains the same creature he has always been and will always be: a being born for the immortal empyrean of the spirit.

NOTES

1 See, e.g., the recent study of R. Nisbet, *History of the Idea of Progress*, (New York: 1980), in which he brings a great deal of historical research to bear upon the subject, but which over-emphasizes the Greek origin of this idea.

2 *Moira* and *dyké* are both key Greek philosophical and religious terms, the first associated with the Olympian and the second with the Dionysian-Orphic schools. Both imply destiny, justice or principle dominating the world and responsible for the world's functioning. The exact meaning of the two terms is, however, very different due to the basic differences between the two world views which they describe. See F. Cornford, *From Religion to Philosophy: A Study in the Origins of Western Speculation*, (New York: 1957).

3 On the significance of this event which, from the traditional point of view, implied a new "fall" for man see F. Schuon, *Light on the Ancient Worlds*, trans. by Lord Northbourne, (London: 1965), especially p. 28ff.

4 This theme has been treated by many social, economic and cultural historians, perhaps the most famous works being the classical ones by R. H. Tawney, *The Acquisitive Society*, (New York: 1920), and M. Weber, *The Protestant Ethic and the Spirit of Capitalism*, (London: 1930).

5 Had not Europe rejected its own traditional civilization, it would not have been able to develop all the means and techniques which made the conquest of non-European civilizations possible.

6 On the pseudo-religious character of the idea of progress, see M. Lings, *Ancient Beliefs and Modern Superstitions*, (London: 1980); also Lord Northbourne, *Looking Back on Progress*, (London: 1970).

7 On utopianism, see J. Servier, *L'Histoire de l'utopie*, (Paris: 1960) and F. E. Manuel and F. P. Manuel, *Utopian Thought in the Western World*, (Cambridge U.S.A.: 1979).

8 On Renaissance science see A. Debus, *Man and Nature in the Renaissance*, (New York: 1978).

9 The absence of serious philosophical schools which would lead to intellectual certainty between the end of the Middle Ages and Descartes is studied and described in E. Gilson, *The Unity of Philosophical Experience*, (New York: 1937). See also S. H. Nasr, *Knowledge and the Sacred*, New York, 1981.

10 On how this process of the mechanization of the universe and of nature occurred, see S. H. Nasr, *Man and Nature*, (London: 1976) and T. Roszak, *Where the Wasteland Ends*, (New York: 1972).

11 The classic by A. Lovejoy, *The Great Chain of Being*, (New York: 1960), is still of much value in tracing the history of this perennial idea in the West.

10

CONTEMPORARY GENETICS: SOME ETHICAL CONSIDERATIONS

ERIC L. MASCALL

The great achievement of the scientific revolution was bringing nature increasingly under the control of man. Though it was no doubt true that *natura nisi parendo non vincitur*, the fact remained that, by obeying nature and nature's laws, man had become increasingly more able to manipulate nature in accordance with his purposes, even if some of those purposes seemed in the long run only doubtfully conducive to his true welfare. In consequence, the contrast between man and nature, which had been a commonplace of the European tradition from classical times, even when an affinity between man and nature on the material level was acknowledged, was accentuated, and this in spite of the mechanistic and deterministic character of post-Newtonian physical science. Man was the investigator and the knower; nature was the investigated and the known. Man was the planner and manipulator; nature, under man's domination, was the planned and the manipulated.

The contrast was, of course, never absolute, and man's very control of nature made it possible for him to use nature as an instrument for, deliberately or accidentally, bringing about changes in himself, though he liked to think that those changes were always, or at any rate predominantly, beneficial. Before the Second World War, there was an advertisement which began by remarking that in the Middle Ages the alchemist was looked upon with fear because the changes which he was able to bring about by his magical powers were often very unpleasant, whereas the modern magician, the experimental chemist, was welcome everywhere because the changes which he made possible were invariably beneficial. Since then such matters as atmospheric pollution and ecological imbalance have impressed themselves forcefully upon us, but we need only consider the advances in medical science, agriculture and animal husbandry to recognize the vast benefits that science has conferred upon mankind or, to speak more accurately, that some men have conferred upon mankind through practicing and developing the techniques of science. And in this respect it would not be inaccurate to say that, by means of science, man has brought about changes not only in nature but also in himself, so that, through his manipulation of nature, man himself has become not only the manipulator but also the manipulated. And insofar as this is so, ethical questions inevitably arise.

Nevertheless, until very recently the changes which man was able to produce in himself by the exercise of his scientific insight and inventiveness were almost entirely distant or indirect. (A partial exception should, perhaps, be made for certain advances in surgery and medicine.) The changes in man were the results— the consequences and sometimes indeed the by-products—of the manipulation of nature. The broad distinction between man the manipulator and nature the manipulated still persists. Today, with the development of genetics and, in particular, of molecular biology, we are faced with a radically new state of affairs. For man is faced not merely with pressures, however influential they may be, acting upon him, so to speak, from outside himself, but from modifications which it is proposed to bring about, and which, indeed, in some cases have already been brought about, in the most intimate structure of his being.

This being so, it is remarkable how little attention has been given to these matters by students of ethics and—here of course my own special interest is involved—by theologians. There are two essays by the celebrated German Jesuit Karl Rahner entitled, "The Experiment with Man" and "The Problem of Genetic Manipulation" in Volume IX of his *Theological Investigations,* and there are two chapters with the enigmatic titles "Born to Rule" and "Dying to Order" in Professor G. R. Dunstan's book *The Artifice of Ethics,* but I am only acquainted with one full-length work on the matter by a Christian theologian, the book *Prefabricated Man: The Ethics of Genetic Control* by the American moral theologian Paul Ramsey. In preparation for this work, which was published in 1970, Dr. Ramsey, whose permanent appointment is at Princeton, spent two semesters as visiting professor of genetic ethics at Georgetown University Medical School. It is from this book that I have derived most of my information, and I would remark that if, as has occasionally happened, it has been criticized as over-imaginative and sensational, we have come to see how often the science-fiction of one generation becomes the stone-cold science of the next. What schoolboy today would be thrilled, as I was, by the novels of Jules Verne?

Ramsey begins his discussion with mention of the progressive degeneration of the human gene-pool due to the fact that medical advances now make it possible for many people with genetic defects who formerly would have died before reaching sexual maturity to survive, bear children, and pass on their own genetic defects to their offspring; diabetes is quoted as such a defect. It is recognized that medical, surgical or selective techniques may be devised to counter some of these tendencies, but Ramsey is emphatic that, even if extreme genetic pessimists such as H. J. Muller are correct in prophesying a "genetic apocalypse" such that "there shall come a time when *there will be none like us to come after us,*" Christians too have believed in an apocalyptic termination to human history on earth.

I must confess that I do not find Ramsey's argument entirely adequate here. However, he makes two points which seem to me to be both entirely right and of primary importance. The first—and it is here that modern biological discovery has corrected the speculative views of earlier times—is that it is at the moment of union of a spermatozoon with an ovum that a new human being, whose novelty is guaranteed by the uniqueness of its genetic constitution, comes into being. This is a purely scientific truth which supporters of abortion are remarkably unwilling to recognize with their entirely mythological fiction that until the moment of birth a child is simply a growth within its mother's body and therefore disposable at her desire. Ramsey's second point is that "in relation to genetic proposals, the most important element of Christian morality. . .which needs to be brought into view is the teaching concerning *the union between* the two goods of human sexuality." "An act of sexual intercourse," he writes, "is at the same time an act of love and a procreative act. This does not mean," he adds, "that sexual intercourse always engenders a child. It simply means that it *tends*, of its own nature, toward the strengthening of love (the unitive or the communicative good), and toward the engendering of children (the procreative good)" (p. 32). Ramsey is emphatic that this principle is not affected by the controversy within Christian bodies about the legitimacy of contraception within marriage. "One has only to distinguish," he writes, "what is done in particular *acts* from what is intended, and done, in a whole series of acts of conjugal intercourse in order to see clearly that contraception need not be a radical attack upon what God joined together in the creation of man-womanhood" (p. 34). What Ramsey is concerned to maintain—and this is of special importance in the present context—is that genetic experimentation and the development and application of genetic techniques must never be conducted in a way that detaches man's sexual equipment from its organic place in the whole human and communal setting of marriage and the family. Sex, and all that goes with it, is something human and personal and is part of a greater whole than itself; it must never be reduced to the status of a mechanical or quasi-mechanical technique.

It is perhaps unfortunate, from one point of view, that Ramsey makes so much use of the adjective "Christian" in expounding this view of the union between the two goods of human sexuality. I certainly hold that it is central to the Christian view of human nature and I doubt whether it can in practice be maintained for very long in a non-Christian or, at any rate, in a non-theistic culture. But the fact remains that there are in the Western world a great many people who are not Christians, and indeed many who are not theists, and who nevertheless are firmly convinced of the importance of marriage and the family as institutions deeply rooted in the nature of man. And, I think, many such humanists would stand firmly with Christians on the issues concerning us here.

It is primarily on such grounds as these that, in my judgment, no encouragement ought to be given to the proposal to form deep-frozen semen-banks which could be used to impregnate selected women with selected semen by the methods of artificial insemination which have been applied with considerable success to cattle breeding. There are, indeed, serious problems of a scientific and social kind. It is more difficult with human beings than with cattle to decide what characteristics are desirable in the race of the future. There is the problem of mutations in the frozen genes and of the emergence of undesirable recessives; it is not as easy to dispose of unsuccessful human offspring as it is animal offspring. But the really fundamental objection, which Ramsey underlines, is that to treat human procreation in this way is to dehumanize it in its very foundation. In this realm, more than in any other, it is necessary for us to admit against all temptations to the contrary—and for a scientist these can be extremely strong, as non-scientists sympathetically ought to understand—that the fact that something can be done—some experiment can be performed or some technique can be devised—does not in itself provide sufficient justification for doing it.

The practice of artificial insemination and the use of deep-frozen semen-banks would indeed be unnatural by any ordinary standards but it would not involve any direct interference with the genetic material; it would not merit the description "genetic engineering." This description could, however, apply to proposals to extend to humans the method of reproduction by "cloning" which is common with trees and other plants. When a tree is produced not from seed but from a shoot of another plant, the offspring has precisely the same genetic constitution as the parent; thus, it is possible by this method to grow thousands or millions of trees with identical properties. (In passing it may be remarked that the only case of genetic identity in mammalian species is that of monozygotic or "identical" twins.) The extension of this method to animals presents peculiar difficulties, since animals, except in the case of some very primitive forms, cannot be grown from shoots; what has to be done is to replace the nucleus of a freshly fertilized ovum with the nucleus of a cell from a different individual in a very early stage of development.

Josiah Lederberg, one of the protagonists in this field, argues that it has advantages over the method of attempting to modify or reconstruct the genes themselves, which is genetic engineering in the narrower sense. Cloning seems to him to be a simple and more direct procedure, involving fewer cases of failure and eliminating the long waiting period needed to find whether a particular genetic modification has been beneficial. Clonal reproduction would make it possible to produce colonies of people all of whom were ideally suited for particular types of jobs. There are, nevertheless, objections of a purely practical and technical kind, but they are possibly not insurmountable, and they are, in any case, trivial in comparison with the detachment of procreation from its natural context in marriage and the family.

The general dehumanization involved in such proposals as these is well illustrated by the fact that Lederberg sees an obvious development consisting of the mingling of human and non-human chromosomes and genes. Writing in the 1960s he could assert "Human nuclei, or individual chromosomes and genes, will be recombined with those of other animal species; these experiments are now well under way in cell culture" and could add, "The mingling of individual human chromosomes with those of other mammals assures a gradualistic enlargement of the field and lowers the threshold of optimism or arrogance, particularly if cloning in other animals gives incompletely predictable results" (cit. Ramsey, pp. 77f). I will quote Ramsey's comment at length:

> This brings us again to the same formidable moral objection. In the case of cloning a man, the question is what to do with mishaps, whether discovered in the course of extracorporeal gestation in the laboratory or by monitored uterine gestation. In case a monstrosity—a subhuman or parahuman individual— results, shall the experiment simply be stopped and this artfully created human life killed? In mingling individual human chromosomes with those of the "higher" mammals (given sufficient dosage and "a few years"), what shall be done if the resulting individual lives seem remarkably human? Moreover, Lederberg does not contemplate only experiments "augmenting" animal cell cultures with "fragments of the human chromosome set." The reverse is also to be done. "Clonal reproduction, and introduction of *genetic material from other spheres*" are two

paths already opened up in *human* evolution (italics added).
Lederberg "infers" these twin genetic policies instead of taking
the other, somewhat longer road of genetic engineering i.e. the
attempt to actually alter the genes. But surely these are paths
no less fraught with mishaps knowingly if not intentionally
created. We must face the grave moral question of what to do
with them. (p. 78)

Again, Ramsey writes, very perceptively,

The entire proposal that we should clone a man and proceed
with mixing chromosomes from "other spheres" with human
material is, therefore, simply an extrapolation of what we
should do from what we can do. There are really only technical
questions to be decided. At root, therefore, the proposal denies
that the mishaps constitute a crucial moral problem. . .(p. 81)

The genetic proposal to clone a man, and the minority practice
of artificial insemination from a nonhusband donor, are border-
lines that throw into bold relief and assault *the nature of human
parenthood.* If cloning men had no other consequences, this
alone would be sufficient to fault it. Our consideration of the
proposal should enliven in our minds an important feature of
parenthood which serves "to make and to keep human life
human." Any fundamental assault upon this is an assault upon
the human and the personal element in parenthood. (pp. 86f)

It is important to add that there can be no moral objection
to directly therapeutic action, whether surgical or medical, whose
object is to cure or alleviate genetic defects. But there may well
be moral objections to certain kinds of genetic experiment, performed upon human beings, even if their ultimate purpose is the
discovery or the invention of therapeutic techniques. There was a
parallel in Hitler's Germany. Because of the denial of normal human
rights to Jews, a number of physiological and biological experiments
were performed upon them, we are told, which could not have
been legally performed upon gentiles, and as a result of these,
knowledge was obtained, much of which was of considerable medical
value. But no one would have said that the experiments were

thereby justified. Some of the ethical problems that arise in this sphere are of course highly complicated and it is not surprising that serious and informed opinion may not be unanimous about some of these issues. But this does not warrant our assuming that no ethical considerations are involved. Two tendencies are at all costs to be resisted. One is the suppression of facts, well exemplified by the concealment from women who are contemplating abortions of the precise nature of the object to be destroyed (see Michael Scott, *Abortion: The Facts*, p. 24). The other is the tendency to assume that anything that a scientist can do he has a right to do, or that at any rate, he has a right to perform any experiment that will add to the sum total of human knowledge.

Professor G. R. Dunstan has raised the question—I stress this phrase "Raised the question," for he does not give a definite answer, though one might guess what that answer would be— whether, for experimental purposes, fertilization of a human ovum *in vitro* ("in a test-tube") might be legitimate if the fetus was destroyed before it reached the stage at which a more than chemical dependence on the mother would normally arise. He writes:

> Is there a point when, granted the possibility, to maintain the life of a human organism outside the womb would become morally intolerable? In order to answer that question, I wish to know whether there is a point, presumably related to the neural development of the fetus, at which the fetus becomes relationally dependent on its mother—dependent on her, that is, for more than a chemical environment, oxygen, nutrient fluids, hormones and the like, dependent on her as a person? When does her *presence* to the fetus begin to awaken in the fetus the potential for human response, as awareness of the fetus begins to awaken in the mother the beginning of a *maternal* response? If we could know at what point a mother, as a human being, as a source of specifically human relationship, becomes irreplaceably necessary to the development of the human embryo into a human child, then we should see a threshold at which experiment must cease, a step which must not be crossed. For beyond it lies the life of a man, the image and glory of God; and this is holy ground. (*The Artifice of Ethics*, p. 71)

With all the respect that I have for Professor Dunstan as a

distinguished moral expert, I must say that I find this argument very perverse. If fertilization *in vitro* leads to a situation in which a human fetus needs a maternal environment which cannot be provided for it, the plain consequence would seem to be that it was morally wrong to initiate the process at all; the suggestion that it is all right provided we destroy the fetus as soon as, or just before, the need appears seems to me to be quite literally monstrous. And if once the principle was admitted I could see it being applied with alarming consequences in the post-natal as well as the prenatal sphere.

In man, as distinct from the lower animals, the physical organism is so intimately related to the mental and spiritual aspects of his life that any attempt to manipulate it in separation is both ethically questionable and intellectually unhopeful. I find this truth excellently set forth in another long passage of Paul Ramsey's:

> Man is an embodied person in such a way that he *is* in important respects his body. He is the body of his soul no less than he is the soul (mind, will) of his body. There are more ways to violate a human being, or to engage in self-violation, than to coerce man's free will or his rational consent. An individual's body, including his sexual nature, belongs to him, to his *humanum*, his personhood and self-identity, in such a way that the bodily life cannot be reduced to the class of the animals over which Adam was given unlimited dominion. To suppose so is bound to prove antihuman—sooner than later. . .
>
> We procreate new beings like ourselves in the midst of our love for one another, and in this there is a trace of the original mystery by which God created the world because of his love. God created nothing apart from his love, and without the divine love was not anything made that was made (John I). Neither should there be among men and women, whose man-womanhood (and not their minds or wills only) is in the image of God, any love-making set out of the context of responsibility for *pro*-creation or any begetting apart from the sphere of human love and responsiveness. (p. 87f)

Here, of course, Ramsey the student of genetics and Ramsey the theologian have come together, but there is nothing new in the recognition that there is a very close relation between sex and religion. And far from shrinking from the new questions raised by

recent developments in genetic science, Ramsey welcomes them
for having provided a much needed clarification of the points at
issue. He writes:

> The "experiment" involved in the thought, shall we clone a
> man?, and the technical possibility of doing so on a vast scale,
> may provide the truly propitious opportunity for acquiring the
> knowledge that the link between sexual love and procreation is
> not in us a matter of specific or animal consequence only, but is
> of truly human and personal import. . .The entire rationaliza-
> tion of procreation—its replacement by replication—can only
> mean the abolition of man's embodied personhood. (p. 88f)

But it must be added that Ramsey is in no way opposed to
the use of genetic information in medical practice. He summarizes
his position as follows:

> Applications of our genetic information in medical practice
> should never lose sight of the physician's real patients: the man,
> the woman, and the child to be born. Nor should they replace
> them by nonpatients: the species, or our control of human
> evolution. If these applications include preventive genetic sur-
> gery, it is because such action is required and reasonably may
> be done in the service of these lives. (*ibid.*, 101)

I would add some concluding remarks from the point of
view of a Christian theologian. In all that I have said I have assumed
that there is a peculiar dignity and value in the human species and
that, in spite of his evolutionary origin, man is not to be treated as
simply one of the higher mammals, differing from the rest only in
degree and not in kind. In holding this I shall have the support of
a great many scientists who would not claim any religious commitment, and I am glad that this is so, though I sometimes wonder
whether scientific humanism can justify itself on its own grounds.

All of us have a much less static and rigid notion of a
biological species than had Aristotle and the Medievals, and this
includes in principle the species of man, though it is remarkable
how little, in spite of its variety and its adaptability, the human
species has developed physically since its emergence. Indeed, many

biologists, such as Dr. C. H. Waddington, see in man an entirely new type of evolution—"socio-genetic"—in which information is handed on from generation to generation by a process of social teaching and learning which is far more speedy in its results than the process of biological heredity and natural selection. Evolutionary theory, for all its emphasis upon change, does not seem to have abolished the concept of man as an identifiably persistent species, and very few scientists would hold it to be either feasible or desirable to try to change man into a substantially different species; they would wish to improve man rather than to replace him.

But an orthodox Christian has further reasons for holding that the human species is of unique importance. He believes that man is made in the image of God, in whatever precise way he interprets that famous Biblical phrase. He also believes that the Creator himself has become incarnate in human nature, so that, in the words of a recent writer, "the central point of Christian belief is that the maker of the universe is now a man" (Kenelm Foster, *Summa Theologiae*, Blackfriars ed., IX, p. xxi). And this, so far from implying a static view of the universe, sees it as undergoing a process of continual growth towards its final christification. Not only the much publicized Pierre Teilhard de Chardin, but a scientist as professional as Claude Tresmontant can be quoted to this effect. There is, I believe, vast scope for exploration in the realm where biological science and Christian theology meet and overlap, but I do not think there is any place for antagonism.

11

A SCALE OF VALUES FOR A CHANGING WORLD

JOSEPH BASILE

A rapidly changing society becomes only disquieting when it lacks a scale of values to which we may refer when measuring, foreseeing or redirecting the great transformations. Our exciting and, at the same time, so disquieting world, has an urgent need of such a reassuring model, liable to procure the necessary formula for a continued and highly effective progression. And these notes are meant as an effort to contribute to the search after such a touchstone.

Taking into consideration the natural organic systems as well as the abstract principles studied in the theory of systems, we may state that: in a closed system, composed of several variables, the maximum global effect is reached when the gradients of the various variables are equal. A simplified application of this general principle is found in the well-known mathematical proposition: "The product of numbers whose sum is constant, attains its maximum when these numbers are equal."

Now let us try to apply this simple general law to human social life, characterized by three great variable constitutents: knowledge, behavior and feeling, components now being expressed by: technical growth, social progress and spirituality or inner life.

From the aforementioned principle we can deduce that the ideal would be: the *even* progress of these three components *together*. As soon as the progress of one of these components outbalances the two others, there is danger ahead. This is a new way of thinking then; hitherto, *knowledge, behavior* and *feeling* have always been considered as values independent of one another. It appears, however, that precisely their reciprocal incidence fashions global progress and that their common growth is essential for the success of our destiny. Total life, and not one of its composing parts (for instance, abstract intelligence as it operates in science and technology) will ensure the continuity of mankind's development. Therefore, every trend in the three components of human nature must be carefully considered, to find the ways to regularize their progress and make them converge towards the synthesis of human advancement.

The Growth of Knowledge

Technical knowledge has outgrown all other developments, to the extent that it has pressed its very particular stamp on our way of living. But society, like every living organism, tries to react against unbridled accelerations and to re-establish the balance needed for vital progress. This compensatory and automatic redirecting reaction is presently taking shape. Energy producers, for instance, are now compelled to take anti-pollution measures which are directed towards "clean" solutions; hence, nuclear *fusion* energy (probably thanks to the recent discovery of the implosive action of laser rays on hydrogen), will replace dirty *fission* energy in which we are actually driven because of the shortage in mineral-oil. To meet the constant increase in social demands, manufacturing knowledge and techniques will have to shift to non-robotics solutions, and their most direct concern now goes to the organization, automatization and miniaturization of labor, and to the "job-enrichment" procedures which avoid degradation inherent to irksome work. Even communication techniques and informatics which, as used by the intermediaries of mass-media, constitute a real "world thinking net," will yield to some ethical rules or code to avoid confusion and general spiritual degradation.

It is unlikely that budgets for fundamental research will be cut, but application research will surely have to bend to political imperatives. This tendency in techniques to turn more directly towards the social and human personality, can already be felt in a new kind of research occurring at the fringe of physics. The World Health Organization, for instance, is at this moment studying the effects of the *properties of the soil* on the health of the people living on it. The earth of certain regions possesses physico-chemical properties—an electrical potential, radioactivity, a magnetic field, climateric factors—whose influence on our glands and mentalities is undeniable. And this field is practically still unexplored. Another unusual example is the study of the water of thermal springs.

These waters possess properties other than those which can be inferred from the simple chemical reactions of their mineral components on us. Without falling into ancient magic, it is a fact that these springs have evolutive qualities; (their rH, oxydoreduction potential, varies) they are really alive, and it is not surprising that they create vital exchanges in our cells. This leads us into the zone where science, life and human behavior are merging. This brings us to consider the second component of our future.

The Growth of Social Behavior

Technological growth in itself, cannot dry up the sources of social conflicts. On the contrary, technological growth multiplies these conflicts because it is unable to ensure that the wealth it engenders will be equally shared. As external liberties are gradually restricted due to the necessities of a more complex organization in a continually shrinking space, internal liberties, (those acquired by self-control, intellectual and creative capacities) will have to grow to compensate. This dichotomy, between external liberties and internal liberties is expressed by Betrand Russell, who declares that liberty increases through the tendency towards *creation* and decreases through *possession*. This external and possessive side of liberty must be limited voluntarily in all solidarities. In *War and Peace* Tolstoi states that "As soon as an act is no longer our personal concern, it must lose its liberty." The only limit to personal liberty is the border beyond which others are made unimportant or beyond which the growth of the collectivity will be hindered. Hence, to exert one's liberty means: to limit one's capability "to have" so that a society that increases its capability "to be."

This brings us to the interrelation between responsibility and liberty, an agonizing problem, when one knows that our responsibility increases proportionally with the difficulty to distinguish good from evil and no longer, as hitherto, with the amount of evil that an action contains. In the realm of present-day practice, these views on responsibilities, liberties and new solidarities, find their application in all fields. In nations as in enterprises, participation will become the object of a compromise between "initiated" and "non-initiated," reaching a ceiling beyond which any added participation and liberty of choice becomes too expensive for the collective. It seems, therefore, that today's technicians and jurists will have to give place to the planners of tomorrow, who will fix all new solidarities thanks to a dosage of external and internal liberties, but above all according to intelligent research in the service of common welfare. As for the employment, the demands of labor are ever-intensifying. People increasingly feel the burden of working conditions, having acquired, through more advanced education, a lot of *unemployed competencies* as well as *frustrated tastes*. If, until now, education of the masses has been the lever of growth, now education will compel us to change the very type of growth. Workmen are much more discontent about uninteresting, irksome jobs, submitting to the authority of some "small foreman," and the monotony of the production line, than they are about insufficient salaries.

Many solutions are being tried in industry to cope with this dangerous fact. These solutions generally lead towards the practice of "job-enrichment" the adaptation of work to human welfare, by allowing the worker a greater variety of tasks, more initiative; the right to prepare and control his own work; and the time to combine it with leisure and education. These are not theories of mere idealists. Assembly lines for color television sets now exist where workers participate in the job-enrichment process. Groups of not more than six or seven persons are free to exchange their occupations within their group, every one of them remaining responsible for several phases of the work. Those on assembly lines perform on the same level as those of the past, where twice as many people worked like robots. As Lewis Mumford points out in his *The Myth of the Machine*, had prehistorical man lived in a world so *desperately uniform* as the one with which we are threatened, he would probably never have acquired the varied experience that made him retain images, forge a language and organize great ideas. In the midst of the strange, ephemeral and quickly changing situations that are ahead, we will have to hold onto certain constants, so that technical acceleration may harmonize with the development of daily human contacts.

Among those values that influence action, the *family circle* comes first. It has been definitely established that the family knot deeply affects the child's future life, whatever the conditions of his later life may be. A particular influence of the family on the behavior of the adult has just been discovered by the psychologists: in a constantly growing society, one of the essential needs of the individual is prestige. And it has recently been proven that a man is more sensitive to his family's appreciation than to the appreciation of any other group in the society.

Another value from the past required for the pursuit of social growth is the blessing of trees and natural surroundings; this helps us escape for a while from debilitating concentrations of some surroundings. This is not so much a question of oxygen as of the psychological balance necessary to the innate feeling of autonomy. Everybody has heard of the famous sphere of Sivadon, which extends about one meter around our body and which, when invaded by an alien presence, makes us feel uneasy. This peri-corporal space, indispensable to our feeling of autonomy, has a tendency to come back to shape when compressed. This explains why, when leaving underground trains or the encumbered exits of big stores, we press the pace without any obvious reason. It is the "elasticity" of that fictive sphere that propels us.

Being deprived of the natural surroundings from which we emerged in the depths of unrecorded times; being condemned to live among concrete blocks, makes us believe, even without demonstration, what a recent study has proven: that the percentage of criminality is six times higher in towns with one million inhabitants than in those with 10,000 inhabitants. Aristotle thought that Greek towns should not have more inhabitants than could be recognized at sight.

It has been observed that for any organization, be it a tribe of the Stone Age, which presumably was composed of 200 to 1000 people, or an industrial enterprise or a military group, five hundred people constitute the most natural and the most efficient unit. This corresponds to the number of people we could recognize and with whom we could have social relations.

What is going to happen when, in about fifty years from now, three quarters of humanity live in towns of ten million or more inhabitants? Contemplation of natural surroundings confers an astonishingly benefic condition. Without any effort, solely due to osmosis and ambiance, the mind is prepared for a more harmonious and orderly conception of things and for better understanding. To stroll along the shore, on a deserted and sunny beach, gives a clearer conscience and a more indulgent heart. And here we have come to the third component of our future.

The Growth of Conscience and Personal Values

The foregoing proves that both technical growth with its inconsiderateness, and social growth with its collective troubles and dangers, are unable to create the auto-regulating system that can ensure the constant progress of civilization. Political powers will have to favor a third component, which, when added to the former two, will beget the cybernetic auto-corrector mentioned at the beginning of this paper, and which will produce its maximum effects when the three components are advancing at an even pace. This third constituent to which humanity will have to pay more and more attention, is the conscience, the intimate aspirations, the sense of religion or "reliance to the infinite." These three components are required as a whole, and not merely one of them, and least of all "zerogrowth." We cannot fall in love with a rate of economic growth, or GNP; there are other values: affectivity, aesthetics, meditation, silence, space.

So as to avoid future collapses, or simply in order to survive, political powers will have to foresee a new type of education. This education should simultaneously broaden internal liberties, incite new levels of solidarity and compensate for the unavoidable loss of external liberties. At the crossroads of destiny, this question of liberties and choices shall rise again, as it did so many times in the millenary past. The animals that in their defense against danger have hidden in quiet corners and burdened themselves with shells, have given us but mussels and oysters. The fish, however, who ran the risks of a naked skin and continuous shifting, has prepared the way for the Homosapiens.

Likewise, our society will have to take a "glorious risk" in order to cross a new threshold in the mutation process. But how? By paying as much attention to the inner education as to the intellectual and technical education.

In this new educational program, the implementation of five new areas of instruction, should be foremost. First, *molding character.*

Last year, all over the world, more than one million studies were published regarding the exact sciences and human sciences, but only two or three hundred papers were published concerning the formation of will and character. It should be decided once and for all what is most important: what one *knows* or what one *is.* Besides, the attraction of facility always foreshadows the arrival of some kind of tyranny.

Each of our actions is the origin of some unsuspected chain of reactions bearing the stamp of the first effort or the first "laisser-aller." Dante expressed it in seven syllables: "Cosa Fatta Capo Ha."

Many of us have read *Future Shock* and were enthralled by the passage: "Our new society offers the exalting possibility of mounting the horse of change, to gallop and realize one's self with it. But this needs more strength of character: if that condition is fulfilled, the triumph will be marvelous." But, could Alvin Toffler tell us how to exert and increase this strength of character so essential for the survival of our civilization? Anyway, we shall have to start somewhere with these mastering exercises. "We begin a round-the-world tour by putting one foot before the other," says a Bantu proverb. We shall all have to begin with the ABC's of mastery: stay calm when driving our cars; make reasonable choices before the television screen, make the effort to assist in some cultural debate; take regular evening walks in the vicinity of our homes, regardless of the weather conditions, etc.

Such futilities permit us to create high images of ourselves, to arouse new enthusiasm, to keep our chins up, and to develop the desire for personal elevation.

The second innovation in education: developing a *sensibility about aesthetics* is also a bias permitting us to reach a harmonious growth. This does not mean that we should encourage the semi-culture that pushes the masses into boring museum visits, but rather we should create an ambiance where the unconscious automatically rejects all forms that do not obey the vital laws of unity, rhythm, proportions and balance. This is part of the responsibility of the technicians who conceive and shape our external world.

The only way for our industrial civilization to leave its primary stage, is for us to add to its technicity those goods which reveal the invisible light of things, that open up the kingdom of the spirit, that confer on men the grandeur they ignore in themselves, that permit man to reach a more secret, a more real and cheerful reality. These goods are those of art, among others. Darwin said that to lose the taste for poetry and painting is to lose happiness and "risks to (sic) injure the intellect and more probably the moral character, by impoverishing the affective part of our nature."

Third adjuvant to external liberties: developing *the sense of creativity*. In order to escape from the clumsiness of our tendencies, we must also develop our sense of creativity. The desire to create arises from the depths of our souls. Creativity techniques, are based on observations far from vulgar or selfish feelings. They are all related to the depths of the subconscious and dependent on full harmony between emotion and intelligence, action and inner conscience. Creativity is the supreme achievement of the individual, the plenitude of personality reached by breathtaking expectation. Creativity also requires retreats: nothing can be created in noisy surroundings. Calmness teaches us how to wait, and waiting favors the mysterious arrangement of things to come. Relaxed waiting, a sort of confident expectancy, is the subject of present psychological studies of group dynamics and, curiously, also of new creativity techniques.

Simone Weil, who has studied these states of serene expectancy, of receptivity and controlled desire, pretends that this intellectual humility becomes some sort of prayer and "every time we put ourselves in those dispositions of passive and confident attention, we destroy the evil in ourselves." So we're judged by Simone Weil. In the mystic terms, she has affected the present conclusions of the American sociologists on the efficiency of serene relaxation. In this century of electronics, automation and interplanetary rockets, silent interior *disponibility* becomes an autodefensive process. The permanently agitated are the disorganized individuals who mostly fear to converse with themselves.

The fourth innovation in education: *psychosomatic initiation*. The revelations of medicine and biology regarding the intricacy of *psyche* and *soma* enlighten the path of inner growth. It is actually known that our opinion as to the finality of our acts can influence the DNA (deoxyribonucleic acid) rate, that plans the health of our cells. Behind the nervous system defense exists a humoral defense and it is becoming known that the functions of the endocrine glands are influenced by our views on the finality of our life and our deepest hopes. One might even say that physical health is influenced by our somewhat religious conception of the universe. This leads to the fifth attention required: developing *the sense of the sacred*. This is that little-known zone, the innermost recesses of our hearts, where physical forces are in accord with the infinite; that zone which contains the sense of mystery without which, as Pasteur said, "one can be a very good technician but never a great scientist."

The irremissible mistake would be to look at the future with the eyes of the past, and not to understand the evolution that operates in sudden forward leaps, after millenary maturation, and always projects into the world where ancient values gradually take on the hue of that famous "supplement of soul" (Bergson). The growth of civilization will in the future be expressed in terms of inner values rather than in quantitative terms. In the great turmoil of ideas and events that is ahead, our action, more than ever, will bear the stamp of what we think and feel deep in our heart. A new renaissance will not appear in our civilization unless the inner dimension of man equals his exterior dimension, when Power and Wisdom shall again be allies. That future renaissance shall emerge only in the triple unity of science, service and inner fervor. The unity of the intellectual, social and spiritual disciplines will fulfill the plenitude of life. To that effect one must, in his inward silence, develop his culture to enrich his action; one must color, with a touch of human warmth, the rigor of science, in order to facilitate for himself and for others cognitive, social and emotional harmony.

The nature of man derives from a synthesis of rationality and irrationality. To achieve a balanced unity, it is imperative that we newly introduce time-honored values in our post-industrial civilization: values such as, an inner freedom derived from strength of will and character, aesthetic sensibility, a creative attitude, a respect for psychosomatic effects, and religious sense of the sacred. To ascend this luminous scale, there are adjuvants called silence, contemplation, family ties, softness in manners, and friendship in heart. In our age of rockets, informatics and telecommunications, we must search and find a unity of thinking for the entire world, because the hope of men is immense and we are at the crossroads of civilization. We are destined to build a great era or to see our world collapse.

12

SYSTEMATIC INTERRELATIONS OF DIFFERENT TYPES OF VALUE

J. N. FINDLAY

Since this paper bristles with as many small points as a porcupine, I shall first list the points, then try to push them in singly. Out of such pressures the fuzzily simple, relatively rounded shape of value-theory should emerge: the difficult but important art or science which tells men and societies how to live and choose.

First, I shall maintain that there is no real problem in drawing up a list of values and disvalues that will have a necessarily shareable, interpersonal appeal: they will merely be such values and disvalues as arise out of an aspiration towards interpersonality and shareability as such and are, in fact, specific forms of the latter. They will simply represent what anyone, who himself has his own personal desires and interests, can consistently desire for everyone, taking account of their own personal desires and interests, whatever these may be.

Second, I shall hold that such an aspiration after the interpersonal is not formal and vacuous, but necessarily begets a whole brood of higher-order interests and counter-interests, among which a number of interesting analogies, complements, contrasts and other relationships can be seen to hold. All our old friends will make their appearance here: the agreeable, the powerful, the free, the uncontaminated, the just, the likely, the insightful, the lovely, the loving and the loveable, and last but not least the morally good. And of course we shall meet all our old enemies, though I shall avoid the bad omen of listing them. These too have their own curious correspondences and affiliations, their entailments and oppositions, as well as their systematic relations to the forms of good.

Third, I shall argue that there is no way to impose such a list of interpersonal values and disvalues on anyone who simply does not want to draw it up, nor to follow it in his choices, but merely to draw up and follow some wholly private list of his own, and perhaps use force or persuasion to impose this on others. There is no superior rightness in the interpersonal over the personal except insofar as we take rightness to be equivalent to interpersonality: if we take up a purely personal stance, it is, in fact, wrong to try to be interpersonal. The interpersonal list will, however, have a superior rightness insofar as a tendency towards necessary agreement is normally taken to be a mark of attitudes that are right, and also insofar as the desire to share stances with others is a contingently strong and perpetually self-reinforcing aspect of human nature.

Fourth, I shall hold also the values and disvalues which are thus necessarily communicable to all who want such values and disvalues, are all to a large extent discrepant in practice: they are not discrepant in their being values and disvalues, but in the possibility of implementing them concretely. Discrepant values can only be implemented in practice and opposed disvalues avoided, by an elaborate set of arbitrary compromises and preferences, which vary from person to person and society to society. The necessity for such practical compromises is often taken to be a sign of the radical relativity or subjectivity of values and disvalues, which of course it is not in the least.

Finally, I shall add to this that the difficult art of compromise is not without a set of guiding maxims and principles, which while not decisive, certainly reduce the problems of decision. These principles bring in context and depend to a large extent on person and situation. In given personal and social situations there is often, happily, only one really right resolution of some difficult personal or social impasse.

I shall now try to elucidate and also to provide illustrations of my five Pythian paragraphs. As regards the first, I shall simply stress that there is a side of ourselves that wants to transcend the personality and contingency of our goals and interests, wants to substitute variables for constants, and to conceive what, if anything, one might want, no matter who one was, and no matter what concrete contents one *happened* to desire. We want, in short, to find goals that will be invariant and necessary for the individual's private choices, no matter who the individual may be, and no matter what he may *chance* to want; we also want to find goals that will be invariant for individuals conferring with other individuals, no matter who these may be, or what they may want, so that one may arrive at practical policies and decisions which will have to be satisfactory to them all. The aspiration I have sketched is certainly one that arises in all animals that are reasonable and political, and that as such want to be guided by ends that anyone could pursue for anyone. I shall presume that we all are, in fact, in at least one segment of our being, such Aristotelian beings. I myself believe that such interpersonal reasonableness is in some manner geared to the deep structure of the universe, but no more of that here.

It might, however, be argued that the aspiration is quite void of substance or content, and that it at most directs us to look for goals that we all *happen* to agree in pursuing, and in pursuing for everyone. Kant thinks that happiness is but a general name to cover contingent goals of this sort, and a modern man might take the satisfaction of the ego or the libido to be an invariant goal of this sort. I think, however, that there is nothing necessary and invariant about either the ego or the libido, and I have met men very uninterested in one or both; quite possibly the angels are wholly free from either. Whatever one *happens* to want, one must also, however, to the extent that one reflects on the matter, necessarily want, *not* because it is the silly concrete thing that it is, but simply *because* one wants it; reasonable beings, who love universality, want things not only because they are the things they are, for example, having children, winning races etc., but for the higher-order reason that they are wanted things, and the progress to this higher wanting is not a tautological but a rational entailment, one which imposes itself on beings concerned to universalize. There is an invariant want to have whatever one may want which grows out of and presupposes the particular, concrete wants out of which it grows, but which, owing to its generality, is capable of coordinating and harmonizing these concrete wants, and which also can, to the extent that we desire the further universality of a coordination of our wants with those of others, be extended to those others, so that we can come to want for every man that he should have what *he* personally desires. This generalized want is for the interpersonal goal of happiness or satisfaction, the lowest of the interpersonal values, since the content to which that happiness attaches may be variable and discrepant for each time or person, and have nothing interpersonal about it. Nevertheless, be it pushpin or poetry or twiddling one's thumbs, let every man or woman or beast have what he or she or it wants.

And I think it clear that the goal of happiness or satisfaction subsumes the goals of everything that is instrumental to such happiness: the *freedom* to achieve whatever one happens to want without let or hindrance from outside, and also the *power*, the facilities, the opportunities, the material and financial and other wherewithal towards all that one wants. Not only satisfaction, but also freedom and power, are necessarily goals that beings concerned to universalize must want for everyone, provided that they all have specific wants of some sort. (The sort of abstract universality which would try to realize for everyone what no one wanted is not one we need consider.)

But of course at this stage, when one raises the alluring prospect of trying to get for each man whatever he wants and whatever will get him what he wants, we become aware of the conflicts to which it will inevitably lead, since what is satisfactory to A may be painful and unsatisfactory to B, and since even A alone may have wants that clash with one another. If one now desires to speak to others or oneself from a stance which cannot be varied no matter what variable desires anyone may have, one must necessarily desire some sort of higher-order accommodation or harmonization of the personal stances in question, which will involve the frequent subordination or sacrifice of one to the other. According to one's prevailing orientation one can then proceed to the Platonic Justice and Temperance and seek, as far as possible, to *integrate* the wants of different members of society, or the wants cherished by a single person, into a *close* union of communal or individual self-love, or alternatively to proceed to a less exalted laissez-faire justice and temperance which would allow individual wants within persons or among persons to develop as freely as possible, and to seek only to restrain them or integrate them where they interfere or come into conflict with one another. Both Platonic Love Justice and Self-Love Temperance and ordinary common or garden laissez-faire justice and temperance thus arise, as new forms of interpersonality, difficult higher-order compromises among personal wants, which are often not only in conflict with primary wants but also with one another, and which then require yet higher forms of compromise. Exaggeratedly totalitarian and exaggeratedly libertarian social dispensations are our modern version of this problem, with the difficult demand to find something which satisfies the values of both, something which would be a sort of remarkable laissez-faire totalitarianism, both for society and the individual. I have no inkling as to what it could be like, but that is the direction in which the value-dialectic is now moving.

I wish now to suggest that our values necessarily proliferate in three independent but complementary directions, corresponding to three necessary differentiations in the human psyche. These are, somewhat traditionally expressed, the aesthetic values of essence, the scientific values of real existence, and the moral values of action or praxis. The values of essence are the values we explore when we merely look at things or consider them thinkingly, and try to be clear *what* they actually are: they are indifferent to the reality or unreality of what is thus considered and as to whether it ought or ought not to be practically realized. To consider the *what* of things is basic to conscious life and is evinced both in regard to the sensuous and the conceptual, the real and the imaginary, the familiar and the strange, the disorderly and confused as well as the well-ordered and calm. Everywhere we desire to be lucid as to what something is or would be like, how it is assembled or put together, and our joy in such clarity is of course proportionate to our success, a success not easily attained in ridding what something is of all that confuses and distorts and interferes with our seeing it as it is.

But this essential and necessary interest in the *what* stands opposed to the complementary interest in the *that*, which is above all concerned to demarcate the real from the unreal, the true from the false or imaginary; this basic interest is not merely concerned to look over structural possibilities and see what they might involve. It is only satisfied in establishing the one possibility which happens to be actual, and to which it can then adjust itself in its thought and action, and in relation to which it can see all that is fanciful or possible.

In addition, however, to this basic interest in the *that* is the basic interest in the *should*, which seeks to use its view of the possible and the actual to decide which of the many possibles it will use its limited power to realize.

I shall attempt no further clarification of the three dimensions of the *what*, the *that* and the *should*, except to say that they are as basic to conscious life as to grammar. However, I want to stress that each has its own peculiar extension into the interpersonal, that each contributes its own peculiar constellations to the value-firmament, and among them there is often a difficult problem of choice. From the interest concerned to envisage particular natures springs the invariant interest in the clear envisagement of *any* nature *whatsoever*, an interest which can be called in the widest sense 'aesthetic,' whether what it tries to envisage are sensuous patterns or natural objects or mathematical theorems or types of societies or philosophies. In the same way, one's interest in the *that* can and must free itself from immediacy and contingency; from a concern about what one's neighbor is doing or what one's landlady will charge, it can become an interest in *whatever* is or must be the case, an interest necessarily shareable since it builds itself on a basic aspect of conscious life. And, in the same way, one's practical interest in the realization of this or that, whether by oneself or others or natural forces, can develop into an interest in active agency as such, an interest necessarily shareable by all who act and strive, and which can then further develop into an interest given concrete content by all the other invariant goals independently established, an interest in increasing satisfaction, freedom, and human power, an interest in essence, existence, and the alternative forms of justice, and, finally, an interest in disinterested, interpersonal practice itself. Here at the apex we get the ultimate narcissism of practical reason's interest in practical interest itself, its interest in its own disinterested pursuit of all disinterested goals whatsoever.

What I am trying to suggest is that granted the *pou sto* of an interest in universalization, one can transcendentally deduce all the recognized forms of the good: the agreeable, the liberated, the powerful, the pure, the loving, the equitable, the lovely, the true and the probably true, and, finally, very virtue or disinterested activity itself. And, all deviant and bad forms of interest can be shown to involve the retention of some element of unwarranted constancy in what is pursued, or in a refusal to carry on the mandate of free and open variability as far as it can be carried. Introduce one element of the empirically or factually constant or contingent into the axiological structure, and it all collapses in ruins.

Further, the profound parallelisms and homologies between values occurring in very different regions of the value-firmament are very interesting. I can only give a few examples of such homologies. For instance, the interest in the personal satisfaction of *each* individual, no matter what he may happen to want, takes the form, in the aesthetic sphere, of the interest in portraying *each* individual detail, no matter how trivial, with profound respect and truth, and in the scientific sphere, in the interest in *each* lone fact, no matter how shattering to established theory, and no matter how confined to a fragmentary papyrus or the spectrum of a remote star, it may be, while in the sphere of practice it becomes the concern, not only for every individual or class of individuals, but also for divergent patterns of value none of which should be missing in a complete life. In the same way, the interest in a just and fair balance to be struck between varied personal and social interests takes on, in the aesthetic sphere, the form of a sort of equity towards elements and aspects of what one is portraying, whereas, in the sphere of science, it becomes the equity of the calculus of probabilities, where no datum is given a privileged position over any other. It is important to stress that science can be regarded as a sort of aesthetics, where one's material is facts and not portrayable characters, and that it can also be regarded as a sort of morality, where one's concern is with pieces of evidence and not with the divergent interest of individuals.

I think it established, then, that all the main heads of

values and disvalues admit of something like a transcendental deduction from the desire for invariance and interpersonality in the sphere of the practical, as in all other spheres. I have given such a transcendental deduction not because I reject the view that they may also admit of a more august, but more dubious, metaphysical or ontological deduction, but because I believe that even if our world is the product of chance and necessity and is hopelessly indifferent to anything rational and good, the absoluteness of the values and disvalues I have inadequately deduced remains unimpugned. They are the goals and countergoals which satisfy the conditions of invariance and intersubjectivity, and must necessarily govern the practice of those concerned for the invariant and interpersonal as such. If one is a follower of Reason (and one cannot but be such in the deeper strata of one's being), one has no choice but to shape one's actions in the light of the goals and countergoals in question.

At this point, however, apparent obstacles obtrude: itself since our interpersonal goals are irreducibly plural, many of them cannot in all circumstances be implemented together, and some of them tend in intrinsically different directions, and cannot, in their purest, most intense form, be realized in one case. There is nothing self-contradictory in this: if X merits interpersonal approval, it does not follow that the contrary of X will not also merit interpersonal approval, and that it may not be true that when both are most utterly irreconcilable that they are also at their purest and best. Obviously, for instance, austere and simple integrity is as admirable as sophisticated tolerance, though they cannot both be readily realized in the same individual or epoch. The problems of practice are different from the problems of evaluation; they involve a choice among alternatives which are existentially, but not axiologically, incompatible. All this means that, while the highest values can all be present together, qua values, in the Reason that *recognizes* them all, they cannot be all together in the realm of instantial implementation, and that the simplest practical decision, whether for man or society, necessarily involves sacrifice.

The situation is not, however, as bad as it sounds. For we are not making choices in vacuo, but in a historical context, in which our own interests are already stabilized, and in which the society in which we are living has itself advanced to a certain stage or type of interpersonality, and has made certain basic choices as to the values which are to be preferred. In such a context it is possible for us, singly or in parties, to make constructive use of our powers, and to see where and how the interpersonal can most profitably be pursued. In such choices our own personal preferences will always be significant, for a person, being only an *instance* of Reason, will necessarily be more devoted to some aspects of the reasonable than to others.

But there are, nonetheless, general principles in such matters and the most important of these is that one should always turn *from* the already over-produced, over-estimated value and *towards* the under-produced, under-appreciated value. Not only the economic but the axiological sphere can suffer from overproduction; there can, for example, be too much efficiency and too little compassion, too much logical rigor and too little obedience to intuitive thought-trends, and vice versa, and the obligation of the man or the society is then to increase the strength of the under-produced, neglected value at the cost of its burgeoning, self-cheapened neighbor. There is a sort of justice among types of value as well as a justice within one type of value, and this is the inspiration of all the fruitful revolutions in taste, politics, scientific ideas, etc., in which human progress has consisted.

At present, we are in quest of a revolution which will curb the self-assertion of certain organized groups which is ruining *some* of our societies, and which will at the same time relax the rigid organization of other societies which is likewise ruining *them*. For Reason has subjected us one and all to an eternal dialectic of discovering ever new and higher accommodations of values and disvalues, an exciting task as long as one can endure the pace.

I do not know whether my attempt at a transcendental deduction of the heads of value and disvalue was an effort suitable for the conference. You have seen how deeply I have been influenced by Kantian ideas, how I believe in the magisterial deliverances of Practical Reason, though for me it does not set up exceptionless imperatives but rather, manifold goals which everyone can and should pursue for everyone, though there will always be difficult personal and social choices in their implementation. And I also believe with Kant in the primacy of Practical Reason, that it obliges us to follow certain principles, for which there is no warrant beyond the fact that they are reasonable, and that we are obliged to follow them I should say, not only in our actions, but also in the construction of our theories. And I finally venture to hope and believe, with Kant, that we shall one day be rewarded by a closer fellowship with reason as such or with reason itself, and that this will as much surpass our present sources of satisfaction as it altogether surpasses our present comprehension.

PART THREE

CONTRIBUTIONS OF SCIENCE AND TECHNOLOGY

13

WHAT DO RELIGION, POLITICS, AND SCIENCE EACH CONTRIBUTE TO THE CREATION OF A GOOD SOCIETY?

HERBERT RICHARDSON

This paper deals with the question of what religion, politics, and science contribute to the creation, maintenance and improvement of society. This paper will argue that they play different, though concurrently essential, functions. Religion creates the unity of society; politics creates the justice of society; and science creates the truth of society.

I

Religion creates the unity of society. Every society is the creation of many institutions, individuals, and symbolic patterns. This unity is experienced as a common bond which allows members of the society to identify with one another. This identification is not, in principle, the immediate knowledge and love of the members of a society for one another. It is, rather, their common recognition that they identify with something that transcends them all. By virtue of their acknowledgment, or love, for this higher reality with which they all identify, members of society affirm their unity with one another.

Because the identification of members of a society with one another is mediated through the shared acknowledgment of a higher unity and good, a society can exist which is larger than the range of immediate personal knowledge and communion. The range of immediate love and knowledge is limited to those people one can know directly. Such immediate face-to-face relationships, valuable as they may be, are not the form of the larger society (although modern contractual/nominalist thinking uses precisely such immediate relationships as a model for society as a whole). Society is, rather, a *mediated unity* that comes into being when persons and groups which do not have face-to-face relationships identify with one another on the basis of their shared identification with something greater, or higher, than them all.

This acknowledgment, that society is a mediated unity, as ritualized in social behavior and articulated through symbols, is a society's "civil religion." That every society has a religion (that is, something that binds its people together) is a commonplace of contemporary sociology. The idea has been popularized recently by Robert Bellah; previously it was espoused by Parsons, Durkheim, and Comte.

From the social-functional point of view, even atheistic societies have a civil religion, for this term refers simply to the values, rituals, and symbols that mediate to people in any society the sense of unity. From this functional point of view, the symbol of a society's unity is its "God-term." The serious question, therefore, is not whether a society calls its God-term "God" or whether it calls its God-term by another name. The theist/atheist controversy is irrelevant from this functional point of view.

What is relevant, however, is whether a society's God-term is *universal and inclusive*, or whether it is *non-universal and exclusive*. If a society's God-term is exclusive, then the identification of its members with one another requires their non-identification with people outside their group. In this situation, war and competition with others can be seen to be essential to a society's identity and existence. Modern nationalism (for example, Americanism), which affirms that a particular nation-state is an ultimate unit of loyalty, is such a non-universalistic civil religion. For this reason, modern nationalism thrives on war and economic competition.

The world needs a universal God-term so that all people can identify with one another as part of a single human society. A world society would mitigate competition and war among particular social groups and provide a framework for justly resolving conflicts. There are two serious options today with regard to a *universal* religion and world society: communism and Christianity. Communism is based on the universal acceptance of a single order of society, articulated as a world view or general ideology. Christianity is a world religion based on the universal acceptance of a single personal God. Christianity, therefore tolerates a variety of orders of society and world views. The basic issue between communism and Christianity is whether the unity of a society is best established by means of a shared ideology (reason) or a shared personal loyalty (faith).

Communism, by raising a philosophical theory to absolute status, requires that all the members of society think alike and that all functions of a society be based on this common ideology. Thus, communism leads to homogenization and the despising of individuality, that is, to the exaltation of human thought over human faith and human freedom. Communism gives an immanent principle a universal function, thereby closing itself to the realm of *future possibility*. Thus, it is intrinsic to communism that it generate a closed bureaucracy, technologism, and behaviorism. In America, the universalizing of a democratic ideology also has this homogenizing effect. This occurs whenever a society's universal principle derives from human reason rather than from faith in a transcendent person.

Only by finding a principle of unity that *transcends reason* (and, therefore, the immanent order of the world), can a society be universal and also open to human freedom. Such a transcendent principle is affirmed only by an act of freedom, that is, by the act of *faith*. The object of this act of faith is, strictly speaking, not a "principle," for the object of faith transcends thought and reason. Moreover, the object of an act of faith must be a transrational reality to which and through which a person can relate *without contradicting* the act of faith itself.

In Buddhism, which affirms the reality of the transpersonal

realm, the object of faith contradicts in principle the act of faith itself. That is, the personal act of faith encounters not a personal God but an impersonal reality which is the *oneness* of all substantial being. Within the oneness of all substantial being, the act of any *individual* is relatively insubstantial. For this reason, Buddhism is a universalistic religion that fails to provide a basis for substantial action in the social order.

In Judeo-Christian-Islamic monotheism, on the other hand, the act of faith is ordered to a transrational being who meets our freedom with a free act of his own. In this way, the *substantial* reality of human freedom is confirmed in the act of faith and the religious foundation for substantial action in the social order is laid.

A transcendent personal God is related to the universal human society when he is identified as the Creator of all things. The world has its unity with respect to, and in relation to, its Creator; it does not have an immanent unity or a unity from itself. What this means is that the world is radically plural, lacking any immanent unity. Moreover, it means that the world contains distinctive spheres of reality that do not have any *rational* relation to one another, but which are, nevertheless, *one* with respect to God. On such an understanding, we see that there may be *several* orders of truth or several dimensions of reality (for example, physical, psychological, and spiritual) which cannot be systematized within any *single* type of reason, but which are united through their common reference to a single Lord. Such an affirmation resists the attempt to have a single bureaucratic or scientific style dominate all human life.

In this way, a personal Creator God is both the transcendent unity of the world and also the principle of its immanent *plurality*. God is, to use the Bible's metaphor, a King to whom many different nations have a personal loyalty, so that they are united through their shared loyalty to him. But such nations need not have the same homogenized culture. They themselves can be distinct spheres of culture and human action.

The way in which this shared loyalty to a transcendent personal God is institutionalized in society is not by the affirmation of a common world view or ideology. A common world view is necessary only where an exclusively immanentalistic view of reality is held. A personal God, however, transcends the immanent order of the world. From the epistemological point of view, we say that God transcends reason. Philosophy, science, and ideology are not, therefore, adequate ways to conceive the unity of a world where oneness derives from a shared relation to a transcendent God. Rather, the unity of the world is affirmed through the shared act of faith.

The institutionalization of this shared act of faith, a shared loyalty to a transcendent personal God, is not a common world view or political vision. The institutionalization of the shared act of faith is liturgy and prayer together. Faith expresses itself in prayer, the act whereby we relate to the transcendent personal God. The sharing of this prayer by many people in a community is their liturgy. Liturgy and shared prayer are, therefore, the institutions by which the oneness of a society united by faith in a transcendent God is expressed.

A society united by shared prayer is different from a society united by shared ideology in that it can be politically pluralistic. That is what Christianity offers as an alternative to the immanent universalism of communism.

To summarize: (a) the contribution of religion to society is to create its unity; (b) society is based not on immediate relationships but on a shared and mediated identification with something higher; (c) this shared identification should be universal rather than non-universal; and, (d) this identification can be universal, without being a threat to the integrity of particular groups, only if it is an identification with a universal-personal God which is institutionalized as common prayer, or liturgy.

II

Religion is not politics. Politics has its own special task. The responsibility of politics is to create the *justice* of society.

Justice is not the same thing as unity. In traditional Christian social theory, this is recognized by distinguishing justice from love. Merely to say we should love one another and recognize that we all are brothers does not solve the problems of the world. The problem is that even where people love one another, their love does not tell them specifically how to act.

Justice is concerned with how to act in a relationship, or a social unity, that includes more than one party. Wherever there is a society, there is a need for justice. Since a society is not just a unity, but a unity of many individuals, institutions, and goals, it is necessary that the good of all these parts of society be ordered and maintained. *The good of all these parts of society can only be conceived as their good with respect to one another.*

Weighing the good of each part of society in relation to the good of the other parts of society is justice. Justice is a comparing, balancing, and harmonizing of different claims in relation to one another to maintain a right unity of society. The creating of justice in society is especially the task of *politics.*

The task of politics is threatened by both anti-religious individualism and hyper-religious communalism. An extremely individualistic society, like the United States, fails to give adequate acknowledgment to that experience of common unity which the political concern for justice presupposes. (Hence, in the United States, there is too much concern for individual rights and not enough for social justice.) On the other hand, an exaggerated emphasis on religion and the principle of unity ("love") can lead to the disparagement of justice and the need to maintain the integrity of society's constituent parts with respect to one another. In any society, love and justice should be distinguished. Therefore, religion and politics must make separate, though equally necessary, contributions to the social good.

Now, what is justice? The first thing to say is that justice is *no one thing.* There are several kinds of justice, and the observance of each kind of justice is equally necessary. Just as there is a rationalistic universalizing which reduces the unity of society to a part of that unity, and thus homogenizes the rest of life, so there is a rationalistic politics which reduces the justice of society to one kind of justice, and thereby overlooks many other just claims. For example, there is a totalitarian democracy which reduces all justice to *equality* (one kind of justice) and overlooks the just claims of excellence and order. Justice requires, therefore, that there be a just balancing and equitable harmonizing of the several different kinds of just claims.

These several kinds of justice cannot be subsumed under a single rational type. Each kind of justice expresses an ultimate social value, so that conflicts among the different kinds of just claims cannot be resolved by reasoning from a more general concept of justice (to which these claims could be reduced in order to be mathematically solved). Conflicts among kinds of justice cannot be resolved by science, for scientific thinking deals only with *terms* that can be related *as the same type*. Conflict among different kinds of just claims requires a harmonizing, or compromising, through a political *act*. Politics, therefore, is an *art*. The attempt to make politics scientific shows a misconception of all just claims as claims of one single kind.

Politics cannot be scientific because there are at least six different kinds of just claims, or ultimate values. Here is a brief description of each one.

The Justice of Proportionate Recompense

First, there is justice in a society where there is proportionate recompense for social contributions, and there is injustice where there is not. Workers should be justly paid. Karl Marx, for example, did not argue that poverty *per se* was unjust, but argued that workers are not justly paid for their labor and, therefore, provide more than their share of labor and taxes in proportion to the remuneration and services they receive. Workers are exploited wherever they are not proportionately recompensed.

The Justice of Consistent Application

Second, there is justice in a society where there is consistent application (or extrapolation) of the law, and injustice where there is not. For example, no matter how we feel about the draft, we can see that the draft laws are unjust if they are not or cannot be consistently applied to all persons. The same rule also holds for abortion laws. No matter how we feel about abortion, we see that a law opposing abortion must be consistently applied; and if an abortion law can only be enforced among the poor, then it is unjust. Moreover, an entire legal system may be unjust if it does not apply the law in a consistent way.

The Justice of Common Equality

Third, there is justice in a society where there is the acknowledgment of common equality. Insofar as things are ours in common, then we have a right to equal access or use of these things. A society is just which enforces this equality and is unjust when it does not. For example, if a swimming pool is paid for by municipal taxes, then it is common property for all citizens of that city and they have a right to equal access. Again, since life (in the basic sense) is common to us all, a society should seek to provide equal access to medical facilities for all citizens, and should not discriminate in favor of any particular group. Finally, and most importantly, since the law of a society is preeminently common, a society must provide equal access to the law and the courts for all its citizens.

The Justice of Proper Order

Fourth, there is justice when a society maintains the integrity and proper order of its constituent groups. For example, it is just for a society to affirm the integrity of the family and to protect the privacy of the family's place, time, and functions. The family is part of the proper order of any just society. In the same way, it is just for a society to defend the right of doctors to make medical decisions, and of law courts to settle legal issues. Only if various functions are performed within their proper groups and at their proper times is there due order in a society. It is therefore, unjust for the police to engage in politics or for the state to set itself up as a church. Such things are unjust because they violate the proper order of society.

The Justice of Honoring Justice

Fifth, there is the justice of honoring justice. When, for example, a person does not honor a judicial citation, then he dishonors justice and is in *contempt* of court. Or if citizens in the society generally disrespect the demands of justice, then that society is in contempt of justice itself and is an unjust society. A just society, or a just person, strives to honor justice by seeking to act justly in all that is done. It is by this seeking to do justice in all things that we honor Justice Itself.

The Justice of Full and Fair Deliberation

Sixth, there is justice in society only if issues of justice are decided by full and fair deliberation. Hence, the just punishment, or proportionate recompense, for a crime must be decided in a just way, that is, by full and fair deliberation. Again, what constitutes the proper order of a society, or how our common equality is weighed against other just claims, must be decided through a process of deliberation that is full and fair. The justice of a society is just only if it is justly judged to be justice. Justice must be decided justly. This explains why even the best intentioned protest groups or world minorities cannot *justly* decide what social justice is. Those groups, including the church, represent only a small part of society; and the just determination of justice requires the full and fair deliberation of questions by society as a *whole* or through its just representatives. Unless a society's justice is decided by its legislatures, courts, and politics—rather than by its prophets—that society is unjust. Prophets may be right; but it is not just to decide justice by doing what prophets say.

How, then, is this full and fair deliberation institutionalized in society? The answer is: *through politics.* But what does this mean? And how is it to come about?

Let us begin by noting an important fact: the creation of justice in society can only come about by a process of full and fair deliberation about the conflicts among the varying claims of justice in every situation. Conflicts over justice in society are not about what is right and what is wrong. Rather, these conflicts are over one thing which is right and another thing which is right. The conflict over abortion laws, for example, is a conflict over whether the right of a woman to control her body and its issue is greater than the right of the fetus to life. It is a conflict not between right and wrong, but between two kinds of just claims. From one point of view, it is just for a woman to control her body and unjust to prevent it; from the other point of view, it is just for the fetus to live, and unjust to prevent this. So *two* kinds of justice and *two* kinds of injustice are at stake.

In this situation, full deliberation requires that advocates of *both* kinds of just claims have a fair share in shaping the final decision. Ideally, one seeks some way to harmonize both claims without detriment to either. Where this is not fully possible, one must balance out the various claims by accepting a degree of injustice for the sake of maximizing justice in the total situation.

The sole justification for accepting any injustice is that it is the only available means for attaining a specific justice which is greater. Injustice is not acceptable on any other account.

The theological question which is crucial to politics, that is, to the task of creating justice in society, concerns eschatology. There are two sets of questions in this regard. First, should we anticipate that a fully just universal society can be created in human history, or should we anticipate that human propensity for evil is ineradicable? Second, should we anticipate that, were there a perfectly just society, the task of politics would pass away? We shall deal with both these questions, since both are important to our exercise of political responsibility today.

The faith and the prayer of the Bible is that the kingdom of God (a reign of perfect justice) will be established *on earth*. Where this faith is lacking, politics is seen as having primarily a negative function: the restraint of evil and sin, (for examples, refer to Augustine, Luther, and John Stuart Mill). Where the purpose of politics or the law is seen as the restraint of evil and sin, the argument follows that we must accept injustice as part of the human condition rather than as the specific temporary cost of attaining a more perfect world. Where evil is postulated as inevitable, injustice does not require specific justification. In such cases politics is separated from its eschatological vocation: the creation of the kingdom of God on earth.

In the failure of Christianity to maintain its faith in the kingdom of God on earth, communism has taken up this theme and rediscovered the true function of politics: to create a more just world. Communism recognizes what the churches have denied: that the universe is open to human action such that no possibility for perfection can be regarded *a priori* as closed. On this view, every situation is open to *eschatological fulfillment* and, therefore, the eventual perfectability of every situation is a real possibility no matter how difficult it may be to realize that possibility.

Faith in the possibility of the kingdom of God on earth gives politics a creative and world-transforming function. It adds to the political task of balancing actual justice against injustice a second task, namely, the creation of *new possibilities for action* in the future. Faith in the kingdom of God on earth is a way of affirming that not merely new actual situations can be created, but also *new possibilities* for action. Freedom, like faith, transcends the realm of reason and existing possibilities; freedom, like faith, creates new possibilities: it reaches beyond the present to what utterly transcends our imagination of what is possible. The Kingdom of God on earth exceeds all that can be imagined as possible, but it does not exceed the power of freedom, for freedom creates new possibilities to imagine.

This concept has a practical application for politics. It means that, in every situation, we should not simply aim at balancing and compromising just claims, but also should aim at the creation of new situations within which competitive just claims may be harmonized rather than compromised. The vision of a better society— an analogy to the kingdom of God—is the vision of a new social arrangement where competing just claims can be harmonized without compromise. The vision of the kingdom of God is the general faith about the possibility of *creating* new possibilities for *resolving* just claims more harmoniously.

An eschatological politics aims in all its decisions at two things: to create the most possible actual justice, and also to create the most possibilities for creating more actual justice at a future time. Various rules for such an eschatological politics can be enunciated, for example, the choice which creates more future options is preferable to the choice which closes off future options, and the maintenance of just procedures for deciding takes precedence over any just claim in the present. Such rules for eschatological politics articulate its two-fold goal: to create a more just world today and also to create a future world in which there are more possibilities for creating justice than there are today.

With the above considerations, we have implicitly answered the second of our questions: would politics (or the state) wither away should a perfectly just society be established on earth? The answer explicity is no. The reason is that even in a perfect society there are multiple claims of justice that can compete with one another and which, therefore, must be harmonized and ordered. Society, even a just society, contains many different value-claims.

The unification of these value-claims is a creative moral activity which requires the envisioning of ever new possibilities for harmonizing and developing the social good. An undifferentiated, limited society may be perfectly just, but so may a differentiated, universal world society. Justice-creation is not merely the balancing of good against evil, but is the creation of evermore developed patterns of social cooperation and productive good. This is why politics, as a human activity, will never be absent from even the most perfect world.

To summarize: (a) the tasks of religion and politics are different; the one creates social unity, the other social justice; (b) there are several kinds of justice and, therefore, politics is not a science, but an art or practical activity which seeks to balance many kinds of claims; (c) the concept of the kingdom of God (or an equivalent symbol) is needed to orient politics to its eschatological responsibilities to create new *possible situations* for creating more actual justice in the world; and, (d) because its essential function is to create greater social harmony, cooperation, and productive good rather than merely to restrain evil, politics will always be necessary, even in a perfectly just world.

III

Science maintains and increases human freedom. The goal of premodern science was simply to increase human knowledge and satisfy man's sheer desire to know (*theoria*). But modern science has a pragmatic goal. Modern science aims at increasing our knowledge of the *principles* of action so that we may both (a) know how to act in order to attain a desired end, and (b) know the full consequences of our action in order that the result we intend will be the result we actually attain. We must know both of these things in order to be free; we must know both the right *rules* of action and the full *consequences* of action. A science that concentrates on one of these, without attending to the other, is not a true science. Science, like justice, cannot be reduced to a single principle. One must pursue both functions of science and strive to keep both in balance.

The contribution of science to society is to increase human freedom. But what is freedom? Freedom is a capacity to act such that one can control one's future situation or actually affect the world so that things become congruent with one's desires. Freedom is not a mere spontaneity of willing, or mere willing what one wants. Freedom is rather the capacity to act such that one can control one's future. If one cannot control one's future, one cannot be said to be free even if one is filled with a sense of inner freedom or is always acting in a totally spontaneous way. These two things are part of freedom, but they do not define what it essentially is. Freedom is man's capacity to control his future through his own activities. It has an objective, and not just a subjective, character.

There are "rules of action" one must follow if one wishes to act freely. These are presuppositional rules for *every* action which is free, such as consistency, goal-seeking, truth-telling, knowing and choosing all the consequences of one's action, and persevering in action. If any one of these rules of action is broken, one cannot be free; for only by acting in such ways can one control one's future.

Science increases our knowledge of the rules of action with respect to specific goals and specific situations. It helps us ascertain, for example, how specific chemicals react with one another so that we can better use them to achieve specific goals. In this way, science increases our freedom. Or, science helps us understand the psychological principles by which people read so that we can better teach reading. Or, it helps us understand how money supply affects economic productivity so that we can better control the economic system. In all these ways, science contributes to the moral good of increasing human freedom.

This concern with freedom rather than with sheer knowing is important in modern science's *pragmatic* conception of truth. Pragmatic modern science like classical theoretical science, seeks knowledge. But the kind of knowledge it seeks is a knowledge not merely of constant conjunction of events, but of their very operative mechanisms. This pragmatic knowledge is expressed, therefore, as scientific rules that can be read as instructions about operations to be performed in order to permit or impede any given effect. We may call such instructions "laws of nature" rather than "rules of action" only if we keep in mind the difference in verifying procedures between assertions that intend to be understood as instructions, and those to be understood as descriptions.

There is, too, a difference in experimental attitude between the theoretical and pragmatic approaches. The model of the pre-modern theoretical experiment was to "stand outside" the natural process, observing it and allowing it to run its course. The goal was to be able to predict this course. The model of the modern pragmatic experiment, on the other hand, *requires* that the scientist interfere with the natural process at some point, manipulating it in order to gain a knowledge of the mechanisms that cause or prevent a particular outcome from taking place. The goal of modern science is operational effectiveness. This is why modern science increases human freedom. What this means is that pragmatic science pre-supposes that we go to nature with specific goals in mind and seek the mechanism for attaining these goals.

Modern science presupposes that man is within nature, seeking to steer and control it. Pre-modern science, on the other hand, took the outsider's point of view on nature and sought merely to understand it. For this reason, pre-modern science did not formulate its knowledge of nature as rules of action ("instructions") which, if followed, would increase human freedom. But this increase of human freedom is precisely the goal of modern science and explains its moral value to us.

There is, however, a second function of science that is essential to its purpose of increasing human freedom: the gaining of ever-fuller knowledge of the consequences of our acts. If we do not know the consequences of our acts, we are not free, since we cannot control future situations through our acts. To be free we must not only intend a future goal and act to attain it, but the action must be appropriate to the attainment of the specific goal intended; and the action must not effect *other* consequences that contradict our intended goal. But this can be the case only if we fully understand and choose all the consequences of our acts. For example, if we intend to raise the world's standard of living by concentrating on the exploitation of fossil fuels, we will achieve a short term success, but fail in the long run. The full consequences of our action, in this case, would prevent us from attaining our goal. Or, again, if we employ an antibiotic to kill a bacteria, but actually introduce a factor that develops a stronger bacterial strain, then the full consequence of our act may be counterproductive. An act can be truly productive, that is, truly free, only to the extent that *all* the consequences of the act (and not merely the specific short-term results) are known and chosen.

Of course we never know all the future consequences of any single act, nor do we know all the factors in a present situation. But there are degrees of knowledge of both the rules and consequences of every act, and to the extent that this knowledge controls our choices we are capable of controlling our future situation and are, therefore, free. The purpose of science is to increase our capacity to act freely by increasing our knowledge of these two factors. A knowledge of both these factors is necessary to human freedom; a concentration on either one at the expense of the other not only does not increase our freedom, but actually deprives us of it.

Let us consider the situation today, where we expend great effort and funds to increase knowledge of the rules of action, but little effort and funds in knowing their consequences. What happens is that we have come into possession of great new powers to act, but lack a knowledge of the full consequences of these new acts we can perform. To use our new powers, therefore, does not increase our freedom. It allows us to do dramatic and exciting things, but that these things will actually effect what we seek to achieve is not something that we *know*. We hope they will; but more often our acts merely change our situation so that we are confronted with some new problem of similar magnitude. Some argue that this only shows there is no human progress, especially no increase of freedom. They say that science merely replaces one problem with another problem. Others suggest that science is not responsible for choosing ends (consequences), but only means (rules of action). If things do not work out well, it is politics, not science, that is to blame. But these judgments presume that science should concentrate primarily on the rules of human action: they assume that a science which merely increases human *power*, is normative science.

A science that concentrates simply on the "how to" and

which, therefore, merely increases human power is not true science. It is mere technique, and mere technique cannot increase human freedom. Technique cannot increase human freedom because it does not increase our knowledge of the consequences of our actions, and because it causes our acts to become increasingly *irrational*. A science that concentrates on this one aspect of the scientific task gives us increased power to act, but generates a social process wherein we merely replace one problem with another problem. So today we are on a treadmill, seeking increased power to effect short-term results, although the results themselves become problems for which we will seek ever more power.

Classical science was disproportionately theoretical, that is, overly concerned with *prediction* and knowledge of the future consequences of acts. Classical science did not give sufficient attention to the pragmatic rules which give human beings the power to effectively change their situation. But modern science is disproportionately pragmatic and technological, that is, overly concerned with formulating rules for action that will be effective in changing our situation. Classical science aimed at pure *knowledge*: modern science aims at augmenting man's *power*. But true science must have as its goal and its work the increase of human *freedom*.

The increase of human freedom is a moral good, both personal and social. Human freedom is different from knowledge and power. It is our capacity to be responsible for our lives and responsive to our world and other people. It is the way we grow and perfect ourselves, coming finally into a direct and freely chosen relation to God, our Father. Without freedom we remain irresponsible, unresponsive, unable to grow, unable to act with political creativity, and cut off from the visible universal divine-human family. True science helps us increase our freedom. This is the essential contribution of science to society.

To summarize: (a) true science seeks to increase human freedom, to perfect our capacity to control our future situation; (b) the two tasks of science are to increase our knowledge of the rules of effective action and to increase our knowledge of the implications and consequences of our acts; (c) a science that does not keep these two tasks in balance not only does not increase human freedom, but can actually diminish human freedom by creating a more and more irrational world; and, (d) modern science, dominated by a preoccupation with rules for our effective action (technique), increases human power but not human freedom and is a threat to society at large. Science must rediscover its moral purpose and institutionally restructure itself to serve that purpose.

IV

To this point, the discussion has focussed on the essential contributions of religion, politics, and science to society, but not on their relation to one another. The argument above clearly implies that not only does society need the particular good which each of these three provides, but that each one needs the others. Therefore, no one of these three should be reduced to one of the others. When, for example, religion is confused with politics or politics with science, not only is society-at-large injured, but these distinctive institutions also become distorted. For example, science becomes politicized or religion becomes nationalistic.

In the larger sense, this problem can be conceived as the reduction of one value to another. When, for example, a hyper-religionist argues that we will have a good society if people will simply *love* one another, he is *reducing* justice to unity and confusing religion with politics. Or, when someone argues that we can develop a rational view of the world and make faith completely unnecessary, he is reducing unity to freedom and confusing science with religion.

Every human society includes more institutional orders than the three discussed in this essay. For example, the family, business, the arts, and the communications media all make contributions no less essential than science, politics, and religion. But, within the parameters of this essay, we can distinguish *six* confusing reductions common today—any one of which threatens the integrity of human life.

The Reduction of Politics to Religion

The traditional form of this reduction is the identification of justice with love, arguing that since all men are one, we should regard the differences among them and their behaviors as irrelevant. This confusion leads to a misuse of the law to promote commonality rather than to protect and weigh differences. Today where politics is reduced to religion, all justice is reduced to the justice of equality. In fact, within this reduction, people do not want justice; they want *love* (pietism) or *brotherhood* (secular nationalism). The danger of this reduction is that the *ultimacy* of human *difference* (and the variety of gifts and vocations) will be disparaged, and that efforts to create true justice will be despised as "rationalistic" and "calculating." In America, the most recent attempt to reduce politics to religion is Robert Bellah's *American Civil Religion.*

The Reduction of Religion to Politics

This reduction occurs when the need to *create* social unity, and especially a society that is universal and embracing the whole human race, is neglected, and religion takes as its primary task the creation of social justice. Theologically, this is the confusion of love with justice; and the Jewish and Calvinist traditions have been most prone to this error in the West. Both of these traditions have defended anti-universalism by arguing that justice is a higher value than unity. So, for example, Calvin replies to Sadoleto's charge that he is destroying the unity of Catholic society by replying that justice is more important than unity, and that creating social justice rather than creating social unity is the essential work of religion. The problem with this view is that it becomes a way of *excluding* those who do not act according to your society's conception of justice. This destroys the possibility of true politics. True politics arises only where your social group includes people who disagree with your conception of what is *just*. The contribution of religion to politics is to insure that the social unit includes people and groups whose conception of justice in particular cases differs from your own. To reduce religion to politics, or subordinate the value of social unity to social justice, generates exclusivist partitions in society. It is, for example, not by chance that racism has been a special problem in societies where this reduction has taken place.

The Reduction of Politics to Science

This reduction takes place whenever the task of politics is seen to be the creation of a single social order within which there will be no more value conflict or conflict among different kinds of justice. The presupposition of a "scientific politics" is the reduction of differing value- and justice-claims to claims of a single type, so that all conflicts can be resolved scientifically by an impersonal cost-benefit analysis. But even in a perfect society there will be multiple value- and justice-claims that cannot be harmonized by scientific technique. The harmonization, or balancing out, of value- and justice-claims is always an act that requires not the mere application of a rule, but the employment of a political process that aims at the creation of a new legislation, or a new social order, within which plural and divergent value-claims can be co-affirmed in a just and maximally harmonious way.

Politics presupposes difference and value conflict (which is not the same as *personal* conflict). It therefore assumes that *no* situation is like any other and that no conflict can be resolved according to a pre-existing rule. Science, on the other hand, presupposes that every situation is essentially like every other, and that all value conflicts are to be resolved by the application of a preexisting rule. This explains why the modern reduction of politics to science is institutionalized as *bureaucracy,* and the bureaucratic method of dealing with persons and situations. It explains, too, why people who reduce politics to science tend to believe that, in a perfectly scientific world, politics and the state will pass away. This is the view of communism, though the ideal of "scientific politics" is also well developed in America today.

The Reduction of Science to Politics

This reduction occurs whenever science is conceived to be not rational knowing and acting, but creative legislation, or even "artistic insight." There is literature on the market today, for example, Watson's *Double Helix*, which suggests that scientific activity is essentially a poetic harmonizing and creative balancing of conflict factors. In this view, the scientist is essentially an artist arranging nature.

It is, of course, the case that the *psychological processes* of working scientists are contingent, subjectively creative, and even analogous to political or poetic activity. Nevertheless, science does not create or legislate the nature of the world, as politics does. Rather, science discovers truth that is rooted in reality. Scientific truth has an objectivity and permanence about it that political legislation does not. Unless we see this, we will not understand how science can increase human freedom by increasing this knowledge of, and ability to live within, objective reality. Unless scientists see this, they will not understand the moral purpose of science in human life.

Science is neither simple human desire to know or human desire to create, be poetic, or play. Whenever scientific knowing is confused with political or poetic creating, the scientist misunderstands his essential dignity and role, and society at large is injured. It is, therefore, understandable that American scientists, so many of whom are employed primarily to increase military power or corporate profits, might find it consoling to advert to a poetic-subjectionistic conception of their discipline, rather than keeping foremost in their minds the true function of science: to increase human freedom.

The Reduction of Science to Religion

Whenever science takes as its goal the building of a metaphysical community rather than the increasing of human freedom, it is confused about its true goal. It is not uncommon today that science has become a faith, and a crusading faith at that. There is a dogmatism in some scientists that is similar to the worst medieval dogmatism. This occurs whenever the attempt is made to construct a "scientific world view," a world view whose negative function is to deny the possibility of events or human actions that are not susceptible to scientific examination. To identify science with a unified world view in this way actually leads to its becoming the enemy of human variety and freedom. Good current examples of such an efforts to make a religion of science are B. F. Skinner's *Beyond Freedom and Dignity* and *Walden Two*.

The Reduction of Religion to Science

Whenever a personal Creator God is denied, and whenever faith is reduced to reason and prayer to morality, we lose the transcendent dimension of life. Then religion is reduced to science and the potentialities of man are reduced to those he can attain in space-time by his own freedom. In this way, religion is lost, and the whole dimensions of grace and providence, which themselves *suggest* the possibility that man has a *supernatural destiny* beyond space-and-time, are given up. Much of modern Protestantism, especially Unitarianism, is guilty of this reduction.

In summary: we have considered the social consequences of the reduction of either science or politics or religion to something other than itself. Each of these institutions has a proper contribution to make to society, and so each must respect the integrity and right of the other institutions to play their own proper roles. Of course, society is a system, and these institutional activities must be coordinated; but they are all equally essential and must all be respected and maintained. Moreover, other institutions—especially the family, business, the arts, and the communications media—have their distinctive and equally important contributions to make to society. The principles enumerated above are also applicable to them. That this paper's scope does not include room for these other institutional spheres does not mean that they are less urgent matters of our concern.

V

In this paper, we have been interested in describing the contributions of religion, politics, and science to society, therefore, there has been no discussion of those dimensions of life that utterly transcend space and time. It would be a serious omission not to mention this supernatural and superhistorical world. True religion not only functions to unify society, but also testifies to that God who is Spirit and who has made us for eternal life in Him. In this way, true religion reminds us that the end of man is not only our life in history, but our life beyond history. This belief has important *political* consequences, for it is the principle on which we base our assertion that life in the state—or in any other historical society—cannot fully encompass the whole good of man.

When this fact is acknowledged, then it is seen that politics also has a superhistorical referent. True justice requires that the spiritual destiny of man be acknowledged and provided for. This means that the state must guarantee time, space, and property dedicated to the service of transcendent purposes. For example, it must maintain within the political calendar a Sabbath Day, a day of rest from temporal labors that allows, positively, an occasion when persons may be free for God alone.

God is that reality which transcends historical society and natural spaces. And God has created us for everlasting life with Him. Hence, human beings are immortal souls. Their hearts are restless not only for His kingdom on earth, but also for life with Him in Heaven. Our hearts are filled with eternity, even while we also live here in history. In our every temporal activity—religion, politics, science, art, communication—we reach *through* what we are doing towards our eternal goal. Hence, God is the principle and finality of every aspect of our lives. God is equally close to art, science, and politics as He is to religion. The whole of creation, and not just the church, must testify to the glory of God. This means that, in the final analysis, the values of unity, justice, and freedom stand in relation to another value: *Spirit.* Spirit is not to be reduced to any of these. This means, too, that the final goal of man is not universality, but supernaturality. Not catholicity, but holiness is the higher destiny of man.

One might, at this point, undertake an analysis of the multiple factors in true spirituality just as we have already discussed the multiple factors in true religion, politics, and science. But, it is sufficient here merely to enumerate them: mystical indwelling, universality of identification and identity, living from eternity, and imitating in all things Jesus Christ. These are, from another point of view, the oneness, holiness, catholicity, and apostolicity of the Creed. True spirituality forms all these virtues in us and keeps them in balance. When this occurs, human unity, justice, and freedom are ordered to their chief and proper end. What is this chief end of man? To glorify God, who is our eternal happiness.

14

THE EUROPEAN EXPERIENCE
OF NATURE

ALISTAIR C. CROMBIE

There is a story, perhaps well known but one which I heard only recently, about the great Japanese admiral Isoroku Yamamoto. He had to summon before him a good but careless young officer guilty of some misdeed. Instead of the expected reprimand, the young man found himself invited to sit down. He did so, and immediately sprang up again. The admiral had placed a number of drawing pins pointed upwards under the cover of the chair. He dismissed the officer with the single comment: You have had a useful experience of the element of risk and fantasy present in every situation.

The characteristically Western tradition of rational science and philosophy can be dated from the ancient Greek commitment to the resolution of questions by argument and evidence, as distinct from custom, edict, authority, revelation, or some other source. The Greek philosophers and mathematicians at the same time committed the Western tradition to the belief that, among many possible worlds, the world that exists is a world of exclusively self-consistent and discoverable rationality. These rational commitments have been applied formally as much to decisions about moral values and principles showing what ought or ought not to be done, as to the decisions of science about what is or is not the case. Aristotle meant his ethics to be derived as systematically from a theory of human nature as his physics was from a theory of matter and causation. It was the generation of Galileo and Descartes who finally clarified and defined science as a mode of rational thinking in the modern world and who gave it a recognizable and enduring identity in relation to other fields of inquiry and decision. The act of definition required first a restriction, the delimitation of the questions as well as of the answers to be admitted. The questions had to be answerable by acceptable means, eventually if not immediately. Later came the expansion of this initial restriction to such exclusively answerable questions, into all realms of experience and thought. The first half of the seventeenth century is a genuine turning-point in the potentialities of Western culture, throwing light on what came both before and after. Since then a scientific community has come into existence with conditions of education and communication providing for both agreement and disagreement by a specific kind of rationality. How does this bear on moral values?

The purpose of this brief contribution is to introduce some examples, if not of risk and fantasy, at least like the drawing pins meriting attention, in this relation between beliefs about existence and beliefs about values. By treating the European experience of nature historically, as a kind of intellectual anthropology, we may look back to the origins of our culture, and relate this to the diverse experiences of different societies the common problems of mankind. The modern West on its part, has not only brought to other societies its science, medicine and technology, it has brought about the confrontation of our time: to determine the meaning men give to existence as a whole and to life, with its decisions and diseases.

An obvious characteristic of the Western scientific tradition is that, from the beginning, it was a moral enterprise as much as a means of solving physical problems. This has had a profound effect on the specific character of Western science. Plato saw rational philosophy as the progress of knowledge from the material particulars of physics through mathematics to the eternal truths and laws which, while abstracted from all matter, provided the model and reason for its behavior. These truths were highly charged with moral values, such as proportion, harmony and fitness, for example in the perfection of the circle which dominated ancient cosmology. The world was a work of art. Plato's scheme of education sought to lead the mind of the virtuous youth up through these stages to the contemplation of the true harmony of existence, which fortified and sustained the human endeavor, and towards the harmony of the soul and of society. This Platonic goal of education was widely used to justify the systematic introduction of mathematics into schools and universities in sixteenth-century Europe. The Italian Platonists and the Jesuits, especially, gave mathematics this moral role in their educational policy, seeing its certain demonstrations also as refutations of then current skepticism, and its applications as essential for the practical arts. Mathematically-minded Platonists and Jesuits were to be the principal educators of Galileo and Descartes.

The consequences of this view of nature as both a deductive system and a moral order have appeared most dramatically when it has encountered other sources of cosmology in the widest sense. Historians have seen the deepest consequences both for scientific thinking itself and for the potentialities of science in Western culture in encounters at the level of theology. Aristotle's theory of the world as a necessary and eternal emanation from the First Cause carried with it the powerful belief that men could discover not only how the world was constructed, but also the necessary reasons derived from the First Cause, why it must be so and was best so. When this doctrine was famously condemned in 1277 in Paris, the theologians responsible acted, not out of any special interest in science or philosophy, but to defend the Christian (and Hebrew) doctrine of God's absolute, omnipotent freedom as creator of the world. God's reasons were hidden from men except insofar as he himself had revealed them either by word or by the discoverable, providential design of his creation. Creation as the realm of secondary causes was open to human science but its ultimate cause was not. Theology, so to speak, secularized the world. At this time something like the modern conception of "laws of nature" appeared, for example in optics, as distinct from "natural law" as developed by the Stoics which had overtones of moral justice. It has been argued that the effect of this defense of divine freedom was to make natural philosophers free to explore hypothetically the possible

worlds God might have created. Following this paradoxical liberation
there was, in fact, a burst of speculation, putting the Earth rather
than the heavens in motion and postulating infinite space containing
other worlds like our own; and the principles of 1277 were later
cited in defense of Galileo.

Moral tension in one form or another, sacred or profane,
has remained an enduring feature of Western intellectual culture.
It must accompany any framework that gives meaning to existence
and values. Perhaps without it any society would disintegrate into
meaningless boredom. Clearly the tension has not involved only
science, but the emergence of science as a rational norm in the
Western search for universally and exclusively true principles in all
regions of thought, has made it a notable source of conflicting
certitudes. The medieval issues were parallelled in the public
controversies and private thoughts that have made Galileo, beginning in his own lifetime, an historical symbol of the conflict of
loyalties that can take place both internally, within the minds of
individuals, and externally, in the relation of free inquiry to the
habits of society and its institutions. Galileo assumed that freedom
to find and state the truth was an established right with precedence
in all policy, and in the long run essential for good policy. "In the
matter of introducing novelties," the words he wrote during his last
Copernican dispute have an obvious application to many later
situations:

> Who doubts that the novelty just introduced, of wanting minds
> created free by God to become slaves to the will of others, is
> going to give birth to very grave scandals? And that to want
> other people to deny their own senses and to prefer to them
> the judgment of others, and to allow people utterly ignorant of
> a science or an art to become judges over intelligent men and
> to have power to turn them round at their will by virtue of the
> authority granted to them—these are the novelties with power
> to ruin republics and overthrow states. . .Be careful, theolo-
> gians, that, if you want to make the propositions concerning the
> movement and the rest of the Sun and of the Earth a matter of
> faith, you will expose yourselves to the risk of being in need of
> condemning perhaps in the long run as heretical those who
> asserted that the Earth stays at rest and the Sun moves from
> one place to another: I say in the long run, when it has been
> demonstrated by the senses or by necessity that the Earth

moves and the Sun stays fixed. . .[it will will be demonstrated
that] Your doctrines are the new ones that harm, as you
want. . .to force the mind and the senses not to understand and
not to see. . . .With novelties you cause great ruins in religion.[1]

Galileo's assumption of the right to intellectual freedom
and truth represents perhaps the greatest moral contribution of
science to the humane conception of a responsible, rational man.
But this moral conception itself came neither from science nor from
nature. Galileo in fact began to make nature something new in
modern experience by dismissing its fitness and design as a moral
norm. Nature was "deaf and inexorable to our entreaties." With
this change came also a systematic change in that other guide to
the meaning of existence, the view taken of time and history.

Of the great originators of civilizations it seems to have
been the Greeks and Hebrews in the West, and the Chinese in
the East, who mainly found their meaning primarily through history.
By contrast, the Egyptians, Babylonians and the Hindus seem to
have turned to the creation of myths rather than to history. It is
true, of course, that every national historiography has myths
designed to influence attitudes and actions, but these are something
different.

In the West, a profound change in the meaning of history
was brought about eminently by St. Augustine when he rejected
the Greek view of time as an eternal succession of cyclical returns,
and replaced it by the Hebrew view that cosmological and human
history fulfilled in a linear time the providential purpose of the
creation. This conception of the benevolent destiny provided for
responsible man must surely have given an evangelical flavor to
the European sense of mission in science as well as religion.

The mechanistic philosophers, social as well as natural,
geologists and biologists from Descartes to Malthus, Darwin and
beyond, whose thinking dismissed design from time and history,
inevitably gave the mission of science a rather different flavor. If
the order of nature and the order of society were simply successions
through time of states of statistical equilibrium, and something like
this was the whole truth about existence, moral values could be
regarded only with profound frivolity or profound despair.

Modern science has developed its power to solve problems

through its selectivity and through its program of reduction of more and more classes of phenomena to increasingly general theories. In this it has made itself explicitly neutral to all values except truth; the aesthetic qualities of theories must also pass this test. If science, as the truest available account of nature, offers us no moral guidance, where are we to find reasons for restraint? Most of us, as individuals, live by custom, varied more or less rationally. Science can show us, as individuals and as societies, the consequences our actions may have for our well-being or our survival. The risk, alas without fantasy, at which both our environment and ourselves, the whole biological and human ecology, are put by present technological, commercial and political exploitation is only too well known. But what reasons can be offered to restrain the powerful from doing whatever they have power to do for their own selfish advantage, against nature, against rivals, or against the weak? Why should those with the power not feel entitled to exploit all opportunities? It is a bleak question in the present world, in which the so-called developing, weaker societies are no more virtuous in intention than the developed.

    We might look for a way to justify an answer to this very old question in the relation of the fundamental methods of modern science to our understanding of human nature itself. By its program of selection and reduction, science inevitably eliminates all data irrelevant to its current problems and theories, but these may be the most relevant to existence and experience outside a confident scientific scheme. There are many examples of this in the study of perception.

    The scientific understanding of human nature built up from biological, neuropsychological and psychiatric theory inevitably falls into the pattern of any general system, which must logically eliminate from consideration each individual's sense of attention, intention, thinking, anticipation, recognition of principles, decision, responsibility. These are irreducible, yet they belong to our experience.

    Sometimes it seems almost as if in our scientific culture people felt a need to use the discovered regularities of human psychology and psychiatry to deny individual responsibility, to treat all human acts as caused, all sin as sickness, all social injustices as products of the system. Why should we believe this about evidently healthy persons? It lacks a sense of proportion, or even humor. Would we really expect a sophisticated savage, bureaucratic, technological or raw, caught in the act of pollution or aggression, to plead diminished responsibility except as a device to escape full retribution.

It is as if the whole of modern industrial society was in the grip of a vast theory, a reflection of the specific rationality of science, gearing its program of selection and reduction to the competitive acquisition of material advantage and power. It is no accident that rational science and rational power have arisen together in the experience of nature. But must we accept the commitment of our society, whatever the political system, developed or developing, towards this single goal? The specific rationality of science, mirrored in industrial society, has imposed on free men the need to recover and retain the responsible decisions from which the individual is eliminated by faceless organizations. It seems that human life is not all comfortable; it seems that the price of freedom is vigilance. Obsession with power and achievement is only one expression of science, and science is not the only way our culture relates itself to nature and existence. We can modify and multiply our rational choices as long as we are alive.

The most difficult choices are, as always, not simply between good and bad, but between various combinations of good and bad. Science, by liberating mankind from a purely biological existence, focused on food, health, energy, transport and so on, has made these difficult choices part of all practical life, whether in medicine or in industry. How fortunate we are to be able to choose! And how better may I conclude these moral thoughts on truth than by quoting the words addressed by Monkey to his future subjects when he claimed the Kingdom of the Mountain of Flowers and Fruit: "Gentlemen! With one whose word cannot be trusted there is nothing to be done!"[2] This I believe comes from Confucius.

NOTES

1 Galileo Galilei, *Opera*, ed. naz., vii (Firenze: 1897), 540, 541, 544; cf. A. C. Crombie with the collaboration of A. Carugo, *Galileo and Mersenne: Science, Nature and the Senses in the Sixteenth and Early Seventeenth Centuries.*

2 Wu Ch'ēng-ēn, *Monkey*, translated by Arthur Waley (London, Penguin Books Ltd.: 1961), 11; Confucius, *Analects* ii.22.

15

FRONTIERS OF SCIENCE AND TECHNOLOGY

ADAM SCHAFF

We are now living in a period marked by a striking paradox: on the one hand, we are very sanguine about the triumphant advances in science and technology, advances unprecedented both qualitatively and quantitatively, and on the other hand, we are growing more and more skeptical, and even pessimistic, about the social consequences of that trend. In the nineteenth century mankind cherished the hope that rapid advances in science and technology would make human life more and more happy and immune to all disaster. The twentieth century has discovered the sad truth that under certain circumstances this progress abounds in calamities that affect both societies and individuals. Advances in science and technology have obviously escaped human control and have started to operate not only independently of man's will, intentions, and aspirations, but even against them, and have come to threaten the very existence of mankind. To resort to philosophical terminology, we are witnessing the alienation of such products as science and technology. The liberation of atomic energy, which gave men the power of ancient gods, has become an event that hangs over the head of mankind like Damocles' sword. The increased productive power of industry, which makes it possible to satisfy human needs on a scale unprecedented in human history, may use up all of our raw materials, throwing the future of mankind into question. This becomes even more evident if we consider other factors such as the population explosion, the pollution of the natural environment, and the threat of adverse genetic consequences due to the thoughtless abuse of chemicals in the various fields of human life. This syndrome of negative effects of advances in science and technology shows us *limits* of those advances: the point is not to deny the possibilities of a further increase of our knowledge of the universe, but to consider the parameters connected with the *social* consequences of that increased knowledge. What does scientific progress offer to man? What are the relationships between the goals man sets himself when engaging in research, and the real effects of that research in the sphere of social life? These are the questions which delineated the content of the increasingly popular and pessimistic thesis on the *limits* of advances in science and technology.

While I am fully aware of the *social* dimension and meaning of that thesis, I wish to focus my attention on a selected issue which, in my opinion, is becoming the principal, or at least one of the principal, problems of our times, and which is obviously relegated to the peripheries of social consciousness by our psychological defenses because it is socially troubling and very difficult to solve. The problem is the social consequences of following our current microprocessor revolution.

Various elements come, in turn, to the forefront of social consciousness within the syndrome of the adverse social effects of advances in science and technology, depending on the nature of the particular crisis which is becoming more acute at a given moment and its relation to other elements. Today, everyone thinks of the energy crisis because it is present and annoying in our everyday life. That, however, is neither the most profound nor the most important problem on the social scale among those resulting from advances in science and technology. The crisis connected with the approaching triumph of the full automation of production and services certainly penetrates deeper into our social life and is more difficult to solve. It is true that we are still in the initial stage of that process, but it is easy now to see its impact and to foresee its social consequence.

In what does the problem consist?

Advances in micro-electronics and the related miniaturization of instruments used in information processing have led to the invention of microprocessors. Their information power has been growing fantastically: between 1975 and 1978 the information power of one 'chip' (one square centimeter in size) increased from 1 to 100,000 units of information; in 1979 the information power of one chip increased to 250,000 units, and the first 'mega-chip,' with one million bits of information power, is planned for 1981. In this way a microprocessor of the size of a human fingernail will have more information power than the biggest cathode-ray tube computers had a quarter of a century ago, computers which were as big as large rooms. At the same time, the economic costs of producing microprocessors has been decreasing unbelievably: in 1978 it was one thousandth of what it had been in 1975. The process has been momentarily stopped by the creation of monopolies, but this is a transient phenomenon.

The combination of miniaturization, extraordinary increases in information power, and growing economic efficiency caused by the product becoming cheaper and cheaper to produce, has turned microprocessors into extremely efficient, both technologically and economically, elements of progress in the automation of production and services. The technology of automation, known earlier but impracticable because unprofitable, has become profitable now. At the same, time miniaturization has eliminated the problem of the size of the instruments indispensable for automation. Thus, obstacles to automation have been removed, and incentives due to competition on the national and international scale will lead inevitably—as can be seen even now in the growing number of branches of production and services—to full automation in twenty to thirty years, at least in highly industrialized countries. If we consider the implications of that process for the armaments industry we can expect that the last obstacles that might hamper that process will be removed and the industry will spread on a scale that will exceed the differences in political and economic system of the various states and societies.

When the discussion of the future of automation and its social consequences began some thirty years ago, it was still mainly a futurological speculation, which made it possible to adduce argument for and against it. Today the situation is much simpler:

complete automation of production is inevitable, and one can merely quibble about when it will occur, within a margin of ten to twenty years. But, as compared with that period of futurological speculation, the present day witnesses an enormously important change which makes us face new undesirable consequences. In the past it was believed that people who lost employment in the production sector following its automation would find employment in the services sector which, theorists predicted, was supposed to grow both qualitatively and quantitatively, in the post-industrial society. Now these calculations have been cancelled: as our experience to date shows, the service sector is being automated more rapidly than the production sector is, and the process is expected to continue in the foreseeable future. Hence, not only will the service sector not be in a position to absorb former production sector workers, but will add to the army of the unemployed. In other words, the coming automation will be *complete*.

The foreseeable resulting society will be one in which work in the traditional sense of gainful employment will have disappeared. Next to its residual forms there will be creative activity (scientific, artistic, etc.) on a much greater scale than it is observable today. This will be a great achievement of science and technology, ending Jehovah's curse that man will his bread in the sweat of his brow. But this revolution—the most far-reaching social revolution we can imagine—which reopens the gates of paradise to man also implies problems which, if left unsolved, may be much worse than the curse of the Maker who became angry with his creature. The principal problems are the following:

First, how to ensure living for men who no longer work in the traditional sense of the word;

Second, the most essential issue, how to ensure for mankind a new sense of life in lieu of the lost one linked to work;

Third, how to prevent the threatening bureaucratization of social life, with the resulting danger of totalitarianism;

Fourth, how to prevent the tragic consequences bureaucratization can have for the Third World if no adequate measures are taken to prevent it.

As we can see, this is an ominous, if only selective, list of problems and dangers. We shall briefly discuss them in the order that they have been mentioned above. But before we do, we shall say a few words about the causes of the astonishing secrecy in which public opinion veils knowledge of the nature and dimensions of the approaching crisis. This is necessary because otherwise the erroneous belief that all this is a matter of pure speculation may prevail, fed by those interested in having it prevail. This does not change the course of events when it comes to advances in automation, but can delay comprehension of its consequences and the use of possible preventive and therapeutic measures.

In my opinion, the cause of the silence concerning as important a problem as the social consequences of full automation is to be sought in the psychological defense mechanism known as cognitive dissonance. As Leo Festinger claims, if there is a conflict between human beliefs and the facts to which those beliefs pertain, and if facts cannot be adjusted to beliefs, nor the beliefs abandoned because of the threat of ideological bankruptcy, people tend to isolate themselves from the facts, to insulate themselves against the information from the outside that could make them feel uneasy. In such situations we observe what has been experimentally confirmed: a quasi-schizophrenic attitude develops. That is a given individual comprehends a given item of information intellectually, but dismisses it on emotional grounds. This applies not only to individuals, but to entire populations as well. This is exactly what occurs in the case of information concerning the inevitability of full automation in our times and the social implications of that process: for the time being it is still a matter of the future, but it is so disquieting and difficult to solve that we willingly drive it beyond the sphere of our consciousness. The differences in socio-economic systems of the various industrialized states does not play any role here: while in one case the decisive psychological factor is the fear of the need to change the socio-*economic* system, in the other case, that of the socialist countries, it is the fear of the need to change the socio-*political* system, which would have to be transformed as a result of full automation. The phenomenon is thus a supra-systemic one, and the tendency not to notice it is universal. Nevertheless, it is something real and the refusal to see it merely makes matters worse. Let us accordingly examine its adverse implications, in the order in which they were listed earlier.

The first problem is: how people earning their living by work will earn their living when there is no work? Note that what is involved here is not unemployment in the traditional sense, but something new: a society that would *not work* in the present sense of the word.

This embarrassing problem is comparatively the simplest in the syndrome, and also the easiest to solve. Of course, society would not be doomed to starvation in the face of an unprecedented plenty of goods, just because of the sacred law of private property. In view of the threatening revolution of the masses, that law will be abolished or at least restricted by the system of taxation and the planned production and distribution of goods to make it possible to ensure to every individual a historically fixed minimum of means of existence, in accordance with that individual's constitutional right. In the United States, a draft of the appropriate amendment to the Constitution was worked out and submitted by the Center for the Study of Democratic Institutions some twenty years ago, when the victory of complete automation was foreseen. In the language of Marxist theory, changes in productive forces necessitate a change in production relations, as reflected in the property law prevailing in a given period. This is an exemplary verification of classical Marxist theory at the time when people so often and so willingly claim that it has failed as proved by the poor effects obtained in practice in socialist countries. We should not hurry with such verdicts, and, in any case, we should not confuse a negative assessment of a theory with a negative assessment of its faulty applications. However it may be, the advent of complete automation will have to bring about changes in existing property laws and the acceptance, whether we like it or not, of some form of collective economy. This does not mean in the least that we will have to copy patterns that already exist. I do not claim that the process will take place painlessly and without strife, but I do claim that the problem itself is relatively simple, as is also its solution.

The second problem is incomparably more difficult. When gainful work ceases to be necessary, mankind will lose its most common, even if primitive, sense of life that pertains to every individual. For if by "sense of life" we mean primarily the *goal* man sets himself in his life, there is no doubt that gainful work (though not necessarily gainful employment in the technical sense of the term) has for most people determined, of necessity, that fundamental and most common task. All other goals, including the "higher" ones, have been based on that fundamental goal. It is obvious that if the goal vanishes and is not replaced by something equally common and fundamental from the point of view of human life, we will be faced by disaster in the form of decomposing societal life including in its pathology alcoholism, drug-addiction, and crime, even if only motivated by sheer boredom. Let us be not deluded by the fact that people who work creatively—and their number will largely increase—will not experience that shock: for them work has always been creative. The point, accordingly, is to make that a universal phenomenon, to replace, on a *universal* scale, gainful work by *creative* work. This is not to say that we shall force people to become scientists, poets, writers, painters, composers, etc., which would mean frustration and hardships for most people, who lack adequate inclinations and abilities; the point is to find for all some *occupations* in lieu of work, occupations that would be obligatory and would contribute to a given individual's internal and external discipline. These occupations would have to be differentiated so that we could offer every person something of genuine interest to him. This would solve the problem of finding a substitute for that sense of life which has been fundamental so far. The issue is not an easy one, and we should focus our attention on it and use our ingenuity, because the problem has been programmatically disregarded.

And here is an idea in that sphere, fundamental in my opinion: let us revert, under new conditions and with new possibilities and objectives, to Plato's utopian society of people who learn. Of course, we would not confine that to any single social group, but make it universal for society *as a whole*: the obligation to learn until one's old age would be accompanied by the obligation to teach others, either younger ones or those to whom a given field is alien. If society offers every individual the right to the means of material existence, it may, and should, require something in exchange: to learn and to teach others. Of course, societal life would not be confined to that, there would be thousands of other occupations and duties that would animate man by forming his

individual sense of life, but *that* would ensure the sense of life for
all, which is necessary.

Of course, this solution would require a specific and entirely
new program, extending beyond the elementary or secondary school
for children. Working out such a program for people who would
permanently be both students and instructors, a program covering
not only the spheres traditionally contained in school curricula, but
in the whole societal life of individuals, is a gigantic and novel task
not yet undertaken even in a rudimentary form. And time is pressing
as it is limited to the said twenty years. It will be the young people
who first experience the shock of the shrinking labor market. The
point is not to let ourselves be lulled by taking cultural differentiation
into account. There may be other ideas about solving this problem,
the most difficult of all, and we should look for them, but the one
I have outlined seems the simplest and is based on common sense,
which does not make the solution easier and does not absolve us
of the duty of tackling the problem at once.

The third problem carries a specific memento. The abolition
or strict limitation of the right to private property, combined with
the planning of production and distribution of goods on the societal
scale implies the dangerous expansion and consolidation of the
bureaucracy. When the issue of bureaucracy is discussed people
often disregard the fact that bureaucracy, in the sense of an apparatus
run by officials, is indispensable in every advanced society and in
every system. But the domination of society by the bureaucracy is
not a given, even though it tends to occur. Experience in existing
socialist states shows that the elimination of the class composed of
the owners of means of production, inevitably accompanied by an
expansion of the bureaucracy and the growth of its power, increases
the pressure toward domination by the bureaucracy and increases
the threat of totalitarianism. No society is immune to this danger,
even in the new economy: democratic traditions, important as they
are, do not alone suffice to ward off the danger. Hence the point
is to devise institutional countermeasures, which can and should
be differentiated according to existing conditions. This is why I
have emphasized that the problem carries a specific memento as
there is no single recipe for its solution, which is a shortcoming,
but this is also a possible guarantee of the effectiveness of the

solutions to be adopted in various cases. It seems that for the time being it is important, and sufficient, to draw attention to the problem.

Finally, a few words about the implications of the trend toward complete automation for the prospects of the development of the Third World. Even though the problem directly affects the highly industrialized countries, it indirectly involves a special danger for the Third World: the automation of production will undermine the investments now being made in Third World countries because of the cheap labor available there. Automated production is beyond competition regarding labor. Exporting products from the Third World will become much more difficult for the same reason if production there retains its traditional forms; if production is adjusted to the new order, the problem in those countries, already grave unemployment will increase. The point is that the highly industrialized countries are so rich that with collective economies they can easily ensure high living standards for all their inhabitants, but Third World countries cannot. Thus, on one hand, complete automation will add new and tragic problems to those already existing in the Third World, if adequate measures are not taken in time. But, on the other hand, global production will increase so much that it will be possible to extend assistance to the Third World that would be both much greater and of a different kind than that now offered. Of course, there is the good will to do so. Otherwise we would face extremely dangerous complications. But in this case, like in the previous ones, it is better to realize that and to act with an awareness of the situation, than to turn our eyes away from the facts. I mean here not only the highly industrialized countries, but also Third World countries whose representatives, as I know from my own experience, not only develop specific cognitive dissonance mechanisms to protect themselves from information about upsetting prospects for the future, but often, when offered that information, respond to it with unconcealed fury, as if their informant were their enemy. I understand the frustration motivating the fury, but I also know that neither leads to reasonable solutions.

We have been discussing one aspect of science and technology. In my opinion, this aspect is of special importance, and its dimensions and dangers must be understood. We have to understand them above all because we must undertake actions which, by removing the dangers, can turn advances in science and technology into what they essentially are—blessings to mankind.

16

UNIFICATION AND FRACTIONATION IN SCIENCE: SIGNIFICANCE AND PROSPECTS

DUDLEY SHAPERE

Listen: there's a hell of a good universe next door; let's go.
—*e.e.cummings*

I

One of the most striking features of the history of science* is that, despite numerous setbacks along the way, there has been an overall tendency toward the development of a more and more comprehensive unification of the various fields of science. Newton fused terrestrial and planetary motions into a unified theory at the end of the seventeenth century. But it was in the second half of the nineteenth century that unification of scientific fields began in earnest. In spite of the differences between electricity and magnetism (and between various types of electricity) which had been noted by investigators beginning with Gilbert, Faraday was able to provide a unified treatment of those types of phenomena.

---

* Some of the scientific ideas discussed in this paper—particularly in the portions on elementary particle physics and cosmology—are by now outdated, the paper having been written in 1976. However, the more general points I made here remain valid, embodying as they do features which have been characteristic of the scientific approach throughout recent times, and remain so despite the dramatic advances of the past seven years. Since those points, and the features of these scientific cases on

His approach was developed and given a mathematically precise formulation by Maxwell, who was also able to extend it further by incorporating light into the same theory. The study of heat too was assimilated to other areas, partly to the theory of radiation and partly to the theory of the motion of particles. As if in protest against what Einstein called the "profound formal difference" between the nineteenth century's treatment of electromagnetism and light by a continuous (wave) theory on the one hand, and of matter in terms of a discrete particle theory on the other, the twentieth century provided a unification of those domains in the quantum theory. With that theory came, too, an understanding of the periodic table of chemical elements and of the bonding of those elements into larger complexes, as well as of the spectra of chemical substances.

The years between the development of quantum mechanics in the late 1920s and the Second World War were concerned largely with extension rather than with unification of pre-existing areas: the period saw, among other things, the beginnings of understanding of the electromagnetic force (beginnings of quantum electrodynamics), of radioactive decay, and of the nuclear force (Yukawa exchange-particle theory). Postwar physicists generalized these results in a clear recognition that there are three fundamental types of forces important in elementary particle interactions, the electromagnetic, the weak, and the strong. In particular, physicists developed the theory of the electromagnetic force, quantum electrodynamics, into the most successful scientific theory ever devised. (The fourth recognized force, gravitation, is too weak to play any effective role except where large masses are involved.) But the vast number of particles discovered during the postwar period, and the existence of four apparently independent fundamental forces, again

---

which they rest, are important for understanding the scientific enterprise and human knowledge more generally, I have therefore left the article in its original form. There would have been little point in bringing the scientific discussions up to date only to find them again superseded in a few years, unless it could be shown that science has changed so drastically in the past seven years that those features are no longer found in it. And even then, as always, there might be important lessons to learn even from such ancient science as that of the mid–1970s!

awakened the urge toward unification. Regarding the multitude of elementary particles, Gell-Mann and Ne'eman showed that the hadrons (particles interacting via the strong force) fall into well-defined families which are representations of the symmetry group SU(3). A further representation of that group, corresponding to no known particles, constituted a family of three; when appropriate quantum numbers were assigned to the members of this family, it was found that the quantum numbers of all hadrons could be obtained as the result of adding the quantum numbers of this family in pairs (mesons) or triplets (baryons). These "quarks" could therefore be considered to be the constituents of hadrons. More recently still, the addition of further quantum numbers ("charm" and "color") and of a fourth quark, in order to account for the stability of the ψ (or J) particle, has produced the suggestion, at least, of an analogy between hadrons and leptons (particles not participating in the strong interaction): as there are four fundamental leptons (electron, muon, and their respective neutrinos), so also there are now four fundamental hadrons; like the leptons, the quarks appear to be dimensionless points and therefore true candidates for the status of being "fundamental" (that is, with no further internal structure); and the leptons and quarks have the same spin (1/2). The analogy is far from complete: for example, leptons do not combine to form composite structures, as do quarks; further, leptons are observed in experiments, while quarks, if they exist as free particles, seem somehow to evade all attempts to observe them. (The fact that the charges of quarks are fractions of those of leptons may not be a serious disanalogy, as Han and Nambu have shown.) Nevertheless, the analogy is there, and its existence, coupled with increasing experimental success of the four-quark hypothesis, cannot help but suggest some deeper relationship between those particles which interact via the strong force and those which do not.

As regards the four fundamental forces, after enormous obstacles had been overcome, a unification of the electromagnetic and weak interactions is now available (unified gauge theory of Salam and Weinberg), and there is hope of extending that theory to cover the strong interactions. The unified gauge and colored- and charmed-quark theories are bound together, so that the prospect of a giant step in the direction of a unified theory of elementary particles and three of the four fundamental forces now lies before us. (The possibility that there are further forces—and indications are growing that there are at least two others, a "superweak" and a "semistrong" force—could not detract from the significance of such unification as has, hopefully, been achieved, but would only set a challenge for further unification.)

The application of spectroscopy to analysis of chemical composition made it possible—despite Auguste Comte's pronouncement of the impossibility of our ever knowing the composition of the stars—to ascertain that the stars are made of the same substances as are found on earth. The development of an understanding, in terms of quantum theory, of how spectra are produced, together with the theory of elementary particle interactions, has provided an understanding of the processes of stellar evolution, and has, with the further occasional cooperation of the theory of general relativity, led to an understanding of the synthesis, evolution, and relative abundances of the chemical elements. The alliance of general relativity and elementary particle theory, especially when coupled with recent observations, has even made possible reasonably-based theories of the origin of the universe in a "hot big bang."

Thus far I have surveyed some examples of unification in the physical sciences, but I will not omit the biological sciences from this picture. Despite the apparent conflict between Darwinian evolutionary theory and Mendelian genetics at the beginning of the twentieth century, those areas were shown to be consistent by Fisher, Haldane, and Wright; further integration at the hands of Dobzhansky, Rensch, Simpson, Mayr and many others, produced a "Synthetic Theory of Evolution" which was at least consistent with, and to a considerable degree explained evidence from a number of fields which had hitherto seemed incompatible.

Chemical understanding of biological inheritance began to be achieved in detail in the mid-twentieth century, and has begun to penetrate the area of organismic development. The work of Oparin and his successors showed that Darwin had been too pessimistic in forecasting that the origin of life could never be an object of scientific investigation, and numerous mechanisms are now known for the production of at least the basic constituents of self-replicating macromolecules. The study of the animal brain, though still rudimentary, has produced associations of various conscious functions with specific regions of the brain, giving us reason to expect that improved understanding of, for example, human psychology ultimately will come from such investigations. (Except for this remark, I will limit my discussion in this paper to the physical and biological sciences.)

Taken together, the developments I have described provide a broad and coherent picture of the universe and man's place in it. In outline, the picture goes something like this. The universe—at least the one we know—began (or at least had become after a fraction of a second, when our present theories became applicable to it) in a hot (of the order of 10^{12}–10^{13} K) dense (around 10^{14} g/cm^3) soup of elementary particles. From this state, after a few minutes (for which period the detailed calculations that can be made are nothing short of mindboggling), a matter-radiation equilibrium emerged in which the matter consisted of roughly 75 percent hydrogen (protons) and 25 percent helium (alpha particles) by mass. Further cooling enabled electrons, after a few hundred thousand years, to combine with these nuclei, ending the matter-radiation coupling.

At some time a few million years later, inhomogeneities developed in the cloud of matter; these inhomogeneities, or at least those of an appropriate size, collapsed gravitationally to form clusters of galaxies, sub-inhomogeneities (or at least those of an appropriate size) collapsing within the larger inhomogeneities to form galaxies. As the galaxies took shape, stars began to form and evolve within them; under the conditions of high temperature and pressure existing in the interiors of those stars, hydrogen and helium underwent nuclear reactions which produced many of the heavier elements; those stars which ultimately died in violent explosions (and which, in the process of exploding, created further heavy elements) spewed those heavier elements into the interstellar medium, where they became available for the birth of later-generation, heavy-element-enriched stars.

Some proportion of those later-generation stars can be expected to be born with planetary systems; on some of these planets, under favorable circumstances, the production of complex molecules, and ultimately of self-replicating macromolecules, will eventuate in the evolution of higher forms of life. The transmission of hereditary information from generation to generation of these living creatures, as well as the variations in that information which lead to evolutionary changes, and the development and functioning of individual organisms, can be understood in terms of chemical processes and the physical processes which affect and ultimately explain them.

We thus obtain a coherent view of the evolution of the universe and of life in it as a continuous process understandable in terms of the same ultimate laws. Not all of the parts of this picture are equally well-grounded. I am not thinking here of the fact that the "details" of the picture are far from being worked out, or that the picture has yet to be extended to many areas; although the working out of details often produces surprising problems which ultimately upset the grander scheme, the difficulties I am thinking of are known ones which cannot be dismissed as due merely to lack of detailed knowledge. Nor am I thinking of the fact that parts of the picture may ultimately come to be looked on as mere "limiting cases" of some larger theory.

Let me explain the sorts of problems I have in mind by beginning with an example of a difficulty that *can* be considered to be the result of a need to "fill in details." This difficulty concerns the birth of stars from an interstellar medium. Small dark globules and highly localized infrared sources have been observed which are presumably "protostars," stars (or at least stellar "placentas") in the very early stages of birth, fragmenting from a larger cloud of gas and dust and collapsing toward a stage where nuclear reactions will be initiated in their interiors. And certain stars are observed which, there is reason to believe, are only relatively recently born. However, how the protostars uncouple from their environment, and what happens between the observed putative protostar stage and the emergence of the fully-born star is unknown. Though the critical factors can be listed, their precise contributions are uncertain and the problem is highly complex. Nevertheless, there is good reason to believe *that* the general "fragmentation-and-collapse" account of stellar birth is "on the right track," and that it is only the details of *how* this takes place that are not yet understood.

The situation is presumably the same with regard to the

transition from laboratory synthesis of relatively small constituents of DNA (or some presumably primitive analogue) to the production of the giant self-replicating macromolecule itself: the gap is enormous and not yet understood. Here, however, there is a hitch that was not present in the case of the "gap" between protostars and stars: in the case of stars, observational evidence indicates that star formation is relatively widespread and therefore has at least a decent probability of occurrence given a proper interstellar medium and proper conditions which are themselves fairly common. But in the case of the evolution of life from inorganic molecules, we have only one planet to look at—one case in which such evolution has actually occurred. And in the absence of an understanding of a mechanism for evolution from relatively small macromolecules to huge self-replicating ones, we do not know what the probabilities of such an occurrence are. In spite of the overwhelming statistics that astronomers like to throw at us about the probable numbers of planets in the universe having conditions favorable to life (once produced), the probability of nature jumping the gap from chemistry to biology may yet be so low that earth's life may be unique or near-unique in the universe, vast as it is. The "filling in of details" in this case thus has ramifications beyond those of the star-formation gap: there, the probability of gap-jumping—the existence of a mechanism, however little understood, which is widespread in the universe— was not in question; here, it is.

Yet a third level of difficulty, this time by no means reducible to a matter of "filling in details," occurs in the case of the birth of galaxy clusters and galaxies. Luckily for theoreticians, observational evidence (such as the apparent black-body character of the 3° K microwave background radiation) indicates that the universe is, in the large, homogeneous and isotropic, and that such conditions held in the early universe, before galaxies and clusters of galaxies fragmented out. Where, then, did the *in*homogeneities postulated in our picture of the origin of galaxy clusters come from? (The theoretician no longer seems so lucky.) In a universe in which quantum theory holds, fluctuations would arise spontaneously; these *might* be amplified in the relatively dense conditions of the early universe, and inhomogeneities of the proper size (galaxy-cluster-size and galaxy-size) *might* be selected out as ones which would collapse rather than be washed out. But thus far, no good theory of galaxy (or galaxy cluster) formation along these or any other lines has been forthcoming.

However, the situation here is potentially more dangerous than mere lack of a good theory might suggest. Two independent considerations in particular make this so. First: evidence is now very strong that the nuclei of galaxies are regions from which enormous amounts of matter (and energy) are expelled, presumably periodically. Ambartsumian and others have suggested that the expelled matter is the source of new galaxies. The nuclei of the new galaxies might in turn carry the matter-producing capability. (There is even some hint of evidence that some small galaxies may have been ejected from larger ones.) On this view, the collapse theory of galaxy (or galaxy cluster) formation, already burdened with the problem of the origin of appropriately- sized inhomogeneities, would be rejected in favor of a "little-bang" theory of their origin. The second relevant consideration is this: why are clusters of galaxies still in existence if, as the cosmological inhomogeneity theory alleges, they were formed several billion years ago? If they are to have the gravitational stability required for such a long life, the clusters would have to have a certain mass to counterbalance their motions. The observed masses, however, fall short of the minimum required in every specific cluster for which mass-estimates are available, and by factors ranging from five to fifty or more. (Needless to say, estimating the total mass of a cluster of galaxies is a risky business; but could the observational uncertainties be of such a magnitude? And all in the same direction, of underestimation?) Is the missing mass present in "invisible" form—black holes, dead stars and galaxies, for example? There are difficulties with such proposals, and one must remember with soberness that once before when there was a "missing mass" problem (the advance of the perihelion of Mercury), the problem was solved not by finding the missing mass but by revolutionizing physics.

Taken together with the problem of the origin of inhomogeneities, these two considerations cannot but lessen our confidence in the "collapse of cosmological inhomogeneities" part of our picture; they suggest that Ambartsumian's alternative cannot be dismissed out of hand. Indeed, were it not for the black-body character of the microwave background radiation, the observed helium abundance in the universe, and some other difficulties, one might be tempted to reconsider the Steady-State theory, with matter being continually (or at least sporadically) created in galactic nuclei rather than in intergalactic space. Nevertheless, although the history of science has often witnessed supposedly dead theories rise, phoenix-like, from their ashes, the objections against the Steady-State theory seem at present insurmountable; and Ambartsumian's suggestion is too undeveloped to be called a theory. (And how are we supposed to account for the huge amounts of matter and energy somehow produced out of the galactic nuclei? Would it be genuine creation *ex nihilo*? What would then become of the principle of conservation of energy? An alternative that has been suggested—not easy to swallow—is that matter comes through a "white hole" from another universe.) Hence, despite its difficulties, and in view of the slim observational evidence in its favor (distribution of globular clusters and of older stars), the cosmological theory of the origin of galaxies and galaxy clusters remains the best available. (However, that theory may be in for further trouble if small-scale anisotropies in the microwave background radiation continue not to be detected. Such anisotropies would be expected, on the cosmological theory of the origin of galaxy clusters, as relics of the original inhomogeneities.)

In this instance, the nature of the difficulty may be summarized as follows: (1) contrary to the "lack of details" kind of problem, in this case the initial (or relatively early) conditions (the inhomogeneities or their relics) are not observed; (2) it is difficult, in light of other considerations, to see how the appropriate conditions could be realized (how the appropriate inhomogeneities could arise); (3) there are other independent considerations which suggest an alternative possible explanation; and, (4) that alternative, however, is not as palatable as the theory available (in the present case because it has not been developed in detail, and because its development would seem to call for radical revision of other well-grounded ideas, or else for the introduction of radically new ideas for which there is little or no other warrant). This is one type of difficulty that might be classified under the heading of a *fundamental theoretical problem*—as opposed to the star-formation "filling in details" type of difficulty, which appears almost certain to be a *problem of theoretical incompleteness.*

These are far from the only known reasons for hesitancy about the picture I have drawn. One can of course expect a sensible caution about the cosmological portions of the picture, involving as they do such enormous extrapolations; and one can expect a tentative attitude toward the most recent attempts at synthesis. Heisenberg went to his grave opposing the quark theory, and we must remember that quarks are, after all, unobserved; and one would suppose that a scientific theory would have to be very good indeed if it is to maintain that the fundamental postulated entities are unobserv*able.* And as I remarked earlier, the symmetry between quarks and leptons is very incomplete.

But there are also difficulties in parts of the picture that are of longer standing. The strong interaction borders on the intractable; the origin of planetary systems is still shrouded in obscurities; the origin of taxa higher than the species level remains something of an embarrassment for evolutionary theory; the problem of development in biology remains complex and very incompletely solved; and the later stages of stellar evolution are still unclear, as indeed is the ultimate fate of the universe—whether it will go on expanding forever (as seems to be the slightly favored view at present) or will ultimately collapse again to a singularity, and, if so, whether it will "bounce" to produce yet another in a possibly continuous train of successive universes. These and their ilk can perhaps be said to be merely open questions, problems of theoretical incompleteness—matters of detail or extension of present knowledge and theory—rather than fundamental theoretical problems, overt threats to present theory (though some may have larger philosophical ramifications than others).

But there are more serious difficulties too, which, though in some cases they differ significantly in general character from the problem of galaxy cluster formation, deserve to rank with the latter as fundamental theoretical problems, as dark clouds on the horizon of contemporary science.

Whatever happens to our interpretation of quasars, something drastic may well happen to current physics. If quasars are "local"—relatively nearby—then we must account for their very large red shifts in some way other than as indications of great distance—possibly as effects of a large gravitational field (but then why are no other effects of the field observed?), or in terms of some entirely new law (but will that affect our interpretation of other red shifts as indicating an expansion of the universe?). If they are "cosmological"—very far away—we are faced with the problem of explaining energy production that appears to put even nuclear fusion to shame. In particular, if quasars turn out to be related to galactic nuclei (and there are strong indications that they are), then we again face the problem of the origin and nature of galaxies. There are difficulties with either alternative. In every problem in science there is the possibility of the unforeseeable; but in this case, unlike most others, we can as it were see that the unforeseeable is a *significant* possibility.

Again, the failure to detect neutrinos from the sun has cast doubt on our theories of stellar evolution, and some have suggested that it indicates some shortcoming in our grasp of elementary particle interactions. Quantum theory and general relativity remain apart, and years of trying have not produced agreed-upon progress toward their synthesis, or even general agreement as to how to try. For all its success in dealing with phenomena in a wide range of domains, the quantum theory has in the past decade or two been subjected to a revival of controversy as to its interpretation. Is a deterministic hidden-variable theory still feasible? Is precise determination of simultaneous position and momentum of a particle really impossible? One interpretation (Everett-Wheeler "relative state" interpretation) of quantum theory, which has the virtue of consistency if not of initial plausibility, has it that the universe splits into two independent universes on the occasion of every measurement, the two universes corresponding to the alternative possible outcomes of the measurement. Given that, we have flirted in this survey with the possibility of parallel universes, successive universes, and now with possible universes being actualized. The past history of science has time and again produced new ideas that far outstripped prior imagination; speculation about other universes, though still on the border, has entered the domain of science. We must be prepared for the possibility that there are indeed more things in heaven and earth than are dreamt of in our present picture of the universe.

But while we must keep an open mind about possible

radical revisions of the picture of the universe and of life in it which I outlined earlier, we must also recognize that it is generally the picture within which the majority of physicists, chemists, and biologists work today. They work within it not in the sense that they accept it dogmatically, but in the sense that they believe it to be, overall, the picture best supported by present evidence; they believe the present task of science to be the development of the details of that picture, its further extension, and its testing and confrontation with alternative reasonable possibilities, especially those parts of the picture which seem weakest. Much of the picture, indeed, seems unlikely to be rejected: what evidence could reasonably be expected that would lead us to deny, after all, that galaxies are stellar systems far beyond the Milky Way? That dinosaurs existed in the past? That DNA is at least implicated in heredity? And so on, for a multitude of details which form the basis of much of our present picture. It is possible, of course—as philosophers since Descartes have been fond of reminding us—that these and indeed all facets of the picture may ultimately be rejected. But the logical possibility that we may be wrong, though it may be a reason for open-mindedness, is not itself a reason for skepticism or even for timid and indiscriminate caution. (This is the reason why I have emphasized that the difficulties I have been concerned with are *known* difficulties, which are, after all, the only ones we can hope to do something about.) And even in those regions of our picture for which we do have positive reasons for worry, we must not forget that, in the light of the available evidence, one picture may well be better than any of the available alternatives.

One final point in this all-too-sketchy survey of some aspects of the unity of the current scientific picture of the universe: there will be some who will claim that my account is "reductionistic," and who will claim that—for example—biology is *not* "reduced" to chemistry because all details of biological processes are not deducible from the chemistry of those processes. In this vein, since the details of the helium atom are not in general deducible from basic quantum-theoretical considerations as is the case with the hydrogen atom, one might as well say that physics has not been reduced to physics. If this is meant to imply that, to the extent that we cannot make such deductions, we do not have an *understanding* of the helium atom in terms of quantum theory (or of biology in terms of chemistry), then perhaps the fault lies in the deductive interpretation of understanding (or "explanation") which decrees that only deduction produces understanding. We do, after all, have such understanding despite the lack of precise deduction; and a more adequate account of "understanding" should allow for this. No doubt there is much in biology that is not understood in terms of chemistry; perhaps it can never be. But if this turns out to be the case, it will be because of specific aspects of the world, and not because of some prior philosophical structures about what "understanding" (or "explaining") means.

II

In the preceding discussion I argued that, as a result of the evolution of scientific thought, there has emerged a broad and coherent picture of the universe and of life in it, a view which, while incomplete and in some aspects open to serious question, is at present the best picture available. In the present section I will argue that this process of unification has not been restricted to the integration of beliefs about the world, but that there has also been a progressive tendency toward unification of those beliefs with the methods employed to attain well-grounded beliefs. That is, I will argue, the methods we consider appropriate for arriving at well-grounded beliefs about the world have come more and more to be shaped by those very beliefs, and have evolved with the evolution of knowledge.

Such a view of the intimate relation between knowledge and the methods of gaining knowledge flies in the face of the traditional sharp bifurcation of the two. For it is, and long has been, commonly assumed that there exists a unique method, the "scientific" or "empirical" or "experimental" method, allegedly discovered, or at least first systematically applied, in the seventeenth century, which can be formulated wholly independently of, and is wholly unaffected by, the knowledge which is arrived at by its means. It is as though scientific method is a set of abstract and immutable rules, like the rules of chess, independent of the strategies of the game but governing what strategies are possible.

Yet the most strenuous efforts of scientists and philosophers have failed to produce agreement as to precisely what that method is. Indeed, general philosophical theories about science according to which there is an eternal scientific method which, once discov‑ ered, needs only to be applied to generate knowledge, but which itself will not alter in the light of that knowledge, have proved to be either empty or false. Consider, for example, the view that science does not (or should not) admit concepts referring to what is "in principle" unobservable. The phrase "in principle" is a slippery one; but on any reasonable interpretation, what is "ob‑ servable," even "in principle," changes with the development of new techniques, discoveries, and theories (think of the "direct observation" of the core of the sun by observing neutrinos). And on the other hand, perhaps the quark theory, if it is ultimately accepted, will have taught us not only something about nature, but also about what to do in explaining nature: about a role for the unobservable that was not allowed for by the straightjackets of philosophies of science that take observability to be something laid down forever. Similarly, what is "verifiable" and "falsifiable" can only be determined by the way things are, and our beliefs about what is verifiable and falsifiable can only be determined by our *beliefs about* the way things are. What for yesterday's science was considered unverifiable (hypotheses about the constitution of the stars, or about the origin of life) may today be a legitimate part of science; what some consider to be beyond the "line of demarcation" of the legitimately scientific (the unobservable, and unverifiable, the unfalsifiable) may at some stage, for good reasons, come to be a legitimate part of science (confined quarks, whose existence is unverifiable—unless, of course, we are willing to stretch the meaning of "verifiable" so that their existence is "verifiable" even though they are "unobservable"; but the philosophy of science has long been acquainted with the bankruptcy of such moves). Observability, verifiability, falsifiability, criteria for being a legitimate scientific problem (as opposed to a "pseudo-problem"), criteria for being a scientific possibility (as opposed to "metaphysics")—all these come, more and more in the development of science, to depend on the substantive content of accepted (well-grounded) scientific belief, and change with changes in that content. A sketch of some important developments in the history of science will indicate some ways in which this has come about.

In the seventeenth century, the boundaries between science, philosophy, theology, and mysticism were not drawn sharply. This fact must not be seen as evidence of some sort of intellectual schizophrenia on the part of the scientists concerned, or as an indication that they sometimes did science "badly." Consider Kepler: he was probably the first thinker to insist that every detail of our experience be accounted for precisely in terms of underlying mathematical laws. All experience was for Kepler interconnected by mathematical (for him, geometrical) relationships, and those interrelationships were clues to still deeper ones. In the light of this belief, Kepler felt compelled to ask not only such questions as, What is the precise relationship between the orbital speed of a planet and its distance from the sun? but also—*and in the same spirit*—What is the relation between the color of a planet and its distance? and, Given two planets forming a given angle at a person's birthplace at the time of his birth, what relationship does this fact have to his later life? and, What is the relationship between the "harmonies" in the motions of the planets and the harmonies in music (and in art and meteorology and. . .)? Angles formed by planets with locations on earth were as much "details of our experience" as, and had as much significance as, the angles swept out by a planetary radius vector in a given time. Within the general framework of his geometrical approach, Kepler knew no constraints on the kinds of questions to ask or the kinds of observable relationships it was appropriate to ask them about. Such constraints would later be introduced in the light of accumulating knowledge.

For Newton, the planets were just further material bodies, obeying the law of inertia and exerting and responding to gravitational forces; their relative positions had nothing to do with either man or music. On the other hand, Newton still regarded theological considerations as relevant to his science: indeed, he saw his science as employing the necessity of periodic miraculous intervention by God in order to preserve the stability of the universe against the continual decrease in "quantity of motion" (momentum) due to collisions, against the disruption of the solar system through mutual planetary perturbations, and against either gravitational collapse in a universe containing a finite amount of matter, or a cancellation of all net gravitational forces in an infinite universe containing an infinite amount of matter (Bentley-Seeliger paradox). Laplace saw the resolution of problems about elastic and inelastic collisions and conservation principles that had plagued Newton's era. Claiming to have shown that planetary perturbations are self-correcting in the long run—but forgetting about the Bentley paradox—he was able to inform Napoleon that science had no need of the hypothesis of God.

In such ways, as science progresses, constraints come to be imposed on the kinds of questions to be asked in science, and on the kinds of possibilities that can be legitimately envisaged. But the development of such "rules of the game" is not all negative— not always a matter of cutting out questions and possibilities that had hitherto been considered legitimate. For at various stages, through new discoveries, approaches, techniques, and theories, the progress of science also opens the door to new possibilities—new questions and new alternatives that were before ruled out as illegitimate or perhaps even self-contradictory or inconceivable. The work of Gauss and Riemann opened the way for thinking of a space with variable characteristics—a possibility which Newton, with good reasons at the time, rejected as self-contradictory in dismissing Descartes' similar suggestion. And no one needs to be reminded that quantum mechanics and relativity opened the floodgates for questions and theoretical concepts which previously would have been rejected out of hand. The idea that quantum theory contains its own theory of measurement, and even refashions the rules of logic in its own image, is completely consistent with the viewpoint I have suggested.

That viewpoint maintains that method not only determines the course of science, but is itself shaped by the knowledge attained in that enterprise. In many ways, scientific method is more like military strategy than it is like the rules of chess: the strategy shapes the course of the campaign, but is itself responsive to the lay of the land, and to the armaments that become available to it; and it adjusts to new situations and new devices. Science has not only tended to move toward unification of its substantive beliefs; it has also tended to move toward unification of belief and method. It has learned how to learn in the very process of learning.

17

PROGRESS AND THE LIMITS
OF SCIENCE

DUDLEY SHAPERE

O ne of the perennial ideas in the history of science, at least
since the seventeenth century, is that science has a
"nature," and that this "nature of science" consists of a
method, "the scientific method," by application of which science
achieves the goal of finding out about the world. Since this "method"
characterizes the very nature of the scientific enterprise—the very
meaning of the word "scientific"—it must be employed at all stages
in the development of science, whether past, present, or future.
According to this view, the method was discovered at some point
in history, say at the beginning of the seventeenth century, and
has been applied ever since to generate the progress of science.
Perhaps we have become clearer about that method as we have
gone along; but insofar as any inquiry in the history of science has
been *scientific*, it has employed that method. The method itself,
though it leads to scientific results, is itself immune to change in
the light of those results. It is therefore no wonder that many have
believed that the method itself could have (and indeed should have)
been discovered and applied long before the seventeenth century,
by purely rational or logical analysis of the concept of an inquiry,
so that it is surprising and unfortunate that it was not.

267

I will not be concerned here with reviewing the enormous variety of attempts to lay out explicitly what this method consists of. For, however the "nature" of science has been conceived, and however that "nature" was supposed to be discovered, the views I wish to examine have held that the nature of science consists of its method; and it is this general supposition that I will examine.

More specifically, according to the views I will consider, that method has three major characteristics.

1. It provides the *criteria* or *strategies* by which science, at any stage, goes about its tasks of observing, collecting data, raising problems, developing lines of research, proposing possible solutions, and adopting some one of those possible solutions as the best.

2. Although the application of these criteria or strategies leads to knowledge or well-grounded beliefs about the natural world, the method itself, once discovered, is not subject to alteration in the light of the knowledge arrived at by its means. Thus, it provides the distinguishing characteristic or essence of science, marking the *boundaries* between science and other areas of human activity in a definitive and final way.

3. The analysis of the method of science provides the basis for discussing such broad questions as whether the goals of science are achievable—that is, whether there are *limits* to the extent to which knowledge of the way things are in the world we experience can be found by application of the scientific method. There is a broad implication, not always adhered to consistently, that the question of the limits of science can be discussed solely in terms of the method and goal of science, without any reference whatever to the knowledge that has actually been acquired through that method.

In what follows, I will question this view that there exists a set of criteria or strategies which are applied in the scientific enterprise, which are independent of the content of belief arrived at by their means, and which distinguish science from other activities. My approach will be to point to cases in science in which the criteria for being an "observation," a "possible theory," and a "problem," among other things, have changed, as a result of new scientific beliefs or conceptual breakthroughs. Through examining these cases, I hope to show that method, rules of reasoning, strategies, criteria (for example, of what can count as explanation) go hand-in-hand with the beliefs arrived at by their employment, both leading to and evolving with those beliefs, on occasion being altered, sometimes radically, in the light of the beliefs arrived at by their means. In short, I hope to indicate that, far from consisting merely in a process of rejecting false beliefs and arriving at correct ones—a process simply of learning—science is also a process in which, in the very process of learning, we learn how to learn. At the end of the essay I will return to the question of the limits of science.

Considerations of time and space, among other things, restrict the scope of my discussion of these issues: only selected aspects of the interplay between method and belief can be illustrated here. Further, there are certain questions with which I will *not* be concerned here: for example, I will not ask whether the "boundaries" or "limits" of science include or exclude (or can come to include or exclude) ethical or religious claims. I will be concerned only with the scientific enterprise as an attempt to discover what there is in the world, how those things are related to one another, and how they came to be as they are—in short, with science as a knowledge-acquiring enterprise. I will not be concerned, either, with whether this is the proper way to characterize science.

But now let me proceed to the cases.

I

What counts as an observation in science is not limited to what can be perceived with the naked eye and other human senses. Beginning with the invention of the telescope and microscope, the possibilities of "observation," and what is counted as an observation, have been progressively extended to a high degree of sophistication. Thus astrophysicists for the past two decades have regularly spoken of making "direct observations" of the center of the sun, despite the inaccessibility of that region to the naked eye or even to the telescopically- or spectroscopically-aided eye. Indeed, the eye, and

the human senses generally, are now regarded as receptive only to
a limited range of events which are part of an ordered series of
types of events, namely (to restrict ourselves only to the electromagnetic spectrum), the electromagnetic spectrum, ranging from
extremely high-frequency gamma rays, with wavelengths as short
as a billionth of those to which the eye is sensitive, to very long
radio waves, of the order of a billion or trillion times the wavelength
of visible light. Thus a total range in wavelength of roughly the
order of 10^{22} is encompassed, of which a range of only about 3 or
4000 Angstroms—about 10^{-19} of the entire known range—is accessible to human vision. And besides the electromagnetic interactions,
physicists now recognize three other fundamental types of interactions, the strong, the weak, and the gravitational. The notion of
"observation" has been refined and extended to cover the possibility
of "observing" all four types of interaction: one can define a general
notion of an "appropriate sensor" or "receptor," in terms of the
instrument which is capable of detecting the presence of a given
type of interaction, and therefore of the entities interacting according
to the precise rules (in particular, the conservation principles) of
current elementary particle physics. And the concept of "observation," in contexts like the one in which the astrophysicist speaks of
direct observation of the center of the sun, can be understood in
the following terms: information is received by an appropriate
sensor; and that information is transmitted directly (that is, without
interruption or interference) to the receptor from the entity said to
be observed. (A fuller analysis of the idea would require some
refinements in this statement, but for present purposes, this is
sufficient.)

What is important to note is the extent to which specification
of what counts as observed or observable is a function of the current
state of physical knowledge, and can change with changes in that
knowledge. For current physical knowledge specifies what counts
as an "appropriate sensor or receptor," the ways in which information
of various types is transmitted and received, the character of
interference and the circumstances and even the statistical frequency
with which it occurs, and even the types of information there
(fundamentally) are. The physics of the present epoch, for example,
makes such specifications through the whole theory of elementary

particles, their decays and interactions, and the conservation principles which govern such processes; for example, knowledge of the cross-sections of such particles, and the probabilities of their interactions with other particles (or decays of individual particles) in given environments contributes to specifying the notion of "interference" or "interruption." (Thus we can confidently expect the neutrino to travel unhindered through the body of the sun and interplanetary space on its way to its rare capture by our neutrino receptors; the photon, on the other hand, will undergo many interferences as it passes outward from the solar core.) In particular problems, far more enters into specifying the generalized notion of a receptor than just what is contained in elementary particle theory: for example, knowledge of the environmental conditions (such as, pressure, temperature, and opacity at the center of the sun) plays a role.

The case of "direct observation" of the solar interior by means of neutrino receptors (the experiments of Raymond Davis) will illustrate the vast amount of knowledge that goes into the specification of what, in that case, constitutes a direct observation. In the range of stellar masses which includes the sun, the basic energy-producing process is the proton-proton reaction, initiated by the interaction of two hydrogen nuclei (protons). In the ensuing reactions, three alternate chains (each having a calculable probability) are possible. One of these involves the production of the isotope Boron 8 (B^8), which decays and releases a highly energetic neutrino. These neutrinos carry away a calculable amount of energy; and since the probability of later capture (and therefore of detection) of a neutrino is roughly proportional to the square of the neutrino energy, it makes sense, given the technology, to set up apparatus capable of detecting them. Since the probability of capture, as well as the probability of the B^8 branch, are both calculable, information can thus be gained about the processes in the sun, and models of it and its energy-producing processes can be tested.

The "neutrino receptor" used by Davis consists of a 400,000-liter tank of cleaning fluid (perchloroethylene C_2Cl_4) buried deep in a mine to shield it from other particles which might produce effects similar to those of a captured solar neutrino. (Both the material of the receptor and its location are, of course, chosen in the light of prior knowledge.) The isotope Cl^{37} accounting for about one-fourth of natural chlorine, will undergo the process

$$Cl^{37} + \nu \rightarrow Ar^{37} + e^-$$

followed by beta decay of the radioactive argon (half-life 35.1 days):

$$Ar^{37} \rightarrow Cl^{37} + e^+ + \nu.$$

The radioactive argon must be removed from the tank before it decays; this can be done by bubbling helium through the tank; the argon is then separated from the helium by a charcoal trap and, finally, carried by stable argon gas to a detection chamber. There the decays of argon will be registered by Geiger counters, so that the number of neutrino captures are counted; these can then be compared with the predictions of theory.

The temptation of a positivistic philosopher at this point would be to say that the astrophysicist, in declaring this elaborate procedure to be a direct observation of the solar interior, is just misusing the term. For what are *observed* here, he would claim, are not events occurring at the center of the sun, but at best only absorptions of neutrinos in our apparatus, or—perhaps more strictly— the decays of radioactive argon, or—more strictly still—only the clicks of the Geiger counter (or perhaps only the "sense-datum" of a click in our consciousness); all else, properly speaking, must be ascribed to inference. That line of attack, however, would purchase a philosophical dogma at the price of ignoring the long history of reasoning that has gone into the evolution of this concept of observation. With the deep insight that made him both a seminal physicist and a profound philosopher, Einstein (according to the report of Heisenberg) went to the heart of that reasoning:

> It is the theory which decides what we can observe. You must appreciate that observation is a very complicated process. The phenomenon under observation produces certain events in our measuring apparatus, which eventually and by complicated paths produce sense impressions and help us to fix the effects in our consciousness. Along this whole path—from the phenomenon to its fixation in our consciousness—we must be able to tell

how nature functions, must know the natural laws at least in practical terms, before we can claim to have observed anything at all. . . .When we claim that we can observe something new, we ought really to be saying that, although we are about to formulate new natural laws that do not agree with the old ones, we nevertheless assume that the existing laws—covering the whole path from the phenomenon to our consciousness—function in such a way that we can rely upon them and hence speak of "observations."

Two comments must be made about Einstein's remark. First, as we have seen, other knowledge than what is explicitly or even implicitly contained in a single applicable theory may be brought to bear in deciding what we can observe. Second, it is important to note that when Einstein speaks here of a "theory," he does not mean something doubtful, but the exact opposite, something that we can "rely" on. Qualifications aside, however, Einstein has grasped the essence of the concept of observation at which modern science has arrived: science builds on what it has found it can trust. The application of acquired trustworthy belief can be applied to the creation of new types of observations which can be used in the testing of hypotheses about which we require more trust. This is not to say that what we trust is sacrosanct: if the predictions of our hypotheses disagree with our observations (as they have in the case of the solar neutrinos), it is not necessarily the hypothesis that is at fault; it may be any portion of the theoretical and instrumental ingredients in the experimental setup. We begin by testing those ingredients which are most likely to be at fault and least costly to give up; if the difficulty persists, the threat penetrates deeper and deeper into the accepted beliefs ingredient in the purported observation. Thus, in the case of the neutrino experiments, the disagreement has persisted after re-examination of the solar models employed, the chemistry of argon, and a host of other parts of the background of the experiment, until even the completeness and accuracy of our understanding of elementary particles has been brought into question.

But my concern here is not with the doubts that can arise about our observations, but rather in the fact that, as our knowledge, our body of well-grounded beliefs, accumulates, we are able to

extend the range of what we are willing to count as "observational."
Or, to put the point in another way, what is observable is not
something given once and for all, but evolves with the evolution of
scientific knowledge which is itself, at least in part, a result of
observation. And this is a special case of a larger truth about the
evolution of knowledge: the more we learn about nature, the better
able we become to learn about it.

II

But it is not merely the range of the observable that can evolve
through the development of science; the range of theoretical
possibilities—the distinction between a legitimate scientific theory
and one that is not legitimate, or is not perhaps even conceivable,
also undergoes change at times, and occasionally the change is quite
drastic. An illustration of this is the following. In the mid-seven-
teenth century, Descartes proclaimed that all the properties of
matter could be understood in purely geometrical terms. By means
of that identification of matter and extension, Descartes hoped to
guarantee, in advance of any investigation of the physical world,
that complete and precise knowledge of physical nature was, in
principle, achievable. For, according to him, the concepts and
methods of geometry (in his own conception of them) are absolutely
clear and distinct, in that any question that could be asked in
geometrical terms could be answered completely and precisely in
purely geometrical terms. And the goodness of God guaranteed
that there would be, in the physical world, all and only those
properties that we can conceive and understand clearly and distinctly. Such a view of matter, however, was ultimately unacceptable
(even to Descartes himself, as we shall see) even as a *possible* view.
Isaac Newton, in his early unpublished essay, "On the Gravity and
Equilibrium of Fluids," pointed out the fundamental objection: the
parts of space are identical, so that their interchange, if it were
possible, would bring about no change at all; space is, on the

contrary, that with respect to which, in which, things move; and to speak of the points of space themselves as moving would be absurd. Years later, the same argument found a laconic restatement in the *Principia*, where the target of attack is not named:

> As the order of the parts of time is immutable, so also is the order of the parts of space. Suppose those parts to be moved out of their places, and they will be moved (if the expression may be allowed), out of themselves. For times and spaces are, as it were, the places as well of themselves as of all other things. All things are placed in time as to order of succession; and in space as to order of situation. It is from their essence or nature that they are places; and that the primary places of things should be moveable, is absurd.

Thus, to Newton, "space" cannot have the property of moveability that is characteristic of matter. Nor, indeed—though Newton of course does not say this explicitly—could it have inhomogeneities of any kind, since inhomogeneity is judged *with respect to* space. An assertion of space curvature, for example, and of change of curvature, would not have been a *false* view; it was not even a possible view. It was absurd, inconceivable, self-contradictory.

Descartes himself was unable to carry out his program in a consistent way. In his actual description of the behavior of matter and the evolution of the universe, he was forced to speak as though matter were not, after all, identical with space, but distinct from it. It did, it is true, fill space, like a continuous and homogeneous fluid, with currents and eddies and vortices distinguishing the various individual parts from one another. (Hence Newton's criticism of Descartes in a paper on fluids and in Book II of the *Principia*, which is concerned with fluids.) Descartes himself was unable to carry out his projected "geometrization" of physics.

At the root of Newton's view of space was the idea that, if one is to speak of properties of an object such as curvature, one would have to do so in terms of some containing space: a line, a one-dimensional object, can be said to be curved only *in* a two-dimensional containing space; a surface, a two-dimensional object, can be said to have curvature only insofar as it is contained in a three-dimensional space. And since, to Newton, three-dimensional space was the ultimate reference-frame, not contained in any further space of greater dimensionality with respect to which inhomogeneities and changes of inhomogeneity could be referred, it itself could not intelligibly be said to have any sort of inhomogeneities such as a curvature. He would have said the same thing about an alleged expansion of space: the idea is absurd, self-contradictory; what could it expand into?

All this changed with Gauss' theory of surfaces and Riemann's extension of it to spaces of higher dimensionality. Gauss' "Theorema egregium," his "outstanding theorem," demonstrated that a two-dimensional surface has an intrinsic and invariant (with respect to choice of coordinate system) property of curvature which can be characterized and determined solely within the surface itself, without any consideration of a higher-dimensional space in which the surface was embedded. Riemann extended Gauss' results to spaces of arbitrary dimensionality, so that it became possible to speak of the "intrinsic characteristics" of a space of any dimensionality. It became possible, then, to do what was inconceivable and self-contradictory before: to consider physical space to have intrinsic characteristics without supposing it to be embedded in a four-dimensional space; and further, to allow those characteristics to vary from point to point and from time to time. The way was paved for a revival of space theories of matter (a neo-Cartesianism), but also, and ultimately more importantly, for the twentieth century space-time theories which related the characteristics of matter and space-time.

It is important to emphasize that the work of Gauss and Riemann did not merely bring back into contention a view that had been *rejected as false*; their contribution was far more fundamental in its implications. For it admitted into the realm of admissible scientific hypotheses *not* what had previously been conceived and rejected as false: insofar as the Cartesian view had postulated a differentiation of space, that view was rejected as *unintelligible* by Newton, Leibniz, and their contemporaries, and could not even be developed by its founder himself.

The Gauss-Riemann case illustrates a shift in what can count as a legitimate or possible scientific theory due to an innovation in mathematics. In other cases, such shifts are the result of new physical knowledge or beliefs (Faraday's field theory). In some cases, of course, views previously considered possible have been eliminated as possibilities by new scientific developments (nineteenth-century ether theories).

III

Thus far I have discussed cases in which the range of possible observations, and the range of possible theories, were changed as a result of new developments. But it is not only the range of possible observations and of possible theories or explanations that depend on the content of accepted scientific belief and evolve as that content evolves. The very range of problems dealt with in science, and even the conception of its goals, may at times be altered. Undoubtedly the most striking case of such transition was the shift in the character of the study of matter in the early part of the modern era (sixteenth through eighteenth centuries); it was accompanied by a revision of the vocabulary for talking about matter to accord with the new conception of the problems and goals of chemistry.

The Greek philosophical tradition represented by the Milesians, Plato, and Aristotle, among others, enshrined what we today call the physical distinction between the solid, liquid, and gaseous *states* of matter into a theory of ultimate *elements* earth, water, and air (with fire included as a fourth element for reasons that need not be entered into here). Within the context of this general view, more specific theories could be generated, depending in part on the reasons assigned for differences between the various sorts of "earths" and "waters." Thus the differences between the various sorts of earth were attributed sometimes to differences in proportions of the fundamental qualities "cold" and "dry," or to various degrees of admixture of "moist" and "smoky exhalations," or to various degrees of "actualization of the potential" of earth, (lead, for instance, being a very imperfect "fulfillment" of earth, only slightly above dirt—as could be "seen" by the ease with which lead tends to decay into "dirt" on the outside). Such specific theories could then provide guidelines as to what could be done with different kinds of earth, and ways in which those results could be brought about. Thus, for example, in one of the above-mentioned views of the relations between different types of earth, the desired perfection could be brought about by achieving a better balance of fundamental qualities, and this in turn could be achieved in certain cases by driving out some of the "cold" by "heat," or some of the "dry" by "moist" (by processes of heating, solution, or the combination of the two in distillation). However, certain kinds of aims and activities were *not* suggested by this way of thinking. For example, although the idea of separating an earthy substance from other earthy substances for the purpose of working on it alchemically was not inconsistent with the philosophical "perfection" framework, and was certainly present in many alchemical recipes, nevertheless such "removal of impurities" was at best only a preliminary and peripheral procedure. For even where removal of irrelevant material from earthy substances was an initial step in alchemical procedure, what remained was not what we would call a "purified" substance, but rather an imperfect substance that still had to be brought, by various actions, to perfection. The later idea of chemical analysis as the segregation of substances and their breakdown into their constituents was, even where present at all, far from central: a substance was imperfect of its kind not because it contained admixtures of material substances of other kinds, but rather because it was only a partial realization of a perfect or harmonious form of that material substance.

The later medieval and early modern period witnessed the discovery of a vast multitude of hitherto unknown substances and types of substances, as well as increasing sophistication in the capacity to distinguish different substances. There was also, in the early modern period, increasing attention to the breakdown products of chemical action, especially heat. Although there was debate as to whether the breakdown products were constituents of the original substance, or were merely created by the action of fire on it, nevertheless by the eighteenth century it was widely asserted that breakdown products were constituents, and that understanding of material substances was obtainable through analysis of those products.

In this way, the whole aim and problem-structure of the study of matter was gradually altered. The central problem, in the attempt to understand matter, shifted from, How can different kinds of earth be brought to perfection? to, What are the constituents of material substances?

With this increasing focus on breakdown products as the key to understanding matter, and with the discovery of more and more types of substances, a demand arose for a reform of the nomenclature of material substances. Hitherto, the primary method of naming material substances had been in terms of their obvious sensory qualities; now, however, those qualities were mere superficial aspects of substances; the nature of things, the key to their understanding, lay in the constituents. And, as Guyton de Morveau put it, "Denominations should be as much as possible in conformity with the nature of things." With his inspiration, and with Lavoisier's new chemical theories, Guyton, Lavoisier, Fourcroy, and Berthollet collaborated to produce a nomenclature, the first step in the development of modern chemical vocabulary.

This shift of aims, problems, and vocabulary is so spectacular that one is tempted to say that it marks the beginning of chemistry, rather than merely a shift in the study of matter (though the "chemical revolution" is usually identified rather with the overthrow of the phlogiston theory, an episode that seems to me to pale in significance when compared to the developments I have described). Certainly it was a radical change in the approach to matter-theory. Be that as it may, there are many other cases in the history of science in which, though the shifts were not so drastic, new developments in the content of scientific belief brought in their wake new types of problems, leaving others behind.

IV

I have argued that the ways in which we observe nature—the criteria, if you will, for admitting something as "observable"—are not independent of the content of scientific belief, but evolve in intimate conjuction with it. The same is true of the objects of our study: our conception of what the objects or facts are which we are trying to explain depends heavily on the knowledge we have attained, and evolves with it, often leading to a recategorization, reconceptualization, and, in some cases, a redescription of the furniture of the world. Similarly, our conceptions of what a legitimate or "meaningful" problem is, and a possible "theory" or "explanation" is, as opposed to a "pseudo-explanation," evolve along with the evolving content of science. Examples could be multiplied to illustrate further aspects of these points, as well as to extend them to the cases of lines of research that seem promising, or more promising, than others, of what constitutes an acceptable solution to a problem, of what characteristics a theory must have in order to qualify as fundamental, and so forth. But perhaps what I have said is sufficient to illustrate that the boundaries between the scientific and the non-scientific—between the "observable" and the "unobservable," between the scientifically legitimate or possible and the scientifically illegitimate or impossible, between scientific problems and pseudo-problems, between scientific explanations and pseudo-explanations, between science and nonscience or non-sense—are not something given once and for all, but rather shift as our knowledge and understanding accumulates. We learn how to learn about nature in the very process of learning about it; and similarly, we learn how to talk and think about nature, and how to understand it, in the very process of coming to understand it. The criteria of scientific admissibility, the strategies for studying nature, for confronting it with questions, for proposing possible answers to those questions, for constructing lines of research to answer our questions and test our hypotheses, and so forth, which are employed at a given stage of the history of science lead us to new beliefs about nature. But in turn, those new beliefs, at least in some cases, lead not only to the rejection of old beliefs, but also to modification, extension, or replacement of the very criteria or strategies which led to their discovery.

If the portrayal of science which I have given is correct— if, that is, the boundaries of the scientific change as our scientific knowledge grows—then what can we say about the limits of science? This question is an irresistible temptation to us all; its answer, if conceived as an implication of "the nature of science," cannot be more than mere speculation. We cannot know in advance the turns that will be taken in the future development of scientific methods and ideas. If the view that science can learn everything is lack of humility, then so is the opposite contention, that science has definite and unavoidable limits in its quest for knowledge: we should, after all, have learned that lesson by looking at the graveyard of attempts to limit what science will do.

Of course, we may someday arrive at a stage at which we have a few simple laws that enable us to explain whatever comes along, and after which we continually fail to find any reason to reject those laws. We may then have the understanding we seek, even though we cannot be certain we have it. However, we may never reach such a stage. We cannot know in advance, but must investigate the world to learn the methods and limits of knowledge, just as we investigate it to gain knowledge. We may, of course, conjecture on the basis of our present knowledge and strategies as to what we may or may not be able to achieve; but we must recognize that such hypotheses are as fallible as any others in science.

The lack of certainty about whether or not science has inescapable limits is not a license to believe whatever we wish about the way things are. We must, after all, build our beliefs about the world we live in on the basis of the best information we have, wherever possible believing that we have reason to believe and doubting what we have specific reason to doubt.

INDEX

abortion, 177–78, 182, 216, 218
actions, 27
  contingency of, 30
  division of human nature and,
    22–24
  emotions related to, 116, 123
  means and ends of, 20–21
  perfection of, 30–31
  rules and consequences of, 221–
    325
  unintentional, 128–29
"acts, actings," 64
  interrelated, good in, 61–62, 65
  metaphysics of, 72
  as quality of substance, 59–61
Adkins, Arthur W. H., 78–80, 94,
  95, 96, 97, 99n, 100n, 107n
advanced societies, 145–62
  basic assumptions and values of,
    146–50, 160–62
  concepts of modern praxis in,
    157–60
  crisis of, 148, 154–55, 160
  cultural diversity faced by, 152–
    53
  individual autonomy in, 149, 154,
    155, 160–61
  man-made future of, 156–67,
    161

  moral standards in, 151–52
  relativism in, 149–50, 156, 161
  responsibility of individual in,
    151–52, 156–57, 161
aesthetic sensibilities, 193
aesthetic values of essence, 200–
  11, 202
aggression, instinct for, 137
aim of life, 28–32
  actions related to, 30–32
  covenants and, 31
  fulfillment and, 31–32
  as polar reality, 29–30
  satisfaction of desires and, 25–
    26, 32–33
Allan D. J., 81, 96, 99n, 100n
altruism, 42
Ambartsumian, 258–59
American Civil Religion (Bellah),
  226
Americanism, 210–11
anarchy, 155
Anaximander, 19
animals:
  nature of humans vs., 134–36,
    138
  and theory of ideal types, 140
Anscombe, G. E. M., 99n, 105n,
  130

A NOTE ON CONTRIBUTORS

Joseph Basile is Professor of Applied Sciences, Catholic University of Louvain, Louvain, Belgium.

Alistair C. Crombie is Professor of History of Science, Trinity College, University of Oxford, Oxford, England.

Jude P. Dougherty is Dean, School of Philosophy, The Catholic University of America, Washington, D.C., U.S.A.

J. N. Findlay is Bowne Professor of Philosophy, Boston University, Boston, Massachusetts, U.S.A.

Ivor Leclerc is Fuller E. Callaway Professor of Metaphysics and Moral Philosophy, Emeritus, Emory University, Atlanta, Georgia, U.S.A.

Irwin C. Lieb is Professor of Philosophy, University of Southern California, Los Angeles, California, U.S.A.

Eric L. Mascall is Professor of Historical Theology, King's College, London, England.

Masatoshi Matsushita is President, Professors World Peace Academy of Japan, Former President, Rikkyo University, Tokyo, Japan.

Seyyed Hossein Nasr is Professor of Religion, Temple University, Philadelphia, Pennsylvania, U.S.A.

Adriaan Peperzak is Professor of Philosophical Ethics, Catholic University, Nigmegen, Netherlands.

Herbert Richardson is Professor of Theology, St. Michaels College, University of Toronto, Toronto, Ontario, Canada.

John L. Russell is Lecturer in Philosophy, Heythrop College, University of London, London, England.

Adam Schaff is President, European Coordination Center for Research and Documentation in Social Sciences, Vienna, Austria.

Dudley Shapere is Professor of Philosophy of Science, University of Maryland, College Park, Maryland, U.S.A.

Ninian Smart is Professor of Religious Studies, University of California at Santa Barbara and at Furness College, University of Lancaster, Lancaster, England.

Robert C. Soloman is Professor of Philosophy, University of Texas, Austin, Texas, U.S.A.

Roger J. Sullivan is Professor of Philosophy, University of South Carolina, Columbia, South Carolina, U.S.A.